THE PEOPLE OF SHIP STREET

INTERNATIONAL LIBRARY OF SOCIOLOGY AND SOCIAL RECONSTRUCTION

Founded by Karl Mannheim
Editor: W. J. H. Sprott

A catalogue of the books available in the INTERNATIONAL LIBRARY OF SOCI-OLOGY AND SOCIAL RECONSTRUCTION, and new books in preparation for the Library will be found at the end of this volume.

THE PEOPLE OF
SHIP STREET

by
Madeline Kerr

LONDON
ROUTLEDGE & KEGAN PAUL
NEW YORK: HUMANITIES PRESS

First published in 1958
by Routledge & Kegan Paul Ltd
Broadway House, 68–74 Carter Lane
London E.C.4
Printed in Great Britain by
Butler & Tanner Ltd
Frome and London

CONTENTS

CONTENTS

CONTENTS

INTRODUCTION

THIS is a book about the lives of a group of people living in a Liverpool slum. Although much is said and written about slums, Teddy Boys, problem families and so on, there are comparatively few studies made in which the improved techniques of clinical and social psychology are fully utilized. The descriptive part of the book is based on field work done on the people of Ship Street, a pseudonym given to this particular group.

My second objective in the book is to test certain generalizations made previously about the effect of environmental stresses on personality development. This is done through an examination of the field work results taken in conjunction with results obtained from projection tests. Once the observations made in the field have been linked with the assessments of the projection techniques then it becomes possible to make tentative generalizations about the effect of certain social stresses on personality.

The next step is the question of identification. In order to understand clearly why certain phenomena occur the exact problem has to be identified and the correct questions asked. There are two possible ways of doing this. The first is the laboratory method of the experimental isolation of different facets of the problem. Unfortunately this is seldom feasible in social science. The next best method would seem to be situational analysis, which is what I am attempting to do in this book. The problem is concerned with the effect of deprivation on personality structure. The method is to study different peoples suffering from different degrees of deprivation. By doing this I hope to map out tentatively some of the results of deprivation on personality structure in such a way that will make prediction possible. That is, it should be feasible to say that if people are deprived in such a way certain psychological conditions are likely to arise. While this has been rather vaguely glimpsed it has never been stated with any degree of precision.

I am greatly indebted to the Nuffield Foundation for a grant for assistance for a considerable period of our time in the field, and to Liverpool University for a small initial grant. I should like to thank Dr. Margaret Lowenfeld both for her interest in the work and her help with the material, and Dr. Dennis Chapman and Dr. Rosemary Gordon for their helpful suggestions about the manuscript. I want also to thank Professor W. J. H. Sprott very much indeed for his great help and encouragement in the last stages of the work. It is not possible to thank Miss Vera Dantra adequately for her field work. I would, however, wish to thank her particularly for her help during the last half of the work when she was sufficiently interested to work without a salary. My deductions on the work, are, of course, my own and none of these people should necessarily be identified with them.

Efenechtyd,
  November 1956.

CHAPTER I

ORIGIN OF SHIP STREET

THE people of Ship Street live in a nexus of streets all within about ten minutes' walking distance of each other in the middle of Liverpool. The area is a typical slum of today, having been devastated in the past by neglect and poverty, and in the near past by enemy bombing. The people are being gradually moved out of their generally large houses into Corporation flats, this movement gaining some impetus during the last year of this five years' research. This alteration in their manner of living has not led to a related change in their ways of life. The ritual and traditions of the past, carried out in the large houses and streets, are now preserved in the present in the corridors and yards of tenement flats. Ship Street, is, to the best of my knowledge, a pseudonym. All the names of the people appearing in this book have been falsified and any possible identifying mark has been eliminated. Even the initials by which people are called are false.

(A) THE PLACE

The surroundings of Ship Street are somewhat reminiscent of Lloyd Warner's[1] description of Yankee City. It is a part of that area of the city to which immigrants come and in which the lowest strata of natives live. People who are reasonably successful and those who become assimilated to the English upper working class or lower middle class patterns of behaviour move away.

The genuine Ship Street resident has been there for about two or three generations. He does not want to move and resists

[1] Lloyd Warner and Paul Lunt, *Social Life of a Modern Community*, Yale University Press, 1941.

3

vigorously any attempt to make him do so. The people we worked with form a residual core of families for whom the life of the street is the only one they know, and the only one they want to know. Although surrounded by immigrants, near the brothel area of the town, and with their derelict houses gradually being superseded by Corporation flats, they still preserve a pattern of living specific in many ways to themselves.

(b) ORIGIN OF THE GROUP

Historically most of this group originated in Ireland about two generations ago. In some cases Irish ties are still recognized and at times holidays are taken in Ireland. This tie tends to be fostered by the Roman Catholic Church to which the majority of families belong.

(c) THE FINDING OF THE GROUP

The Ship Street people were discovered in the following manner. From an analysis of the field work and projection tests which I did in Jamaica, I deduced a relationship between social pressures, expressed in the form of deprivation, and personality. In Jamaica it was found that the majority of peasant children who did the Lowenfeld Mosaic Test produced a certain type of pattern which is indicative of non-integration.[1] This type of pattern is produced in Europe only by chronologically young children or those suffering from some difficulty which has prevented them forming one type or other of the integrated patterns of behaviour which are given cultural approbation.[2]

I was fortunate enough to find the right sort of group very quickly. The Lowenfeld Mosaic Test and the Rorschach Test were given to all the children attending a slum play centre.[3]

[1] 'Field Work and Projection Tests', paper read to the British Rorschach Forum, 1953, by Madeline Kerr.

[2] *The Lowenfeld Mosaic Test*, by Margaret Lowenfeld, Newman Neame, London, 1954. A description of this test will be given in Chapter 15.

[3] I should like to thank the people running this centre for their help, especially the man in charge of the play group. Names of individuals and of the centre cannot be given as this might lead to the identification of Ship Street.

This group contained children aged 8 to 13 years. So many of them produced patterns so like the Jamaican and so unlike the English groups of the same chronological age on which the test was standardized, that it was obvious that no further search was required. The children, too, responded with such enthusiasm that it was often necessary for one member of the team to lean against the door while the other did the testing.

These children started to visit the experimenters' house and so contact was made with the parents. Intensive field work was done on sixty-one families over roughly a period of five years. Frequent visits were made to the children's homes and in many cases these visits were reciprocated by the mothers. In some instances the parents were also met at pubs. Throughout the time the children provided a sort of continuo, running round to tell us the family news. 'Our Jenny's had another baby'; 'our Billy has had to go away'; or long recitals of injuries received by the children in fighting or wall climbing.

(D) FIELD TECHNIQUE

Contact was made with the parents in the following way. After the initial meetings with some of the children, small groups of them were invited to visit the experimenters' house. The parents were then visited so that they would know where the children were going. The plan originally had been to use this introduction to start intensive field work later. However, the situation was such that no explanation became necessary. Interest in the children gained the friendship of the parents and no difficulties arose during the entire five years of reciprocal visiting. Information was obtained through friendly discussions, the informants often sending for the investigators when anything exciting or important happened. This easy entry into the people's lives, though surprising at first, is quite explicable in the light of our later knowledge about them. They are not interested in abstraction, or in status, but only in personal relationships centred on their family group. Therefore their topics of conversation are inevitably concerned with the doings and sayings of their blood relations. It is perhaps the place to explain here that references to our own conversations have at times been left in the descriptions or quotations from the field notes in cases where this adds to the accuracy and vividness of the description. This acceptance on a friendly basis not only gave us an opportunity to record their opinions but also to observe and participate in their daily activities.

(E) DISCUSSION OF TERMS

Before the field work is presented it is necessary to define rather carefully some of the terms and concepts used throughout the book. Although the theoretical aspects of the work are reserved for the last section it is not always possible to refrain either from some explanations or from use of the terms.

As in *Personality and Conflict in Jamaica* the main explanatory hypotheses are centred round the idea of roles. During the years it has taken to do these two researches, the tendency to use this term has become more frequent and popular, so I shall define briefly the way I intend to use this and related terms in this book. A discussion of the many ways in which it is used would, in my opinion, be premature at this time.

I am using the term role to mean that facet of the personality which is in focus or in action at the time under discussion. The individual plays each role just as an actor plays a part on the stage. In so doing he expresses a facet of his personality relevant to the situation in which he is acting. The roles he will produce will be primarily decided by the pattern of the culture in which he lives, but each person will bring his own unique contribution to the culturally stereotyped part he is playing. From this it can be seen that role is not entirely concerned with motor behaviour. In the sense I am using the term, the man's own ideas, his feelings, and projections of himself as the man playing the role are also included. The total personality could be said to consist of configurations of roles.

Now roles will not be learned singly and are therefore unlikely to exist in isolation. The main role activated at any time will almost certainly be only the one in focus. Other roles belonging to the same configuration, could be activated, were the focus to shift. The effect is rather like picking a piece of seaweed out of the sea; the small piece is found to have the most complicated trailers attached and to be, in fact, merely one part

6

of a large, somewhat amorphous mass. The focusing of the role calls for a very delicate adjustment.

It seems plausible that each person has a minimum and maximum number of roles he can play. If he is forced to try and play more or less than these he can suffer severe mental derangement. The frustrated woman at home helping mother will be an example of the latter. An example of the former would be where society demands more roles of a man than he is able to play. The inability to respond will cause intense anxiety and then gradual disorganization. The man sometimes commits suicide at this point.

In *The Nature of Intelligence*[1] Spearman applied the law of the conservation of energy to psychology. One of his theories was that the amount of energy available to any person would be constant in quantity. Now it seems possible that the number of roles it would be possible for an individual to play would depend on the amount of available energy. Spearman said that at a given time the amount of energy would be constant in quantity though differing in quality. If this is applied to the role theory it would mean that some roles will absorb a great deal of energy, thus leaving less for the others. This is, of course, borne out by everyday observation. Again Spearman pointed out that some people have more energy at their disposal than others. This would mean that it would be possible for some to play more roles, which might be supported, too, by work on mental defectives. These people are only able to be taught a limited number of skills and habits. They are incapable of taking over many roles. This looks as if there would be a correlation with Spearman's general mental energy and the capacity for role development. Support for this hypothesis may be found in Klopfer's formulation of Rorschach hypotheses:

'Thus provided there is an adequate amount of basic security, the available life energy can flow into the construction of a strongly unified, highly differentiated, and hierarchically ordered system of personality organization. . . .

'If there is not a sufficient amount of basic security then part of the available life energy is used in defensive manœuvres to protect the developing organism from being inundated by anxiety. As a consequence thereof, there is less life energy available

[1] C. Spearman, *The Nature of Intelligence*, Macmillan, London, 1923.

for the construction of a unified personality organization. Depending on the degree of early deprivation, the personality organization remains more or less "de-integrated", fragmented, compartmentalized, loose-jointed, or dissociated. In such cases we speak of an impairment of emotional integration.' [1]

While these are not new ideas they provide a most useful reformulation from which to attempt some explanation of the lack of integration among groups of people suffering from lack of security owing to role deprivation or impairment.

Three aspects of the theory of roles are going to be used in this book. The first is role deprivation, the second role impairment, the third role uncertainty. Role deprivation will be caused when an individual is prevented from playing certain roles which the culture decrees should be played. Impairment will result when a man is prevented from playing all the culturally required aspects of the role. Uncertainty will occur when alternate roles are presented which appear to be of equal value or utility.

Role uncertainty can arise from two main causes. The first is where the doubts arise in the mind of the individual because he is presented with a choice of roles and is indecisive which to play. For convenience this type can be further sub-divided. In one case the social perception of the individual is in some way impaired. He perceives the situation with which he is faced only partially and therefore has insufficient data to decide which role to play. In the other case, which is that of culture conflict, he may not know which role to play or, to be more accurate, which role will be acceptable in the situation which confronts him.

The second cause will be operative when the situation itself lacks coherent structure, and therefore it is difficult for the individual to perceive what his role should be. Merton's[2] example of the difficulties which beset the psychologist investigating housing is a good example of this.

It would be expected that the impact of these types of role inhibition would affect the personality with different degrees of severity.

---

[1] Bruno Klopfer, *Developments in the Rorschach Technique*, Vol. I, George C. Harrap & Co., Ltd., London 1954.

[2] Robert K. Merton, 'The Social Psychology of Housing', in *Current Trends in Social Psychology*, University of Pittsburgh Press, 1951.

In role deprivation then, the individual would have too much energy to be absorbed by the limited number of roles. This seems plausible, firstly, in the examination of cultures where role deprivation takes place; not all people suffer equally from it. Some people with a low energy potential would not be affected. As energy cannot be destroyed it must manifest itself in some other form. The second reason for the plausibility of this suggestion could be found in the hysterical behaviour found in the evangelists in Jamaica. In *Personality and Conflict in Jamaica* the suggestion was put forward that deprivation causes such severe distress to the growing personality of the child that maturation is inhibited. In role restriction and role uncertainty the damage will not be so great. The symptoms would tend to be of the neurotic type associated with anxiety.

It is now necessary to try to find why role deprivation or impairment or uncertainty should result in the lack of integration or in anxiety in the individual.

In a relatively simple society the roles demanded from the individual are generally clearly, if not legally, defined, e.g. the roles a Dobuan[1] has to show to his mother-in-law. In a complex society, or perhaps one could go further and say a complex of societies, the situation is not so simple. The functions expected from the individual will have become more and more differentiated and he himself will require to develop his social perception into a very finely discriminating instrument. Unless he can do this he will not know which role to play. In a complex society too it is quite possible for there to be alternative roles which may be equally acceptable. For example, when a junior female member of the university meets the male Vice-Chancellor in the doorway who opens the door for whom? Socially clumsy behaviour will be shown by individuals who are not able to appreciate that there can be several possible roles to play or who are unable to perceive subtleties of discrimination.

Now the person who is non-integrated because of either personal or cultural conflict will have difficulty in acting in an overall manner. He will tend to react in a piecemeal way. Because of this it seems likely that he will miss many role subtleties. He will tend to react in a simple manner and perhaps

[1] Reo Fortune, *The Sorcerers of Dobu*, Kegan Paul, London, 1932.

be rigid in his role playing, at times, comically so. Like the man known to me during the war who always beat his wife on Wednesday if she did not produce steak and kidney pudding for his dinner. He said he had always had this dish for dinner on Wednesday and always intended to, rationing or no rationing.

It might be possible to classify societies according to whether the approved roles were rigid and simple, or complex and discriminating. In the primary stage simple roles would be produced in answer to clearly defined situations. In the secondary stage, configurations of roles would be produced in answer to complex situations. People in the primary stage would be clumsy or have difficulty in producing the roles required by people in the secondary stage. People in the secondary stage would be more liable to role uncertainty. They would require more in the way of education of the sentiments rather than simple role learning. It would, too, involve individuation, used in Jung's sense of the word.

The difficulty in a complex society is that primary and secondary groups co-exist. The Ship Street group are still in the primary stage, e.g. their attitude to the opposite sex (see p. 89). For them it is possible that a sort of threshold exists. This would act as an efficiency bar which the non-integrated personality does not cross.

Finally, one criticism which is likely to be made must be answered at this stage. It is that while it is easy to see that Jamaicans suffer role deprivation because of difficulties over colour, how can this be said of white English people? This is really quite simple to answer. The Jamaican is aware of his deprivation, but the Ship Street man is not so of necessity. It is quite possible to be deprived without being aware of it if you have never known any other state. People have frequently suffered from chemical deficiencies without being aware that their condition was anything other than normal. It is not claimed that the deprivation in Ship Street is anything like as severe as it is in Jamaica. What is claimed is that it is present and similar in kind though not in intensity to that suffered by Jamaicans.

The deprivation of Ship Street people lies in the fact that their arrested maturation leaves them unfitted to play complex or more discriminating roles, even when these are offered to them.

Where hypotheses have been put forward in this chapter they are tentative. Each will be examined in the light of the evidence presented by the field work. This, therefore, will be presented next.

CHAPTER II

SHIP STREET FAMILIES

(A) STRUCTURE OF THE HOUSEHOLD

THE writer on family structure is at once caught up in the problem of whether enumeration can ever bear much relation to reality. The census deals with households, not families, and frequently this has coloured sociological thinking, and in practice social planning, so that in England when we talk of family structure what we usually mean is household structure. Because of this the family has come to mean mother, father, plus own children, which appears to be the usual content of a middle-class household. In this latter case it is almost as if the convention of the small house or bungalow has started to alter some of the functional relationships within the family to suit the building.

It is not very easy to give figures showing the heads of each of the households as where there are a large number of people in the house it is difficult to decide whom to choose. One criterion might be who has the rent book. However, in some cases this can be a very old woman to whom the house 'belongs'. The following figures are based on an attempt to focus on the most responsible people in the household.

In 43 cases husband and wife are jointly the responsible householders, in 10 cases this position is held by a widow and in 4 cases by a widower. In 1 case a divorced woman is the householder. In 3 cases the man 'has taken a walk' leaving his wife in sole charge.

It is relevant here to define the term 'household'. We have taken it to mean a group of people living and eating together and sharing the money earned by one or more of them. In Ship Street these people are always relatives. This definition if rigidly used could blur the true picture of this type of family life. When married daughters bring their husbands home the custom is for the daughters to cook their husbands' evening meal in the communal household kitchen and then 'to take it upstairs'. During the day the daughters and their children feed with the mother.

An attempt has been made to classify the households according to their constituent members. In 19 cases the household consists of parents and own children only; in 5 cases parents, own children plus lodger; in 10 cases parents, own children and adopted, illegitimate or stepchildren; in 2 cases grandmother and grandchildren; in 12 cases parents, own children and a relative of the woman other than the mother; in 1 case parents, own children and a relative of the man other than his mother; in 12 cases parents, own children, married daughter and grandchildren.

(b) STRUCTURE OF THE FAMILIES

These figures have to be considered carefully before a clear picture is obtained. In Ship Street the family is the essential unit and this may spill over into many households. The custom is for married daughters either to bring their husbands to their parents' home, or to go away for a short time when they first marry, only to return when the responsibilities of married life become too heavy. Married sons, too, like to live near their Mums. This is not always so easy for them as they, of course, get absorbed into their wives' matrilocal family units.

The fact that twenty-four households consist of parents and own children only (19 + 5) seems relatively high. But in twenty-one of these twenty-four cases, all the children in the family are unmarried. In thirteen of these twenty-one cases the Mum's mother is also dead. In one case a couple is childless and the woman's mother is dead. So in fourteen out of the twenty-four cases where the household consists of parents and own children only, there are not three female generations alive.

Now in five cases lodgers are included. A Ship Street lodger is not just anyone. If not directly related, he is in some way connected with the older generation of the family. In one case he is the old lady's mother's friend's son to whom an obligation was felt. While it is generally claimed that the lodger is separate from the rest of the family, our observation has shown this not to be entirely true. The special family connection seems to give them the status of relatives. That they are rather special is, I think, shown by the fact that there are only five of them.

Thus the 'ordinary' family occurs in twenty-four cases, and in the other thirty-seven some variation exists, giving a picture more in keeping with the concept of an extended family. In nine cases of the variation there are also stepchildren or illegitimate children in the household, and in one an adopted child. In six cases, there are relatives of the woman present other than the mother. In one case, and in one case only, is there a relative of the man, and the reason for this is because his wife died in her first childbirth. In two cases grandmother and grandchildren live together and in the remaining eighteen cases mothers and married daughters are living together in the same household. In all these eighteen cases there are three generations of the family in the same household. (In six cases where there is a relative in the household other than the mother, there is a married daughter as well.) We have had two informants who told us that at one time four generations lived together in the same household.

(c) THE MATRILOCAL TENDENCY

This ideal custom for married daughters to live with their Mum is not always easy to put into practice. Women in Ship Street have large families and it is not a physical possibility for all the married daughters to stay at home. Many of the houses are large, though decrepit, so it is possible to make some compromise. Mums who had the misfortune to be bombed out and were rehoused in flats come off particularly badly as it is obviously not possible to cram nearly so many people into a flat as into a house. The compromise necessitated by both these snags is made by the married daughters living as near as possible, preferably in the next house or flat, across the street, or 'just round the corner'. If, through circumstances outside their control, they are forced to live further away frequent and sometimes almost compulsive visiting results.

I have attempted to sum up the information obtained in the field about the nearness of residence of married sons and daughters to their mothers. This is rather difficult to present accurately for any one period of time as members of the household do change quite often. For example, a girl gets married and moves out with her husband. An older sister will then take the opportunity to move back. When she produces more children than the house can possibly hold she may move away again, and the other sister move back. 'Near' is defined as within five minutes' walk.

In 44 cases mother and married daughter live or have lived in the same household. In 32[1] cases mother and married daughter live or have lived within five minutes' walk. In 8 cases mother and married son live or have lived in the same household. In 8 cases mother and married son live or have lived within five minutes' walk.

It is interesting to note that in cases where married daughters are not living with or near their Mums some nearly insuperable obstacle exists. In five cases the mother had died before her daughter's marriage. In one case the only child was a son. In one, the informant ran away to become a prostitute and was disowned. In another, the girl married a coloured man against her mother's wishes. Today, in this particular family, even after twenty years, there is frequent visiting between mother and daughter although they live some distance apart. This woman's married sisters all live in the same street as the mother. In another case, the daughter ran away at the age of fourteen because her mother married again and she hated her stepfather.

It is likely that many of the married daughters now reported as living near Mum would, in fact, be living with her if it were not for slum clearance and the effects of bombing.

From this evidence it can surely be safe to say that the pattern of life in Ship Street is matrilocal. Chapter IV deals in detail with the power of the Mum. This is really so far-reaching that it is perfectly justifiable to call this a mother-dominated group, if such a label were considered to be useful.

(d) ILLUSTRATIONS FROM FAMILY RECORDS

In order to demonstrate the complexity of relations and the persistence of family ties, both of which tend to get lost in

[1] These figures do not, of course, add up to 61 as many families contain more than one married daughter living at home.

purely enumerative data, three family units will be presented in detail. These have been chosen to illustrate how the tie to the Mum persists although housing arrangements are different.

In Family No. 6, the tie can be seen persisting for several generations. When Mrs. S. got married she took her husband home to live with her parents. 'As the children came along' (she had 14) she was forced to move. When her eldest child, Mrs. X., got married, she repeated exactly the same pattern. She took her husband home to live with her mother, Mrs. S., who was now a widow, despite the fact that Mrs. S. had all her unmarried children still living with her. Mrs. X.'s youngest brothers, twins, were only four years old at the time. As Mrs. X's children came along, she again was forced to move. She moved near her mother. Eventually Mrs. S. handed her house over to her married daughter, Mrs. X., who returned to it, while Mrs. S. herself went back to live with her yet older Mum, taking her only unmarried child, a son, with her. When this boy got married he brought his wife home. Thus three generations lived together. When his first child was born it made four. Now returning to Mrs. X.'s household, she has succeeded in doing what nearly all the women in Ship Street want to do, that is to have her married daughters bring their husbands and children back to her house. During the five years we have known this family, the eldest daughter has twice taken her husband and children away because of overcrowding and the unhealthy dampness of the house, but has always come back on some pretext. The last time she returned the pretext was that her husband had changed his job and now worked too far away to get home at nights. In fact his work was about half an hour's journey from home and he usually did come home at night.

Her second daughter went to live with her husband's family on her marriage, but in her own words, was 'looking for an excuse' to return to her mother's home. She found it four months later. She moved back while her husband was at sea. On his return he joined her there.

Even Mrs. X.'s second son, who left home on his marriage, returned without his wife six months later, saying he was going to stay at home till he and his wife could find a house. She is an orphan so she went to live with an aunt.

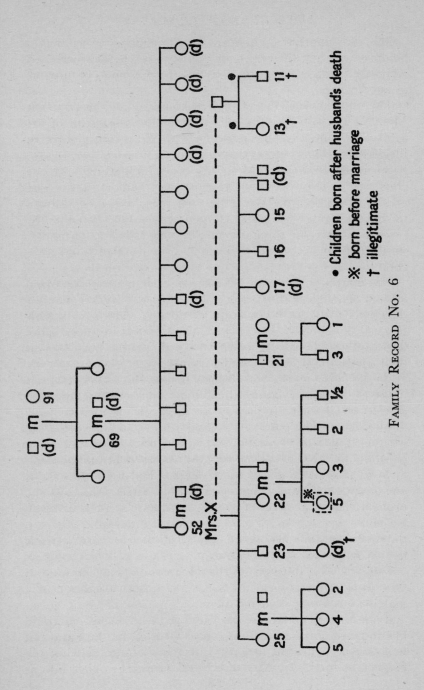

FAMILY RECORD No. 6

• Children born after husband's death

※ born before marriage

† illegitimate

Mrs. X.'s unmarried children are all members of her household except when the eldest son is away on seasonal work and when the younger boys are away at reform schools of one sort or another.

The only unusual factor in this household is the fact that Mrs. X. had two illegitimate children after the death of her husband. While it is quite usual for Ship Street girls to have an illegitimate child before marriage, it is unusual for this to happen after marriage. Mrs. X.'s second daughter had one child before marriage and married the man when she was expecting his second. Her eldest son has had a child by a member of Family No. 18. It is interesting to note that Mrs. X. refused to have anything to do with this baby or its mother until the baby died. The two families then united to give it a good funeral.

The matriarch in Family No. 52 has her relatives arranged around her slightly differently. She does not have her married daughters living at home, but all, in fact, within call. One married daughter lives next door, two opposite, and two more live together a few doors further down the street. They all visit their mother daily and spend a considerable amount of time at the old lady's house. She is one of the most martinet of Mums in this group. One evening when all her married daughters and a selection of their children were there she decided to have music. She would point at a child who would have to sing whether it wanted to or not.

More unrelated people come to this household than is usual as Mrs. Y. is an unofficial moneylender. Because of this she is one of the two leading characters in Ship Street. Although she probably has quite a bit of money she does not use it to make her house, her actions, or food and clothes differ from others in the street. To some extent she epitomizes the Ship Street desire to have more of what you know.

Family No. 39 differs from the other two in being Protestant. One point of interest in this one is the forlorn condition of a male who is being pushed out of one matrilocal family group and not fully accepted into another. Mr. A., a widower, would like to marry Mrs. B., who is separated from her husband but who has been unable to get a divorce. Because of what the neighbours might say Mrs. B.'s mother refuses to have him as

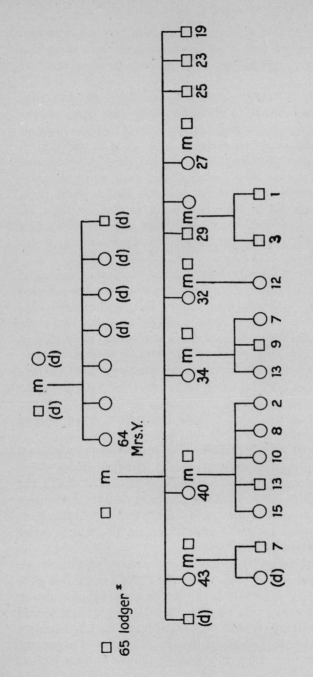

FAMILY RECORD No. 52

* Mrs. Y's mother's friend's son

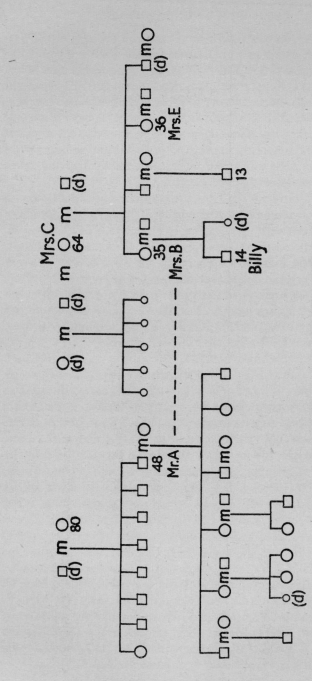

Family Record No. 39

a lodger in her house where she lives with Mrs. B. and Mrs. B.'s son Billy. He goes round immediately after work and has his evening meal there. The only meal he has in his own house is breakfast. Gradually his daughters have married, brought their husbands home and produced children. Mr. A. was moved out of his bedroom one day when he was out at work and put into an extremely uncomfortable back room. Some of his things such as a prized piano have been sold and altogether he is shown that he is unwanted in his own home. His daughters go so far as to refuse to cook for him.

Mr. A.'s position is an extremely interesting illustration of the matrilocal tendencies of the group. As a courting male he should be prepared to go into his prospective wife's household. This he wants to do but is prevented for the reason mentioned above. He has lost his footing with his own family who are absorbed in setting up matrilocal systems of their own. While his wife was alive of course this difficulty did not arise, although she was so tied to her mother that Mr. A. once said, 'I couldn't take me wife to the pictures without taking me mother-in-law. I might as well have taken her to bed with me.'

The other outstanding fact in this record is the way in which Mrs. B.'s mother, Mrs. C., has managed to prevent any of her children having a happy married life. Somehow she always stopped any of them marrying the person he or she really wanted to marry. At present she is making Mr. A. and Mrs. B.'s situation much more difficult than necessary, and at the same time making trouble between Billy and Mrs. B., mainly by telling Billy not to take any notice of his mother and not to tell her things. Her main goal in life appears to be to keep all her relatives tied to herself. Any attempts they make to find other relationships even among themselves are foiled with considerable skill. Her elder daughter, Mrs. E., is unhappily married and lives in the same street. Mother and daughter see each other daily and spend a great deal of time together. Mrs. C. frequently visits Mrs. E. to watch her television. When Mrs. C. is not on speaking terms with her daughter, Mrs. B., Mrs. E. dare not speak to her sister, Mrs. B., in her mother's presence, although both sisters are very fond of each other. The married life of Mrs. C.'s son, Mr. F., has broken up on more than one occasion. He has always then homed to his Mum.

The main points which emerge out of these three records will now be enumerated. They will come up time after time in the field work report and are, in fact, the foci of Ship Street family relations.

The first characteristic which emerges clearly in this group is the central figure of the Mum. Whatever her personal qualities she is the focus of all the family activities. Entrenched in a house, in many cases taken over from her mother, she rules her family through techniques suited to her own personality.

Secondly, because of her dominant position in the family she is able to manipulate the external world around her. If her house or flat will not hold her family, then she sees to it that they get houses or flats as near to her as possible. As she is the holder of the rent book and deals with the rent collector she generally manages to achieve this. A large settled family, spread over the street, is less likely to 'flit' without payment, and usually behaves satisfactorily from the point of view of the landlord.

Thirdly, the married daughters acquiesce to this domination. Outside the radius of their mother's influence they are helpless. Their husbands accept their often uncomfortable fate as this is what has always happened and change is suspect.

Fourthly, the last case, that of Mr. A., shows the anomalous fate of an individual in this group who comes out of his institutional setting. In Ship Street people must play their traditional roles, because owing to the rigidity of the culture pattern alternative ones are unthinkable. Mention of the psychological aspects of this hypothesis will be made in the section on projection tests.

CHAPTER III

THE ENVIRONMENT

(A) THE TIE TO THE LOCALITY

VISITORS from the country or other more desirable areas can see no reason why anyone should feel any tie to the Ship Street locality. The inhabitants, however, do not appear to feel like this. With surprising uniformity they say that they do not want to leave the neighbourhood. The streets consist of rows of dreary terrace houses which were once occupied by more prosperous tenants. Originally well-built they are now somewhat derelict through lack of repair. There was much bomb damage in the area so here and there are gaps used by the children as playgrounds. Blocks of flats are being built and these streets are gradually being demolished. However, many Mums prefer to stay in their houses, although only two or three rooms may be usable owing to damp. Fifty out of the sixty-one families have been in the neighbourhood all their lives.

Before considering the tie to the locality it was necessary to ascertain whether it was possible for the people to move if they wanted to. When houses are in short supply people may have to stay in a neighbourhood which they would be only too glad to leave. In our sixty-one families only three expressed what could be called a genuine desire to move. For example, Mrs. L. said she would be very glad to get out of this house. She would go wherever she could get a house. She would welcome a house in a housing estate with a garden. She would love to have a garden for the children. It would be so good for them to have somewhere they could play and not have to play in the streets.

Two other families express what might be called half-hearted desires to move. In theory it would be nice but in fact it would be too far from work or too expensive. These reasons may be genuine but on the other hand they could be rationalizations. In general, however, it appears that overcrowding, condemned houses, bombing and a host of other inconveniences are not enough to shift a family out of the neighbourhood once it has dug in. The most interesting fact arising out of this is that it is not because of friends or human relations in general that the family wishes to remain. The reason seems to be a vague un-differentiated feeling of belonging and the security of moving around in a well-known territory. This may well be an example of Katz's[1] personal space. The following examples illustrate this feeling.

Mrs. E. said her husband had been offered a better job with more pay, but it would mean his being away a good bit, so he has turned down the job. He would have spent a good bit of time in another northern town. 'So it would mean his having two homes.' Mrs. E. told me she would not move 'far from this neighbourhood'. She had been offered a house in a housing estate, but she would not take it. She would not be happy there. Her husband would move, 'but then he'd be out all day'. She refused. I asked Mrs. E. if she has a lot of friends in this neighbourhood. She replied, 'Not particular. I don't make friends with all. I go to Mrs. F.'s yard sometimes.' I asked her what tied her then to the neighbourhood. She repeated: 'I've always lived in this neighbourhood!'

Mrs. S. was born in a nearby street. She has always lived in this neighbourhood. She hopes when these houses are pulled down they will put up some flats instead, and that they will get one. She wouldn't like to leave the neighbourhood. Yet she has no friends here and is not on friendly or visiting terms with her neighbours. She said: 'They are a rough lot; we keep to ourselves. We keep our front door shut.' On being pressed she said she has no friends who come round to her home and she visits no one except her brothers and sisters and that when you are a large family you haven't the time or need for friends. She sees her brothers and sisters frequently. 'I never go out except to see my relations.' In order to see how far she extended this category, I started talking about the new tenement flats in which her husband's brother and his family live. She said: 'To tell you the truth, I have only been in their kitchen.' She very evidently

[1] David Katz, *Animals and Men*, Penguin Books, London, 1955.

does not include her husband's relatives in her frequent visits. From Mrs. S.'s conversation there seems to be one exception to this 'no friends'. She says that the old lady who was their tenant is very fond of Barbara. Every Sunday Barbara now goes to visit her in St. X.'s Home, and when the weather is better in the summer she expects the old lady will come up to visit them. However it was clear that Mrs. S. does not really regard this old lady as a friend, and that other factors enter into these duty visits.

Mr. T., Mrs. N. and Jill all love the country and feel they would like to live in it. Mr. T. nearly bought a caravan once in which he thought he would like to live when he retires, but Mrs. T. was dead against it. She loathes moving. 'We came into this house when I was 13 [she's now 39] and I remember me mother saying you will have to carry me out in a box. Me mother's only lived in three houses all her life.'

The general picture is that each family has for two generations lived in this small cluster of streets. In many cases the present tenant has taken over the house from her mother. The house is usually alluded to as 'me mother's house' although it is in fact rented. The following statements are typical of the group. Mrs. W. told us that although she has only been 13 years in this house, she has lived 30 years in this neighbourhood. Before, they lived in a smaller house lower down the street. Mrs. L. said they have always lived in this neighbourhood, although they have done a bit of moving. They lived in X. Street—from where they were bombed out, and in two other houses in the same street.

In cases where the woman has married a foreigner the situation is slightly different. The man usually wishes to take his children home and the woman either identifies herself with this wish or else refuses to move, saying the man will go alone if he does.

Mr. and Mrs. Y. both said that when the boys are older Mr. Y. intends taking them 'home' and settling them there as it is a much better life. He said, nodding his head in his wife's direction, 'She won't go.' Mrs. Y. said this is a fact. He went on to tell me that he could get a good job in Australia with their passages paid but his wife won't go. But better than this, his father's brother has a large farm in East Kenya. He is a very old man and he wants to hand over to Mr. Y. He has no one else to leave the farm to on his death, and he would leave it to Mr. Y., but again his wife won't go. Mrs. Y. said, 'Leave England? No.' When I asked her why, she seemed amazed at my question and merely repeated her former remark. I asked her if she did not think it would be worth trying if living conditions were so much better. She replied she could never settle in a foreign country. Her parents are dead and one brother is the only member of her family whom she sees, but she will not leave England. In answer to my further question as to whether she has many friends here with whom she is on visiting terms, she replied in the negative.

It may be significant that in these families where there is doubt as to which country constitutes home, the incidence of personality deviations leading to crime is particularly high.[1] Perhaps many of the difficulties which occur in international marriages arise because the family lacks the security of its personal space.

There are no comparative data obtained from a group of a higher social class and with more education. If there were it might be that the urge for this type of security might be obtained through associations in work and recreation which are not based on the family. Perhaps where these are lacking, security can only be acquired in its more primitive form, e.g. in the personal space around the centre of the primary group, that is the Mum.

(B) HOUSES AND RENT

I have just pointed out that the houses in Ship Street are decrepit and dreary, though sometimes the people try to alleviate this by paint. Thirty-eight of the families live in these houses, eighteen live in flats and five in rooms. It is likely that more will be moved to flats as the Ship Street houses fall under slum clearance schemes. In fact, several of the families now living in flats were in houses at the beginning of the work. The rent of these dwellings varies considerably. The question of rent

[1] Two out of these three families have children in reform schools. The woman in the other case has committed several crimes and one of her children raids shops but has not yet been caught.

was not pressed as it was not relevant to the enquiry. Where information was offered it was recorded.

Rents can be conveniently grouped as follows. Twenty-three households pay between 7 to 12 shillings per week, 8 pay 13 to 18 shillings per week, 20 pay 19 to 24 shillings a week, 2 pay between 25 and 27, and 1 pays 40 shillings a week.

Household incomes in this group vary enormously. One household where several members are working gets a combined income of about £30 a week. Others are down to £4 or £5. There are about three cases of genuine hardship. The interesting thing is, that however large the income, saving is impossible and everyone is broke by the end of the week.

The state of the premises occupied by a family does vary considerably. Only in three cases were the rooms physically distasteful through dirt or smell. The others tended to be reasonably clean and sometimes very clean. Little money is spent on making the home more comfortable to live in, though in some cases a parlour is kept for ritual occasions. However, in many cases the parlour has to be put into more mundane use to accommodate a married daughter who has homed to Mum plus her own family. Suites bought on the cheque system are appreciated but do not appear to have the high status value that they do with a slightly higher class.

Frequently, several rooms in a house are out of use owing to damp, the ceiling having collapsed and caused general disrepair. Few houses have electric light. Most have gas, though one or two still use oil lamps. Most, too, have only cold water taps. In one case, water has to be brought from a tap in the yard. The flats, being newer, are of course better equipped and most have bathrooms.

An attempt was made to find out how long the people had been tied to the locality. Fifty out of the sixty-one households report that they have always lived in the neighbourhood. That amounts to 83·6%.

We next tried to find out more exactly how long this was. In 40 cases the parents of both the man and woman in the households had been born in Liverpool. In 13 cases this was so for the woman's parents only. In 1 case the parents of the man only had been born in Liverpool. In 7 cases the parents of both came from elsewhere.

Again, the length of time people have lived in their houses or flats gives some idea of their tie or otherwise to the neighbourhood. Six households have had their present residence from 1 to 5 years, 5 from 6 to 10 years, 14 from 11 to 15 years, 4 from 16 to 20 years, 3 from 21 to 25 years, 3 from 31 to 50 years. 'A very long time' was the only answer which 7 households were able to give.

Quite often when questions are asked about the house the informant will say proudly, 'It was me Mum's house.' In this group 12 out of 61, that is 19·6%, made this claim. Two only said the house had been their father's. Again, this percentage of women taking over their mothers' houses would have been much higher if it had not been for slum clearance and bombing. Only those people at present living in houses inherited from their Mums have been counted.

The general picture, then, is one of people who dislike change; who cling together in small groups of blood relatives; who have lived in the neighbourhood for many years and in the town for at least two generations.

(c) SHIP STREET AND ITS NEIGHBOURS

Although, as we have seen, Ship Street is considered a highly desirable place to live by the inhabitants, this view is not held by people in other areas of the city. These people frequently make their opinions heard in the local press.

These vigorously expressed complaints are generally about delinquency, vandalism and, in general, the low and degraded habits of the people who live there. As Lloyd Warner pointed out in the *Structure of American Life*:[1]

'Their (the lower lower class) reputation for criminality often is no more than the projected fantasy of those above them; as such they become a collective symbol of the community's unconscious' (p. 7).

In short, Ship Street is the type of area which acts as an irresistible draw to social reformers. Unfortunately these people do not realize that they are dealing with a somewhat different culture pattern from their own. Therefore they do not make much headway, because just as they deplore the habits of Ship

[1] Lloyd Warner, *Structure of American Life*, Edinburgh, 1952.

Street people, so Ship Street people tend to be highly suspicious of them. At the worst they are regarded as interfering agents of the police, at the best a good comic turn.

The isolation of people into groups of blood relations with little contact with the general population is dealt with in Chapter IX. The main point to be emphasized here is that their lack of contact with people other than relatives naturally makes their relations both to the individuals, and to social institutions of the surrounding people, somewhat tenuous.

This isolation from the more general ideas and ways of the town is reinforced by the fact that the majority of the people are catholics. They are, therefore, already subject to two differing types of social control, one set of legal and ethical ideas being held by the state, and the other by the Church. It is, therefore, no new thing for them to be faced with conflicting ideals.[1]

Ship Street, then, is looked down upon by its neighbours. As the people have their social life in family groups the usual contact with people outside the immediate neighbourhood tends to be lacking. People from outside are frightened to go there at night, while Ship Street women, in their turn, will only leave the safety of their streets when accompanied by at least one other woman, nearly always a relative.

(D) WORK

The 61 Ship Street families contain 120 adult males. Of these 37 are dockers, 27 sailors, 11 factory workers, 9 builders, 6 scalers, 5 drivers, 4 old age pensioners, 3 labourers in shops, 2 are unemployed, 2 do casual work in hotels, 2 are fruit porters, and 2 are in prison. Other occupations with one representative are pipe layer, dance band musician, fireman, window cleaner, coalman, linesman, post office, cabinet maker, blacksmith's striker and one is disabled.

The boys in between 18 and 20 are of course doing National Service. Twelve of the boys below this age are in Borstal or some other approved school. Only one girl is in an approved

---

[1] This book is obviously not the place to discuss these discrepancies. Anyone interested will find an excellent description by Paul Blanchard in *The Irish and Catholic Power*; also by comparing *The Pope and the People*, Pope Leo XIII, Catholic Truth Society, London, 1950.

school. It is perhaps interesting to note here that the post office worker is climbing out of the group. He owns and reads books and is able to save money.

A similar classification of the women's jobs is not really possible. With two exceptions the men wish to work and dread unemployment. The older men remember the slump of the thirties and dread anything of this nature happening again. The women's attitude to work is quite different. None of them are interested in it, they do not form the work associations and produce the loyalties to their mates as the men do. When a girl leaves school she takes the first job she can get. This is frequently in a sack factory, or as a tailor's apprentice or some blind alley type of work. She changes the job frequently, often several times a year. Adolescent boys do this too, but this phase is finished for them when they come back from the army. The girl continues in this way until marriage. In Ship Street there was only one unmarried woman of over 25 and she had adopted children. Marriage is, therefore, an almost inevitable step.

After marriage the women work only when they need money. If the man is out of work or if they want something in particular, they will take a job for a short time. So long as they are not in the later stages of pregnancy this is possible as there is nearly always some other female relative to look after the other children. These older women take cleaning jobs generally, or help in restaurants, or laundries. As soon as the immediate need for money has passed they give up. Again there is one exception, a woman who is forewoman at a laundry. She is one of the very few in this group who is interested in status.

(E) RECREATION

The neighbourhood provides all the usual recreational facilities of a large town, e.g. cinemas, dance halls, pubs, a park about one mile away from Ship Street, and the possibility of visits to the river banks near the docks about three miles away. Adults are interested mainly in the pubs and cinemas but the children avail themselves freely of all the amenities. The children visit the cinema very frequently, generally at least two or three times a week. In the summer some organization often takes them to a holiday camp or even abroad. One child got as far as Austria last year. On the nights they are not at the cinema there are several play centres, both lay and church, for them. They also go to the parks and to the swimming baths. Here are some typical examples.

Bill, aged 11, goes to the pictures every evening except Tuesdays and Thursdays, when he goes to the Play Centre. His mother gives him the money to go to the pictures. He had a mate, Jimmy, with whom he used to go to the pictures, only Jimmy expected him to pay for him. His mother did in fact often give him the money for Jimmy too.

Joan, aged 12, continues to be mad about the pictures and to return late from them and to cause her parents anxiety. Her mother said, 'I have no objection to her going to the first house, but she always sits the picture through twice.' The other evening it was eleven before she got home. 'Her father went out to look for her.' She goes with Maggie, but Maggie comes home after the first house. A year later Joan's father complained 'Joan now goes to the pictures every evening. Me wife and I try to stop her but we cannot.' Joan earns the money to go to the pictures by running errands for people in the street.

Ruth, aged 14, with her mate Diana, aged 16, who has already left school, called in to see us on their way to the park. There is a fair on in the park. They were hoping to be picked up by boys and were really out cadging for cigarettes.

Both sisters came in from school. Their mother had their tea ready for them. As soon as Dorothy aged 10 had drunk one cup of tea and eaten a sugar bun and an Eccles cake she asked her mother for the money to go to the swimming baths and tried to take it out of her mother's purse but was stopped. As soon as Dorothy got the money she was off. Her mother said she loves swimming. Her sister Jean, however, only a year younger, doesn't like going to the baths. When her mother suggested it was time she went she said she didn't want to go. Her mother persuaded her and, in a final effort to escape, Jean turned at the door and warned, 'I'll get nits in my hair.' Her mother replied, 'All right, then, if you do, I'll take them out for you.'

Adolescents, too, use what facilities the neighbourhood has to offer. For instance Enid, aged 19, usually goes to the pictures twice a week, on Mondays and then again at the end of the week when the picture changes.

They use the dance halls and also the dances run by the local church. They go to dances with a friend of the same sex whom they call 'mate' and then dance with any boy they meet at the dance hall who comes up and asks them to dance. They say they do not feel so tied to the same partner in this way.

Molly, aged 20, with an illegitimate baby, is mad on dancing. Sometimes when Marian, aged 22, sees her sister getting ready to go to a dance she is envious. Molly says, 'Well, I didn't tell you to get married.' Marian used to be very keen on dancing too, but she and her husband never go dancing now they are married. Before their mother, Mrs. W., married, she also loved dancing. She gave it up after marriage.

It is interesting that just a year later this is what Molly had to say of her younger sister when Molly in turn had got married and given up dancing.

'Sue is now mad on dancing. You remember how mad I was on it? Well you wouldn't believe it but Sue's got it just as bad. She goes dancing every Saturday. There's a new dance come out since I used to go—it goes like this—you should see Sue doing it! Sue goes with her mate Joy just round the corner. A year ago both Sue and Joy were at school and Sue was a blushing, clumsy, unwilling dancer when she used to get up to perform to us.'

Dancing is extremely popular with the girls until marriage, when it is dropped at once. Reference will be made to this in the chapter on 'Marriage'. Boys do not appear to be so keen on dancing for itself. They go to the dance halls to pick up girls and dancing is generally an excuse for this and for petting on the way home. As the roles they can play towards women appear to be limited to those of courting or being relatives it can be seen that they would be suspicious if their wives wished to dance after marriage. For the adolescent girls dancing is a pleasurable activity for its own sake and steps are tried out and practised with mates and a high standard of proficiency is reached. As dancing stops at marriage it means the loss of another group activity which was not restricted to members of the family. For boys, going to football matches and hanging around at street corners appears to have a somewhat similar social function.

The women after marriage seem to do little else in the way of recreational activities except visit members of the family or be visited by them. The men do little more except go to football. Both go to the pub, some regularly and some occasionally. Football pools form an important part of the men's lives and women often do them too. Mrs. G. told me on one occasion that her husband spends 3s. a day on football pools. She can't stop him. Last week he lost 10s. He has won as much as £15. Mr. G. is a football fan. He goes to watch football matches every Saturday —this may well be for his pools. When he was a sailor he used to play for Buenos Aires when there. When at home Mrs. G. said he reads and does his football pools all day. He hardly ever speaks.

A visit a year later to this household when Mr. G. was in a much better job, got this information from Mrs. G.:

'I think sometimes he now spends as much as 10s. a day on gambling, but I don't ask him.'

One old lady of 64 when asked if they manage to save at all, replied, laughing heartily:

'Don't be silly, as long as there is a horse with a leg to stand up on, my husband will back it.'

One very interesting fact has emerged and that is the distinction made between pools, horses and gambling games. The first two are not considered to be gambling. A man will say he never gambles, but if asked if he does the pools, will say, 'Oh yes.' He just does not connect pools with gambling. The following series of excerpts illustrates this. Peggy, the informant, is aged 12.

30.11.52. 'Me mother takes three tickets every week, one in me father's name, one in her own name and one in aunty's name.' I asked Peggy if her mother had ever won anything in this football pool. She replied, 'No, but me mother says you are bound to win one day.' Mr. and Mrs. T. also put money on horses sometimes.

15.3.53. Peggy told us that her father had caught her playing a gambling game called 'toss' with the boys in the street last week. He had given her a thorough beating and told her that if he caught her gambling again 'he would break me legs and fingers'. Her father takes a serious view of her playing gambling games whereas pools and backing horses is regarded as usual for the parents. I asked Peggy if she ever makes any money. She replied that she made 2s. 6d. last week and that the boys do pay up when they lose.

29.3.53. A fortnight later Peggy announced, 'I won 7s. 6d. at toss last week!'

Although Peggy and her friend Betty admit to playing 'toss' neither admits to playing a game called 'bang out'. While they think 'toss' is all right they think the other isn't. The reason seems to lie in the fact that 'bang out' is played for higher stakes and almost exclusively by boys.

Thus the children, like their parents, make distinctions between different sorts of gambling.

It is not hard to see how this habit of gambling grows in early childhood. Here is an excerpt from another Family Record: Mary, aged 11, was absorbed in her Rorschach. Suddenly she stopped, looked at the clock and said with urgency, 'I must run an errand for me Dad. I'll be back in two minutes.' It was 2.20 p.m. and she had instructions to put 2s. on a horse for her father with a bookmaker round the corner in X. street. She had been given the money. The bet had to be on by 2.30 p.m. She had her little sister Mildred, not yet 5, with her. She tried to leave Mildred with me. Mildred howled. Mary picked Mildred up and ran from the house. She returned out of breath but beaming, still carrying Mildred. The bet had been made in time. When asked what would happen if she had forgotten, she said, 'He'd shout.'

In general adult recreation does not show any great variety. Men go to football matches as spectators, though at times young men play. Some of the pubs run their own teams. In the evenings the men go to the pub generally on their own during the week, on Friday or Saturday they may take their wives. Women tend to go with another woman. Two women who would almost certainly never visit each other's home will meet night after night at the pub for a glass of beer. Two old ladies in this group have done this every night for twenty years. It is more general for people to go to the pub with non-relatives, the only instance of this choice of company found in this group. Except for the pub outings the following quotation illustrates the only entertainment the women have outside the family circle.

Mrs. M. said she sometimes goes to 'matinees' at the pictures because she can take the baby with her. She used to go to the pictures every Monday and then again on Thursday when there was the change of programme and she used to take Mary and

Dolly with her—'and we used to go every Sunday', Mary reminded, and Mrs. M. agreed. Mary said she is not really very fond of the pictures. These visits to the pictures are now Mrs. M.'s only outings except for shopping and errands.

Although the Catholic Church offers many associations for its members, these people do not seem to belong, or if they do belong, they do not go very much. The children take part in activities which lead them into groups, but the parents only use the facilities such as cinemas, pubs or football matches in which the individual can either be solitary or just one unit in a crowd. Human relations except on a superficial level, seem to be confined to the family as soon as the individual is married.

(f) HEALTH

The Ship Street person's relations with the police and the social services tends to be one of avoidance. Even the Catholic Church is unable to hold their attention for long away from their intensive family life. However, as everyone has to be born and die and generally gets ill at some time or other, contact with the health services is inevitable. Therefore a short section on health will serve to illustrate the Ship Street people's attitude to health.

As might be expected from the environmental conditions the health of this group is not very good. Just as it is quite usual for one child to be at an approved school, so it is similarly common for one or more members of the family to be in hospital.

Mary, aged 11, told me that she has rheumatism and that sometimes she has very bad pains at the back of her legs. She said, 'We all have rheumatism, it's our damp house.' The very first day she came to tea with us she told us her mother was ill with a very bad pain in her neck, it must be rheumatism. Mary says their house is very damp. Sometimes you can see the water trickling down the walls—especially in their bedrooms.

Birth is included in this section because in this group it generally necessitates an inconvenient visit to the hospital. Most mothers have their first baby in hospital. Whether they go again for subsequent children depends on home circumstances. In many cases where the mother-daughter tie is particularly strong the daughter will prefer to remain at home with her

35

mother in attendance. Among the older generation it was the custom for some old woman in the street to act as an unofficial midwife. This custom is now dying out. The following quotation is about one of these old women who kept her daughter at home. This incident took place twelve years ago.

Mrs. B. brought a bed down into the front parlour for her daughter's confinement. She and Mrs. F.'s elder sister, Gertie, remained present throughout labour, which lasted about sixteen hours. Only right at the end after Lily was born did Mrs. B. run from the room. 'She was born with a veil over her head and me mother thought she was dead.' Mrs. F. heard her mother telling her father that the baby was dead. At that moment she was past caring. Her sister knitted herself a pair of gloves in the time. Her needles were flying to quieten her nerves. Her sister has never had any children. Her comment at the end was, 'If that's having children you can keep them.' The nurse did not arrive till after the baby was born. Gertie went for the doctor who was present at the birth. Mr. F. was in the yard crying. Mrs. F. said that her mother had acted as midwife at many a birth. The neighbours used to send for her when labour started. She remembers once when she was a child she was sent to stay with an aunt for a night. When she came back 'there was a baby in me bed'. It was another aunt's child and she had come to her sister's, Mrs. B.'s home, to have it. When a cousin of hers was expecting a difficult confinement, Mrs. B. went to her.

Among the children, respiratory complaints are fairly common. Some families have a child in a sanatorium and others state that children have spent long periods in hospital and at convalescent homes following pleurisy or pneumonia. The following is typical: Teresa, aged 14, goes to a school for delicate children. Teresa has a weak chest and has always had a lot of trouble with it. She has to go into hospital from time to time 'to have the fluid drained away'. She has just returned from hospital. There is a big scar on her back where the incision is made. Teresa looks healthy, though she's rather gentler than most Ship Street children of her age.

Besides illness the children are very prone to accidents. Their playgrounds are streets or bombed sites so that falling off walls, etc., is common. Here is a bulletin with which the field worker was greeted after being out of the field for some weeks.

The moment June saw me she announced, 'Muriel broke her thumb, Mick broke his thumb and I've been to hospital and had five stitches in me leg and Sam has his leg in plaster.' Muriel had hit a boy and bent her thumb back and hurt it. A boy of 5 threw a slate at June and it cut her leg badly. The same boy had previously cut her head with a slate he had thrown. Everybody is now better.

If a group of children come to visit the investigators, some are always bandaged. Accidents range in severity from cuts and bruises to broken legs and backs.

The following diseases are reported from the 61 families during the investigation (they include members of the family and people included in the household):

Tuberculosis, deafness, constant headaches, cancer, duodenal ulcer, varicose veins, ulcers or abscesses, operations on throat, teeth out, lumbago, bad eyes, pain in ribs, dropsy, diabetes, fibrous uterine growths, kidney inflammation, ear trouble, rheumatic fever, operation on side, eczema, insanity.

These vague diagnoses are as much as the people themselves know.

The following excerpt illustrates the mixed attitudes the mothers have towards the doctors' advice and the hospitals. If the advice goes against the mother's inclinations she just doesn't take it.

Mrs. F. retold me in detail his birth and her illness. She herself was really ill when she came out of hospital. Soon after, her husband got a ship and went to sea. 'He needn't have gone and left me and the baby. He said he had to go or he would be put in jail, but that wasn't true.' Then the baby got ill and she took him to a children's hospital. A doctor 'with a walrus moustache' said he had gastro-enteritis and he must come in but she refused to leave him. She took him for treatment every day but he didn't seem to get any better. It was an awful winter. So she told the doctor she would leave him in. He said he was sorry but they hadn't a bed now. Then she rushed up to another hospital. The matron there had a look at the baby and said, 'Mother do you know the baby is critically ill?' She replied that she knew it, they had made him like that at the other hospital, they had kept giving him injections. They kept the baby in and immediately 'put him on the drip'—i.e. he was

fed intravenously. When she saw this she knew he was danger-
ously ill. She used to go up every day. Then on Christmas Eve
when she was bathing and putting Sheila and Vera to bed a
policeman walked in and told her they had a message for her
from the hospital. Her baby had collapsed. She ran into
'Nancy's next door' and told her and asked her to put S. and V.
to bed. 'Then I ran down to Chinatown and shouted, taxi,
taxi, like a mad woman. I saw a great big fat woman getting
into one. I grabbed her by the collar and jumped into the taxi
myself and told the man quick! the hospital. The woman was
so surprised she said nothing. The driver said he didn't know if
he could drive to the hospital, it was foggy. I said my baby
is dying. I'll direct you. I sat on the edge of the seat saying,
right, left, right, left. I didn't know what I was saying. I didn't
know the way but I got there. I jumped out of the taxi and ran
in the back way across the lawn, the quickest way into the ward
where my baby was. A nurse said, "What are you doing here?"
I pushed her out of the way. When I saw my baby I was
hysterical. I couldn't help it, I didn't know what I was doing.
I was mad. The matron took me away. My baby was not in the
ward where I had last seen him. He was in a great big cold
place with all glass windows. He did not have gastro-enteritis.
He got cold and caught pneumonia. He died of pneumonia. I
know he died of pneumonia. When I had recovered a little I
went home. I went by bus and trams and got lost and walked
a long way. It was Christmas Eve and everyone was happy. I
met the Vicar of the church where the children were baptized.
He was out for a walk with his huge big dog. I said, "My
baby's gone." He said, "Where's it gone?" I said, "He's dead."
He came in with me with his great big dog and all, and we sat
in the kitchen and he said prayers over the kitchen table.'

An extension of the tie to the locality can be seen in the wish
of Ship Street people to die at home. Although this may entail
almost insupportable hardship for the rest of the household a
person's right to do this is never questioned. The patient says
that he will die if taken away and in face of this attitude and
the overcrowded state of the hospitals, doctors do not always
insist. The Mum, supported by daughters if she has any, does
the nursing besides her usual chores. In one case the bedclothes
had to be burned each day, newspaper in the end being used as

a substitute. This attitude is probably more common among the older people and bound up with fear and superstition.

It is interesting to note that the men are more afraid of hospitals than the women. This may be partly due to the fact that most women go there for their first child, but it seems likely that there are deeper reasons for this. The man's attitude is perhaps epitomized by the man who said:

'If I'm going to drop dead this minute, I'm not going to hospital.'

As might be expected, many superstitions about health exist, and the Mum is ready to believe in quack remedies. At times she will quote remedies which appear to be derived from peasant bush medicine. Some of the superstitions will be given in Chapter XII.

In matters of health, as in all other affairs, the Ship-Streeter's pivot is his home. He is born, nursed, brought up, cared for when sick, and eventually dies, under the supervision of the Mum.

CHAPTER IV

THE POWER OF THE MUM

(A) THE WOMAN'S TIE TO THE MUM

'I couldn't get on without me mother. I could get on without me husband. I don't notice him.'

This rather surprising statement made by a married woman of 39 with five children, epitomizes what the Mums in this area feel about the relative values of mothers and husbands.

In the same way this account of beatings by a child of 11 epitomizes what children feel about the relative values of mothers and fathers.

'When me father beats us we hide behind our Mum: when me mother beats us I run out on the street.' I deliberately misinterpreted and suggested, 'So your mother must beat you much harder, Vi?' 'Oh no,' came the spontaneous reply, 'me mother will protect us but me father won't.'

This feeling of the power of the Mum is often instilled into children at an early age by the mother herself. A child of 13 said:

'Me mother says, "You can get another father but you can't get another mother": and that's true, isn't it? You can't get another mother.' Ruth went on to say, that should her mother die and her father remarry she would run away from home and persuade her siblings to do the same. 'I would not have a stepmother.'

Two children of 15 said: 'Me mother always says, "If you steal from your mother you're no good to anyone."'— 'Me mother always says, "If you steal from your mother your hands will wither off you."'

In adult life the general pattern seems to be for a woman to take her husband home to live with her mother. The following quotations from the field notes illustrate this more vividly than any formalized account could do. When Mrs. R. married she asked her mother if she could bring her husband home. Her mother replied, 'You can please yourself but I don't want him.' After a fortnight's honeymoon Mrs. R. was back home with her husband and there they have remained ever since. She has never had nor wanted a home of her own. She has now been married 25 years and her husband and three surviving children are all members of her mother's home.

Mrs. B. said that when she married, 'I went straight back to me mother's home with me husband.' I asked if her husband hadn't wanted to take her away and start a home of their own. I asked what would have happened if he had forced a choice on her. She looked at me in amazement and said, 'My husband loved my mother. He said I couldn't have a better mother in the world.' Mrs. B. said she never would have left her mother as long as she lived. 'When she died I thought I would have died.' Other siblings, although married and with families, also remained in their parents' home. I asked Mrs. B. if she felt the same towards her father as she did towards her mother. She replied her father was all right: 'I mean to say he worked hard and kept us clean, but he drank. There is only one mother.' (A woman aged 53 who says of her marriage, 'My marriage is happy, my husband is good'.)

Here is a husband's experience who tried to break this general pattern, who wanted a home of his own. When Billy and Maureen first married, Billy got her a lovely home. One day he returned from work to find a removal van driving away from what looked like his house. He stopped the van and asked the men whose things they were moving. He learnt from them they were moving his own. His wife had ordered the van and given instructions. Billy went in and questioned his wife. She said, 'I'm going back to me mother. You can please yourself.' Billy returned with her. It's been like this throughout his married life. More than once he has attempted to set up a home with his wife and son alone; it's always ended in the same way. Either his wife has returned to her mother and he has eventually followed or else her mother has come and parked on them. On one occasion he tried to hold out. He refused to go to her mother's to live. He took their son and placed him with his married sister who had a daughter about the same age, while he himself returned to his own mother. He hoped his wife would come back to their home. She did not. In the end he fetched his son and joined his wife in her mother's home and there they are still.

This is what a married woman of 40 with two children, whose mother is a member of her husband's household, says of the strength of the tie:

'I always tell her when she goes (dies), I will not be long after.'

In the section on 'The Tie to the Locality' the generalized feeling of attachment to the place only was stressed. In the cases mentioned this appeared to be the main motivation. However, in some cases there is the fear of leaving the mother. In the following instance the woman's mother was tied to the locality and would not move even with her daughter to another place. Here is what the daughter's husband had to say. Mr. Y. told me that he doesn't really like this neighbourhood or house and wants to move. Twice it was nearly achieved but on both occasions Mrs. Y. ratted at the last moment. The first time he was offered a very nice house on a housing estate. His wife said she wanted to move and they went over the house. She liked it very much. As they were leaving the house 'she burst into tears and said she could never leave her mother'. Later he was offered a house somewhere else. His wife said she would like to see it. Again they went over it together and she was absolutely delighted with it. It was a lovely house, nicer than the other one and would have been very easy to run. His wife would have been saved a great deal of her present chores. When he returned from work a few days after, he could see that his wife had been crying. He asked her what was the matter. She replied, 'nothing'. He told her to come off it, he could see she had been crying. She told him she really liked the house at X. but she didn't want to move because she would have no friends there. Mr. Y. said he knew the truth was that she would not leave her mother. (A woman of 44 with six children, married twenty-six years. In spite of her tie to her mother, the husband said of his marriage, 'If I had me life again, I'd do the same thing again. I'd marry the same partner—mind you the same partner—at the same early age.')

(B) THE MAN'S TIE TO THE MUM

The man too is tied to his Mum, and in disputes between his wife and mother will tend to take his mother's side. In this group, it is not usual for a woman to live with her mother-in-law. It will be seen from the previous pages that the woman expects her husband to go to her mother's home. This feeling is so pronounced that one old lady said: 'A son married is a son lost.' Though another Mum went one better and greeted us with 'I've lost three'. Only on receiving our condolences did it become clear that these three were not dead but married. One of the 'lost' three, in fact, a daughter, was actually a member of her mother's household! In the few cases where the son does try to take his wife to his home, trouble invariably arises. The following instance illustrates this.

Mrs. Z.'s only child who was unmarried lived with her. David is 26 years old. He had an illegitimate baby but he didn't wish to marry the mother. She took him to court and got maintenance. D. wanted to contest the case and get custody of the baby, but the lawyer he went to told him he was unlikely to get it since he wasn't even married to the woman. Anyhow, it would be an expensive business, so he left it alone. The mother of his baby was one of a large family and lived with her parents. Her mother went out to work leaving her to do all the cooking, shopping and housework. One day she came to D. and told him she was fed up with her life and she had decided to go out into service. He could have the baby because she knew he would be good to her. D. told her he wanted her and married her. They had a quiet wedding last week, and he brought his wife and baby home to live with his mother. I asked Mrs. Z. if she was glad that D. had married the girl. She pulled a little face but both she and her daughter said there was no denying that the baby is D.'s—she's the image of him, and the girl is so pleased that D. has married her that she can't do enough for him. She waits on him hand and foot. 'She worships him' and the little baby May is sweet, but she cries all night and Mrs. Z. wishes they would go somewhere else to live. 'The girl is a fat lump of a girl and she's always cooking.' A later visit showed the following development. Nina, Mrs. Z.'s daughter-in-law, has got a 'legal separation'

43

from her husband, i.e. from Mrs. Z.'s son. He has to allow her
£2 a week for herself and child. Mrs. Z. was so impossible to
Nina that Nina had to go. She has gone to a relation very near
the Z. household, taking May, her daughter, with her. Her
husband, Mr. Z. identified with his mother in this row and
not with his wife. He did not go with his wife, but remained
with his mother. Now to get a respite from the whole affair he
has taken himself off to sea—it's ages since he's been at sea.
His wife Nina is expecting his second child. Even Mrs. Z.'s
daughters reported that their mother had been pretty impossible to Nina.

Quite a number of old ladies have what they call 'bachelor
sons' living with them. These men say they will never marry
so long as their mother is alive. One of our female informants
got engaged to such a son. Here is what she had to say about
him.

'I went with him for six years and then one day I found that
he thought more of his mother than he did of me because he
told me he would never get married while his mother was alive,
and so I said goodbye to him. It wasn't easy because I loved
him, and he was a Catholic.'

At times the situation can get extremely complex. In the
following instance the old lady, Mrs. D., aged 74, our informant, has both a married daughter and two bachelor sons
with competing claims. Mrs. H. married at 19. Her husband
was 20. Mrs. H. is now 33, her husband 34 this month. They
have five children but, as already recorded, the H.'s are no
longer members of this (Mrs. D.'s) household, except Albert,
aged 12, who still sleeps here. Mr. and Mrs. H. and their
other four children have moved to a 'luxury flat'. This household was overcrowded with the H.'s and their family, yet in
spite of this and the fact that Mr. and Mrs. H. had their names
down for ten years for another flat, both mother and daughter
regret the move. Joe (Mrs. D.'s bachelor son of 49) rationalized
this by saying: 'I think me sister finds the rent a bit heavy. It's
17s. 9d.'; Mrs. D. by saying that her daughter can no longer
go out to work as there is no one to mind the younger children.
Anyhow, soon after the H. family's departure, Mrs. D. joined
them in their new flat, taking Joe with her. Mrs. H. continued
to work, Mrs. D. continued to look after her grandchildren

and run Mrs. D.'s household for her. George alone (the other
bachelor son of 45) remained here. That was the snag. 'I had
to cook and carry his food to him every day.' This proved too
much for the old lady. 'I got a bit fed up so I came back.'
Joe returned with her. Then five weeks ago one after the other
of Mrs. H.'s children went down with 'flu. Mrs. H. at once
sent an S.O.S. to her mother; her mother at once moved in
again taking Joe with her. Mrs. H. appears to have continued
going to work while Mrs. D. nursed her grandchildren. The
old lady herself told me that Mr. H. helped look after the
children a great deal and that is how he also got 'flu. When I
asked, 'Oh he's good?' she replied, 'He's all right.' He continued to work when he had 'flu. Only when Sammy (one of
Mrs. H.'s children) was better did the doctor tell them that
Sammy had had pneumonia. The old lady finished her story
by saying: 'It's only this week I come back.' Joe, of course,
returned with her. When I said how fortunate I was to have
found her here today and that I supposed next time I called
she'd be away again, she said, 'I hope not. It's a bit too much
for me now.' Since her mother's return to her own flat, Mrs.
H. has had to give up going out to work.

If the bachelor son's work is in another town he will pay
frequent visits to his mother.

One man gets twenty-four hours off every week from Thursday evening to Friday evening when he has to be back at work.
He comes home to spend his day off with his mother every
week. He is not courting and has no girl.

Sunday evening is a time when married sons frequently
visit their mothers.

Married daughters, too, who do not live in the same house
as their Mums either move as near as possible or pay frequent
visits. In many cases these women come to see their Mums
every day. One takes a bus each night to say 'good night' if
she has been prevented from seeing her Mum in the day. This
daughter, aged 25, has since moved back into her mother's
household taking her husband and three children with her.

(C) ECONOMIC POWER OF THE MUM

Besides having this psychological power over the family the

Mum very frequently has economic power too. She expects her 'wages' every week, and will take measures to see that she gets what she thinks is a fair amount. One dad tried to give his wife too little. She started walking with him to work to ask his boss what his wages were. At this threat the dad capitulated and paid up. He tried again later and started getting drunk too, so she left him. The following three illustrations exemplify further the economic expectations of the Mum.

Tom aged 34, who is not married and who still lives with his mother who is a widow, hands her his 'wages' every week. That is how Mrs. R. referred to the money he gives her. He keeps something for himself and gives her the rest. She did not mention amounts, but again she emphasized, 'He is a good boy, he's generous just like his father.'

Mrs. C. said her husband had been a good husband on the whole. He'd always been generous when in work. He'd bring his pay packet back and hand it to her. 'We share it.' He helps her in the home, too, and with the children. Mr. C. said again today that he gives his wife half of what he earns each week. Last week he earned £13 and he gave her £7. This was said in Mrs. C.'s presence and she confirmed it. He said, 'Don't worry, I look after No. 1, and by that I mean the home.'

Mrs. K. told me that during all the years of their married life her husband handed her his pay packet. He would take £1 or so out for himself, but that was all. Every Friday evening 'before he took his coat and his cap off'—he would bring her his pay packet. Sometimes she had £8 or £9 a week off him. He worked on the railway. He used to do the painting and tiling. When he needed new clothes she would give him the money to buy them. He chose his own clothes, and she did not accompany him. In the same way she always chose her clothes and he never accompanied her.—'He would not go into a ladies' shop.' Just as her husband used to give her his pay packet, her unmarried son Doug now gives her his. He puts it down on the mantelpiece. She says: 'Go on, take your pocket money.' Sometimes he only takes 10s. and she says: Go on, take £1.' This information is interesting as previously Mrs. K. had told us that her married son hands his pay packet over to his wife every week, and when asked whether she held with this, she replied, 'Well, I do and I don't.'

Sometimes one or other parent complains that the working son or daughter does not hand over enough. In Mrs. L.'s case both boys used to hand their pay packets over to their mother intact, and she used to give them so much back for their expenses. Recently George got dissatisfied with the amount his mother was returning him for expenses. Mr. L. told him: 'You know what to do then,' and added that as far as he was concerned he was welcome to quit. But his mother got upset, and George offered her £2 10s. for his keep. Mr. L. considered this inadequate, but Mrs. L. said it would do, so he told her she could please herself. Out of this £2 10s. Mrs. L. gives George his lunch money every day. Alfred still hands his unopened pay packet over to his mother, and is not dissatisfied that his brother no longer continues to do so. 'Alfred is a good boy.' Mr. L. explained that he was brought up to hand his pay packet to his mother as long as he was living at home, and he has tried to teach his sons to do the same. He considers it is right that they should do so. He reached up to the mantelpiece and brought down Alfred's pay packet and showed it to me. Alfred had handed it to him yesterday in his mother's absence in hospital.

The excerpt below gives an account of a Mum greedy for both psychological and economic power and shows the rather terrifying lengths she is prepared to go to in order to keep her children. The informant recounted this story twice: it was almost identical on both occasions although an interval of two years separated the accounts.

'Mum didn't want to let one of them go. She told our Maisie, "He'll never be any use to you, I'll see to it that he isn't." And he wasn't her only son either, she had plenty of them living at home. She wanted their wages, they were all handing her their wages. On the day of the wedding she pulled down every blind in the house. You would have thought they was in mourning. She didn't go to the wedding nor the wedding breakfast either. The night before the wedding, the best man—he was a friend of our Maisie's too—he slept in the house. He knew that Mrs. T. would prevent her son from getting to church if she could—she would have locked him in.'

When in spite of all her efforts, Mrs. T. was unable to stop her son from getting married, she said to him, 'I'll see that you are put out of work,' and she did. Her husband was a big one on the docks, he could pull strings and all and she made him see that Freddy got no work. 'For the first two years that Freddy was married to our Maisie he was out of work, and there was no minimum wage then you know.' When I suggested that it was unkind of Mr. S. to put his own son out of work, she shrugged her shoulders and said, 'He had to live with her.'

A 'good' dad therefore hands over his entire wages and is given something back. Children, too, are expected to hand over a considerable amount until they marry—even if they are working in another town they will be expected to send something home. However, not all dads are good and there are some indications that this habit is declining, especially among the younger people. But a Mum does expect to see her husband's wage packet and to know exactly how much he has earned each week, so that she is in a position to judge for herself whether she has received a fair 'wage' or not.

Finally, here is a Mum, Mrs. M., who started putting the power of the Mum into operation, even before her child was born. This is what she said:

'I knew in the first week my marriage was a mistake so when I was pregnant I prayed the child would be a daughter. All the time I was carrying her I kept saying to myself, "Please, dear God, let it be a girl, please dear God, let it be a girl. She'll be my companion, she'll be my companion. I'll never be lonely any more." '

(D) THE GRANNY

The granny in Ship Street plays a very important part, nearly as important as the Jamaican granny. She is, therefore, being given a section to herself, although she is obviously a Mum at the same time. Children show some of the Jamaican child's mobility in regard to the granny, or 'nin', or 'nanny', or 'nanna' or 'gran', as she is often called. Sometimes a child differentiates between its maternal and paternal grandmother by reserving a different name for each. No constant rule has been found about which name is given to which grandmother. A child will go and sleep in its granny's house without previous

48

arrangement with the parents. For example, I asked Tim, aged 14, if he likes his new flat. He replied, 'I would rather be here.' He misses granny. It was 10.25 p.m. when we left. I glanced at Tim and said to granny, 'I think someone intends to spend the night here.' Tim looked at granny and asked, 'Might as well? It's too late to go back now.' Granny nodded her head, Tim smiled. I asked if his parents wouldn't be worried. Both granny and Tim said together that they would know where he is. As recorded, Bill, aged 12, still sleeps in granny's household. The only reason I could gather for this is because Mrs. J. does not want to be without any grandchild. (She has two bachelor sons living with her.) Bill hadn't come in before we left.

Muriel's children, Peggy, aged 5, and Chris, aged 3, are very attached to her. Especially Chris. They call her 'nanna' or 'nin'. Sometimes Chris does not return home with her mother but stays the night with her. She asks to stay. The other day she was being impatient and was jumping about saying, 'Go to nin, go to nin.' Her father said, 'You and your mother live there anyhow.' One day Muriel and the children were round at Mrs. C.'s. When they saw her getting ready to come out, the children asked where she was going. She had to say she was going round the corner for the groceries. She could not put on her coat in front of them. This, in spite of the fact that their own mother was with them.

In a crisis the granny will take charge.

Joe was brought up by his mother's mother. When he was about two he got pneumonia very badly. Granny took charge and took Joe over to her place. When he got well he remained with granny. 'Granny was a woman with a will of her own. Perhaps that is why she had three husbands.' Granny was strict but kind. There were always children about in her household. When they needed beating 'Granny didn't hesitate to beat us'. She never used a stick. 'Granny was always boss.' She died quite recently. Joe continues to live with his stepgrandfather. Joe is now 23.

Besides helping in a crisis a granny gives a lot of help in everyday affairs, such as minding the children, cooking the midday dinner when the mother is out at work, and looking after little children when the mother has gone into hospital to have a new baby.

When Mrs. E.'s husband died and she had to go out to work again to keep her children, it was her mother who came and did the cooking and looked after her children. Mrs. E. would go out to work in the morning locking the young children in the bedroom. 'I had to and me mother would come as soon as she could.'

Another woman said: 'Me mother does all the cooking for me and me children. She's a very good cook although she's 78. I do all the washing.'

In some cases, although this occurs only among the older people, there is a trace of the granny acting as midwife, or being called in to lay out a neighbour. Mrs. G. said that in the olden days, many a time women in labour sent for her when the nurse hadn't arrived. She had attended many births in this street of theirs and brought many a baby safely into this world. Sometimes she went to help the midwife. Of course now it is a different matter, she is getting old and she doesn't go out much. She was present in the room at the births of all her grandchildren.

When Mr. D.'s brother's mother-in-law died they at once sent for Mrs. U., aged 66, to wash and lay out the body, and Mrs. U. at once went although she only knew the woman by sight. What's more she ordered her own daughter's spare bed to be taken across to lay the woman out on—in spite of her daughter's (aged 38) wishes to the contrary. Then she dragged her daughter out of the pub, and insisted that she accompany her. 'When we got there the woman's body was all cold and stiff. She had a heart disease and her body was terribly swollen and full of water. We couldn't lift her and had to send for the men to help. She was lying on the sofa in the front parlour. She must have been dead some time. Me mother washed, dressed and lay out the body on me bed. Me mother's been in on all the births and deaths in our street.'

Just as in Jamaica a granny will adopt one of her grand-children, so Ship Street grannies sometimes do the same. Various reasons are given, including the Jamaican that the old lady simply likes to have a child around the place, whether for company or running errands. In both communities, too, an illegitimate child may be left with granny when the mother marries.

Mrs. R. was living with her mother when Patricia was born. She was born in her maternal grandmother's home; she has always remained there. Mrs. R. never took Patricia with her on her marriage, when Patricia was three. Her maternal grandmother brought her up and paid all her expenses. Patricia is now 21 and contributes financially to her grandmother's household. Her father has since married but has no children. He wants Patricia to join his household, but she prefers to stay with granny, although granny still has children of her own living with her.

Both in Ship Street and in Jamaica the prestige of the granny can become so great that she may be called 'mother' by the children and their real mother is called something else.

'When they want anything they ask me for it, they don't ask their mother. When I'm feeling upset with meself I say, "Oh, for goodness sake why don't you ask your mother." They only smile at her and wait. Her grandchildren call her mother, and address their real mother as mum, thus differentiating between them. They called her mother from the very beginning when they heard their own mother doing so.

Again, as in Jamaica, it is the female head of the family who is so important. A matriarch seems to appear and the family collects. The reason why one woman should take on this role rather than her sister is unclear but probably is specific in each case and the result of a more dominating personality, or special circumstances, or both. This is discussed again in Chapter XVI.

CHAPTER V

THE CHILDREN

(A) PREGNANCY

THE Mums complain bitterly when they find they are to have yet another baby, but when the child is born, it is generally loved and cared for. The mother will deny herself many necessities so that the child will have food and clothes. A child of 16 said, 'Me mother never buys herself any clothes. If dad gives her money and tells her to buy something for herself, she buys clothes for the children.'

The next example from the field notes gives a short illustration of observed behaviour. In spite of Mrs. G.'s attitude towards another child and all she has said about Dorothy, aged 13, and Nancy, aged 10, I have always observed her to be very kind to her children. I have never seen her, either in the streets or on my many visits to her home, without the youngest two, aged 4 and 2. In the summer, any sunny afternoon, the three of them were to be seen sitting on the wall in the square. As I passed she would say, 'I am trying to get a bit of sun to them.'

On one occasion when I asked if she was going out with her family, she replied, 'They're not a family, they're a gang.' She said her children have given her nerves. Yet she has told me, and it is obvious from observation, that she loves her children very much. There is no doubt whatever that she goes without herself to buy for her children.

Since the above note Mrs. G. has had two more pregnancies resulting in three more children, a boy and twin girls. After the birth of these babies some of her other children came to tell us about them with great pride and affection. Mrs. G. herself wished for and had attempted miscarriages, but said she never had such luck. She was 42 at the birth of the twins;

she had vomited during the first three months of the pregnancy, throughout labour and for some days after; and she had been given a blood transfusion and iron injections while in hospital. A short note from a visit to her in hospital says that I found Mrs. G. looking washed, clean and rested as I have never seen her look before. Yet she was champing at the bit to get home.

The hospital insisted on keeping her thirteen days. This is what we saw thirteen days after the birth of the twins, on a Sunday morning at 10. We saw a procession. It consisted of Mrs. G. carrying one twin, of Margaret, aged 16, carrying the other, of Robert, aged 10, carrying his brother John, aged 1, of Maureen, aged 12, leading her sisters Sylvia, aged 4, and Eileen, aged 3, by the hand. The twins were sleeping, everybody else was grinning. Mother was coming home. Mrs. G. looked well and was hurrying. She said, 'Ah, look at him,' and pointed to John, aged 1, whom she had had to leave at home when she went into hospital to have the twins. The twins had on their new clothes that we had taken to the hospital from Dad. Pink jackets and bonnets and fine white shawls. Dad, they all reported with glee, was cooking the Sunday dinner at home. Mrs. G. was returning to a husband, eleven children and three rooms. When she first discovered this pregnancy she told us in utter exhaustion, 'Me love is turned to hate.' Today she was happy, she was hurrying, she was going home.

The Mums love their children but blame their 'nerves' on them. In spite of the fact that Mrs. H. was most indignant at the way the teacher had treated Moira she made excuses for her. She said that she supposed the teacher's nerves were bad through having to deal with children all the time.

Nearly all the families studied possess large numbers of children. Although many of the mothers complain of this, sometimes with great bitterness, as they are Catholics nothing can be done about it. One Mum had just died in childbirth at the time when our field work started, although the doctors had repeatedly warned her that she was not fit to have any more children. She did not even tell this to her Protestant husband. Most look forward to the 'change' as their only hope. Frequently, a great fuss is made by the baby's brothers and sisters, who generally shower affection on it. Spinley,[1] too, made this point about her slum group.

(B) WEANING AND FEEDING

Ages of weaning have been given as anything from two to nineteen months. However, in general the trend is towards early weaning. In many cases mothers put their babies on to the bottle as soon as they get home from the hospital. Many rationalizations are given for this, the most usual one being that they haven't the milk. But from field notes and from observation we have concluded that the mothers have not the patience nor the time to sit with the baby while it feeds. Bottles are propped up in prams or beds and the mother gets on with coping with the other children. As families are large, the mother would not be able to sit peacefully with the new born baby but only be immobilized in the midst of a clamouring throng of small children getting into every conceivable kind of trouble. Only one mother reported difficulties over weaning. It may of course be that in many cases the child was not breast-fed for long enough to create any trouble when put on the bottle.

Again the mothers do not look upon feeding the baby as a time when tenderness might be expressed. It appears to be regarded as just the preparation for another meal.

Mrs. Z. was breast-feeding Barbara, aged 5 months. She augmented this with a little soup or even a bottle during the day. She had plenty of milk. At about 4 p.m. Barbara started howling. I asked Mrs. Z. if it was feeding time. She looked at the clock and said, 'It must be.' I asked, 'Would you rather I went?' She replied 'no' and gave Barbara her right breast. Her eldest daughter aged 17½ was in the room at the time and took not the slightest notice. While Mrs. Z. was suckling Barbara her sons Bob and Henry came into the room. Bob is 14 and Henry is 11. Neither they nor their mother showed the slightest embarrassment, though at first she showed some in front of me. Mrs. Z. kept the child at her right breast most of the time. She put her to the left for a few moments at the end. She did not feed the baby for longer than ten minutes. When

[1] Betty Spinley, *The Deprived and the Privileged*, 1953.

I asked whether the child had had enough, she replied that she had as 'it's not long since she had soup'. While she watched the feeding child, she did not caress her.

Although nurses and doctors give instructions about regular feeding hours, on the whole babies are fed when they appear to be hungry or start to cry. Mrs. I. said that the hospital told her to feed Winnie every three hours and that if the baby is asleep she should be woken for the feed. But she doesn't always do this. Her nephew Gilbert, aged 23, who was present said that in his view a baby should not be woken to be fed but should be fed when it cries. 'The baby knows when it is hungry not the clock.'

Nora was breast-feeding her baby and she said she had plenty of milk. At the clinic they told her that she must feed the baby every three hours, and that if the baby was asleep she must wake her and give her the breast, but she did not do this. Dorothy slept so much. Nora fed her when she woke. Dorothy slept right through the night and Nora did not wake her to feed her. This morning Dorothy woke at 7.30 and she was fed then. I asked if she had had a feed since. Nora thought and then said 'yes', but I doubted this. It was then about midday.

Most training seems based on 'I didn't have the patience'. Mrs. K. said. 'Every one of me babies slept in the same bed with me—every one.' She only breast-fed her babies as long as she herself remained in bed after her confinements. After that 'I didn't have the patience'. She put them on bottles. When I asked whether bottle-making wasn't more trouble really, then, and then only did she say that she would have continued breast-feeding them if her milk had done them any good. She could see it was doing them no good. Her milk was watery. So she squeezed the milk out of her breasts herself. She had quite a considerable amount of pain. At a later visit it was observed that a bottle was less time-absorbing as Mrs. K. left the baby with the bottle while she got on with some washing.

(c) TOILET TRAINING

The following example of cleanliness training was not approved of by the children who told it us.

Sally, aged 12, said Daisy is lazy, dirty and she neglects the children. For instance when little June 'calls for the pot'— she's too young to use the lavatory—Daisy curses. When she eventually fetches the pot she puts June's face in it because she's so cross at having had to fetch it. (Daisy is an unmarried mother.)

Generally, there does seem to be an attempt on the mother's part to make the children clean which is supported by the older children. From the frequent remarks that Mums pass about the dirtiness of other people's children it does seem that cleanliness is not acquired for several years.

Mrs. T. said that all her children had been bed-wetters, 'You would sit up watching them and they would do nothing; the moment you closed your eyes they would wet the bed.' Jack, aged 5, still very occasionally wets his cot.

I was just about to put my arm round Norman, aged 3, when his sister Lucy, aged 14, stopped me. She said, 'His back dirty up.' I looked and saw there was dried faeces on his thighs and leg. His mother had told me a few months earlier that all her children were clean by the time they were two.

(D) GENERAL DISCIPLINE

Sex-training appears to be nil. Mothers express horror at the idea of telling their daughters even about menstruation. The following extracts show more accurately than any description how the mothers feel about it.

Mrs. U. said she thinks her daughter Lily, aged 9, 'knows where babies come from.' Some time ago there was an account in the papers of a boy of 20 or so marrying a widow twice his age and Mrs. U. and Mrs. V. were discussing it. Mrs. V. said, 'I think it is disgusting; how many children has she got?' Mrs. U. told her. Lily said, 'And she'll be having some more now I think.' They couldn't believe their ears and Mrs. V. asked, 'What did she say?' Mrs. U. replied that she didn't know, but if she said what she thought she did, she would rather not hear it.

Mrs. W. told me again that none of her children know that she is expecting another baby. She wouldn't dream of talking about such things with them. In reply to my question she said she will not even tell them later on that they are going to have another brother or sister. There won't be any need to say anything to the younger children as they won't notice anything. She's a little worried about Jimmy as he is nearly 18. She implied that it's not really decent for her to be expecting another baby when she has a son as old as 18. This is her only worry that she is again pregnant.

When Mrs. K. had said she intended telling her children exactly what married life is before they get married, she said at the same time she does not hold with telling them everything when they are young. She thinks that mothers who let their children know when they are going to have babies are 'disgusting. That's disgusting.'

I expressed surprise that they had not told Harold about the coming baby. Both Mr. and Mrs. E. said that they do not talk of such things to the children. Oh no, they wouldn't dream of that. Mrs. E. said especially would they not talk of such things to the boys. Mind you, she thinks they know; all the children round here know everything. When I asked if they did not think perhaps it might be better if the children first heard of such things from their own parents rather than from other children, Mr. E. said, 'Oh no, that would make them rude.' He would tell his sons when 'they are big; 17 or 18'. He would tell them then that they must behave themselves and not bring the family dishonour.

At times one parent will especially spoil an individual child or all the children.

Mrs. Y. said that their father spoils the children terribly, which makes it difficult for her. He especially spoils Pat, aged 9. Pat promptly said, 'He does not.' Mrs. Y. continued that he gives them anything they want. 'He would give Pat the moon if he could.' Last birthday he gave Pat a new bicycle. It's upstairs. It cost £12. Pat went over to her father during this; he smiled, and as usual remained quite silent.

Mums very often spoil the children over food. They will buy what the child wants rather than what would be nutritious, e.g. sticky cakes rather than meat or vegetables.

'Me mother asks us what we would like for tea. Me father says that we should eat what's put before us.'

Mothers tend to accept the word of their children and do what the child wants. If the child does not like the school dinners, then he is allowed to come home. If he objects to the food at a convalescent or holiday home, the mother will go and retrieve him.

One boy wrote the following letter from a holiday school, 'Dear Mum, please fetch me a passley (parcel).' Larry was supposed to have stayed there about five months but Mrs. X. fetched him home after three weeks. He kept writing to say he was not getting enough to eat. There was a riot in the canteen one evening and all the boys threw 'plates and things' at the canteen staff as a protest against the underfeeding. Mrs. X. went up to see the headmaster and he said, 'Mrs. X. I know how you feel; I have boys of my own.' So she brought Larry back. She was paying 15s. a week for him and she didn't mind paying this if he was happy and if the school was doing him good, but she wasn't going to leave him there if he was under-fed. She brought him back that very evening without his belongings, which were sent after him.

Occasionally a 'bad' parent mistreats a child in some way or other. This is much frowned on by the street.

Mrs. Z. said Bill is a nice boy. He should never have been sent away. He did nothing wrong. His father did not want the trouble of rearing him and so he went down to the Court and asked that Bill should be put under care. He said that he was un-able to control him. Bill has been away eight years. Now that he is old enough to earn, Mr. S. wants him back to earn money for him. She said, since he did not have the trouble of rearing him and since he gets his beer money, she thinks the boys are entitled to a bit of peace, at least in the home. She's sorry for them. Last night Bill and his elder brother Peter, aged 17, came and sat on her steps and talked to her. She was sitting on them waiting for Maggie to come back from the dance and they came over and said, 'He's off again.' Their father was drunk and going for them and so they quietly slipped out of the house. But the time will come when they will turn on their father and leave home. 'Anyone in the street will tell you Bill should never have been taken away.'

On the whole children are trained by a mixture of indulgence and shouting and threats. It is interesting to compare the Ship Street threat of 'I'll murder you' with the Jamaican 'I gwine kill you'. They both have much the same effect. Harassed mothers tend to get irritable and complain that the children get on their nerves.

Mrs. W. mentioned that her husband comes home from work in the evenings, has his tea, and then goes out. She never goes with him. 'He doesn't smoke but he likes his beer.' She said, 'To tell you the truth I prefer it when he goes out. When he's in the children keep begging him money for the pictures and he only shouts at them to shut up.' Mrs. W. said she doesn't know what's wrong with children these days, there's only one thing they think of and that's the pictures. They want to go every day. They give Rose, aged 14, and John, aged 13, money to go to the pictures every Thursday, but that's all. John goes with a boy friend, Rose with a girl friend. Some children from this street go almost every day. Nearly every house in this street has a boy away at an approved school. That's one thing she can't grumble about, John is very quiet. But it gets on her nerves and upsets her when they keep asking for money to go to the pictures. She herself hardly ever goes and it is three years since she went taking the children.

Isobel, aged 10, Ivy, aged 4, and Veronica, aged 2, were in today when I called. I gave them small packets of sweets and they dropped the sweets as they opened the packets and ate the sweets off the floor. After some little while Ivy went to her mother, clung to her and then turned and asked me for a sixpence. Mrs. J. told her angrily not to be 'rude'.

Quite often the children know that if they make a nuisance of themselves for long enough they will get what they want. One woman said of a boy of 8, 'I give him money to get rid of him.' Discipline seems generally to take the form of an attempt to get peace for the moment rather than any long-term policy.

In the mornings if Mary, aged 13, and Vera, aged 9, are ready for school before breakfast is ready, their mother sends them to church in order to keep them off the streets. They like church.

(E) CHILDREN'S WORK

As in most large families, the older children look after the younger. Elder girls often wash, dress, feed and take the smaller ones out and to bed with them.

Kathleen, aged 14, was the oldest person present and had taken charge. She was sweeping the floor and generally tidying up and getting tea ready. She told me that her mother had gone shopping with one of the boys and would be back any moment now for tea. Mr. B. and the four eldest girls had not yet returned from work but Kathleen was preparing tea for their return. Phyllis, Tommy and another girl, a neighbour, were the only other occupants of the room. Phyllis, aged 11, was helping Kathleen—under instructions—while the neighbour had been delegated to feed Tommy. She was sitting with him on her lap and was giving him a bottle which he was drinking energetically. She allowed Tommy to slip into a recumbent position. Kathleen immediately hiked him up and said, 'Oh, hold him up, poor Tommy.' Tommy looked very healthy and large for his age. I admired him. Kathleen held him up for me to inspect him better. Tommy remonstrated. Kathleen immediately returned him to his bottle saying, 'Tommy would rather have his bottle.'

(F) CHILDREN'S INCOME

Besides helping at home, children earn pocket money by doing odd jobs, mainly running errands and doing shopping. In assessing the amount of spending money children have, total income should be calculated rather than the conventional pocket money. Most children have several regular and irregular sources of supply. Regular supplies will come from parents and others, in conventional pocket money; and in weekly payments for errand running. Irregular supplies come from windfalls from visiting relatives and from successes in gambling and from the odd errand.

Patsy, aged 13, runs errands for three old ladies in the street and they give her 6d., 6d., and 3d. a week for this. Mrs. A doesn't mind Patsy running errands for old people who haven't any children, but she objects to her doing it for people who have children of their own. Patsy is always ready to run errands for her.

Marie, aged 13, goes to the pictures almost every evening. I asked from where she gets the money. Her sister Jenny, aged 11, replied that Marie earns 4s. a week. 'She runs errands

and fetches her papers on Sundays for a lady in the flats above.'
Marie doesn't give Jenny money or take her to the pictures
with her.

Stella, aged 11, and Louise, aged 7, earned 1s. 6d. each last
week running errands for people in the street. When I expressed surprise that Louise is able to run errands by herself,
Stella said that Louise is very 'crafty'. Louise looks rather like
a little old woman and has a low voice and a slow smile.

Mothers look forward to their children leaving school and
getting jobs, as this will help the family budget.

Mrs. B. said that Muriel, aged 14, 'is as tall as I am and
takes the same size boots'. She leaves school next term. Mrs. B.
said she is looking forward to this as it will mean a little more
money coming into the house. Muriel too, seems to be looking
forward to it as she is already making enquiries to see where
she can earn most money.

In some cases the children give their wages to their mother
who gives them pocket money back. They are sometimes 20
before she lets them buy their own clothes. The amount she will
take will vary, of course, with their earnings. But it seems usual
for a boy or girl to hand over about 30s. by the time he or she
has reached the age of approximately 18.

Most of these children also add to their earned and unearned
incomes by gambling as described in Chapter III. Presumably
like adults they have their ups and downs. Children in Ship
Street are not generally short of money though like their parents they spend it as soon as they get it.

(G) NAUGHTINESS

In Chapter XI on 'Crime' it is stressed that many of the Ship
Street boys attend an approved school at some period of their
childhood. From observation and from information given it
seems likely that most of the boys have committed some technical delinquency, although they have not of necessity been
found out. However, this section is concerned with naughtiness,
not with delinquency. Here are a few examples. The mothers
seem to object to swearing more than anything else.

Beatrice, aged 12, spoke of her brothers, Alan, aged 11, and
Ronnie, aged 8. She said of Alan, 'He's never brought any

trouble home to me mother.' Alan wears glasses and looks as if
he has adenoids. His mouth remained permanently open.
Ronnie, on the other hand, brings plenty of trouble home. 'He
swears something awful and he tells me father to shut up. When
me father beats him he's worse.'

When Molly, aged 10, came in from the lavatory in her
nightie before going to bed, she took something from a drawer
and sat at the table. It was a used lipstick and she started smear-
ing it all over her hands and face. Mrs. D., her mother, tried
to snatch it from her and the lipstick fell the other side of her.
Molly tried to push past her, Mrs. D. blocked her way. Molly
slapped her mother on her injured ribs and said 'c——t' in fury.
Mrs. D. went white and there was silence. She asked me if I
had heard what Molly said. I replied that I had. Throughout
all this an old lodger had sat in the corner smiling, playing
with the cat. He had been dangling the cat's leather collar and
she was jumping at it. Mrs. D. asked him to pass her the collar.
He hesitated, Mrs. D. held out her hand, he passed it. Mrs. D.
said that she should give Molly a good thrashing there and then
in front of me but she wasn't strong enough. She would give it
her first thing in the morning when she awakened her. Molly
was told to wash off the lipstick and go to bed. Presently she
did so, saying, 'Good-night.' Grandma called out, 'Good-night
luv and be a good girl, I know you can.' Mary, aged 8, Molly's
younger sister, came up and kissed each one of us good-night
in turn. She did so with genuine affection, but her expression is
always smug when Molly is being naughty and she is being
good, and when Mrs. D. holds them up, as she frequently does,
for comparison.

Mrs. H. said Frank, aged 10, and Michael, aged 9, are wild
and use awful language. 'They call me b——. You know, not
bugger but the other one.' I suggested 'bastard' and she said,
'Yes, that one. I don't mind being called bugger but I do object
to being called a bastard because I am not one.'

Allied with this quite ordinary naughtiness is a strong tendency to violence. The following rather unusual definition of a
current slang word seems significant.

Margaret, aged 12, is Teresa's best friend. Teresa is the same
age. She said of Margaret, 'She is smashing.' When I asked
Teresa what she meant by this, she promptly replied, 'If anyone

hits her she batters them.' I said, 'I suppose she fights your battles for you?' Teresa replied, 'No, she fights me.'

Children are always fighting and many long and complicated stories are told of their feuds. It seems accepted to 'batter' with your hands, but one girl who is said to use scissors and pins is definitely shunned by the other children. Allied with this violence is fear, which is inordinately strong. One example only is given as this topic will be dealt with at length in the chapter on 'Superstition'.

Mrs. A.'s twins, aged 4, just scream at anyone who comes. Mrs. A. had kept them away from other children and not allowed them to play with the children from the tenement flats because they really do use such bad language. The result is that the twins now scream at any stranger who comes. Mrs. A. realizes that she must break them of this habit and so she is now getting Chris, their elder sister, aged 11, to take them to the park in their pram.

Although the mothers may hit or even beat up the children themselves or get the fathers to do it, any punishment from the school is strongly resented. The following story is very typical. Katie, aged 14, is in trouble again. She had been 'bold' at school and to punish her the teacher told her she could no longer go to cookery lessons. They go out to cookery lessons and teacher well knows that cookery, dancing and singing are the only lessons Katie really enjoys. When Katie came home and reported this at lunch-time, Mrs. B. immediately went up to see 'Sister'. Sister said she didn't know anything about it but teacher had found it necessary to punish Katie. Katie had been 'bold'. Mrs. B. asked to see the teacher but was told she was in class. She waited till class was over and when she saw the teacher, the teacher said it was nothing to do with her, Sister had decided on the punishment. So Mrs. B went back to Sister, who told her she was busy. She could come back later if she wished. Mrs. B. said she could not come back because, as Sister could see, she had the young baby with her and she could not leave him at home and she could not keep taking him backwards and forwards this weather. Sister again said it was nothing to do with her. Mrs. B. then returned to the teacher and challenged her. Teacher replied that Mrs. B. should 'chastise' Katie. Mrs. B. said she could not very well chastise

Katie when she was at school. Since Katie is not being allowed to go to cookery lessons the B.'s are not sending her to school tomorrow. She has to go to school until Christmas. When I asked where she would go to school then, Katie promptly replied, 'Whoever'll have me.'

(h) PLAY

The children play mostly in the streets. Games range from traditional ones with chalked squares, versions of cricket and football, gambling games to 'formless'[1] and rough and tumble types of play. The most general characteristic is that it is very noisy.

One time I saw Frances, aged 4, sitting outside their house on the rubble, playing with her usual stones. She did not see me and I stood watching. A little further down the road I came across her three older brothers aged 10, 9 and 8 respectively, playing in an empty charabanc with some other children. The children were chasing each other through the charabanc. They jumped on at the passenger end and jumped off at the driver's end. Roy said the driver, who was absent, knew they were playing in it. A little later, as I walked on, I heard the driver come and yell at them to get off and all the children hurriedly scrambled off.

The N.'s front door was wide open. Tom, aged 8, David, aged 5, and Harold, aged 3, were standing about on the pavement outside playing formlessly. The house next door was bombed in the war and has been completely pulled down. David and Harold were squatting in the dust and rubble digging aimlessly with their hands. They were scratching the earth as if they were looking for something. They were not together. Tom was standing on the steps aimlessly looking out. He told me that he was at home with a sore throat, and that he was looking after his younger brothers. Their mother is dead. He looked most forlorn and was very ready to talk. All three children's faces were dirty and covered with dust. Their noses were running and sore.

Brian, aged 10, had been playing outside the N.s' household. He was the only child with a toy and whose play did not

[1] Margaret Lowenfeld, *Play in Childhood*, Gollancz, London, 1935.

appear formless. He had a toy car which he was pushing along on the pavement. If the car once wound, it evidently no longer does so. I was struck by the fact that although these children were all aimlessly playing about in the street, they were not playing together but quite independently of each other. They only remained near each other; their games were separate.

Mention has already been made of the high popularity of the cinema. The swimming-baths too, are much used by many children. Parents entertaining their families sometimes, though not very frequently, take them to the Pier Head to see the ships.

Where the family is not so large, mothers sometimes find time to join in their children's fun in the evenings. For example, Mrs. M. is obviously on very good terms with her children. Like some other mothers, she told me I ought to see the high jinks in the evenings. Furniture is moved back, carpets rolled up, and there is dancing and singing. She joins in her children's games. 'It keeps you young.' Mrs. M. has no complaint to make against any of her children. They are all good and cause her little anxiety.

Play centres are very popular and there are usually more children clamouring at the doors to get in than can be accommodated. Tickets are issued and many children will try to get in on one, find excuses to accompany younger or older children, or try a bit of Black Market with the tickets.

Reading is mainly of comics such as *Superman, Beano, Radio Fun,* etc. Quite a lot of money is spent on these.

Alice, aged 19, mentioned that when she was a child she got 2s. 6d. to 3s. 6d. pocket money every week. Her mother and father gave her 6d. to 1s. a week, her grandmother, Mrs. O., gave her 6d., and her Uncle Tony (Mrs. O.'s eldest surviving son) gave her 1s. Uncle Tony still gives her 1s. each week 'and jolly useful it often comes in too'. She said, while her brothers aged 12 and 10 don't get any exact amount of pocket money each week, she's quite sure they get much more than this in kind. Their father takes them out to the pictures and a meal at least once a week. Their mother pays for their comics. They just order what they like; they're delivered to the house and their mother pays the bill each week. Alice is quite sure they have at least 5s. worth of comics each week. They all read them.

Mrs. O. is the only one who will not admit she reads them. If someone comes into the room while she is reading one, she quickly puts another paper on top of it!

The general picture of the social life of the children would not be complete without mentioning the great affection they appear to have for each other.

They were both in the yard. Peggy, aged 7 months, was in a pram, Veronica, aged 5 years, came up to see me. Edward, aged 13, went down to fetch his little sister Peggy and he carried her in with great care and affection. He handed her to granny, on whose lap she sat very happily. She stared hard at me but was a little anxious when I touched her. Granny laughed. Edward sat on his chair making affectionate noises and faces at her. He appeared very fond of her. Mr. J. told me that Edward often takes his little sister out in her pram. Peggy did not cry at all while I was there. Granny said she sleeps throughout the night.

Sheila, Doreen's illegitimate baby, now 13 months old, came running to the bottom of the steps and held out her arms to me to be lifted. She had on no shoes or socks. She looked plumper than ever. From time to time she climbed on Dennis, her young uncle, aged 20, and Raymond too, aged 6, hung around near his brother Dennis. The room was clean, tidy and warm. Eunice, aged 13, came in from school through the back yard. She peered through the window to see who I was. As soon as Eunice came in she picked up Sheila and kissed her.

Older children take the greatest pride in showing off new babies. When the latter are brought to show the investigators for the first time, they are elaborately dressed, sometimes carried for over a mile, and affection is showered on them by the older siblings in charge. It is not an uncommon complaint to hear a girl, from about the age of 13, say, 'Me mother has too many children.' But when yet another sibling arrives that same girl will show the new baby nothing but care and affection. Two visits to the same household within a couple of months illustrates this. At the first visit Joan's mother, aged 43, was in the last weeks of her tenth pregnancy. Joan, aged 14, was staying away from school to help her mother with the children and household chores. She greeted me with, 'I'm fed up. I've been at it since 7.30 this morning.' She was in a rebellious mood. She said openly in her mother's presence, 'Me mother has too many children. I'm never going to get married and have babies.'

During the second visit Joan came in from school while I was there. She went straight to her new, 32-day old sibling, lifted her tenderly and kissed her. Presently her mother asked Joan to go and fetch some potatoes from the greengrocer's. Joan said, 'Can I take her with me?' She received permission and marched out proudly with the baby in her arms. She returned with her sister in one arm and a large bag of potatoes in the other.

CHAPTER VI

ADOLESCENCE

(A) JOBS

THE general pattern in Ship Street is for the boy or girl to leave school as soon as he possibly can and to get a job. Therefore, for the adolescent, this is a time of external as well as internal conflict and change. There are plenty of blind-alley type jobs available and it is not surprising that the Ship Street adolescent usually takes them. This is yet another example of his inability to take a long-term view or to plan for the future. Both the boys and girls, as a rule, do not stay long in any one job but move around. For instance, Shirley, aged 15, who hasn't been out of school a year, is now in her third job. She left her second after four months work. Both Ted and Sam, aged 16, have been out of school and at work just on a year. Ted is now in his fourth job since leaving school, Sam has just left his ninth.

The reasons given for leaving a job are usually the flimsiest. Personal likes and dislikes play a large part in influencing the adolescent. If he feels any injustice has been done him, he immediately 'walks out'. He sees no alternative behaviour as possible. The girls often give ill health as an excuse for leaving a job.

Jimmy, aged 16, is now working as a builder's apprentice. He said he thinks perhaps he will stick to this job. He likes the chap he is apprenticed to and the chap treats him decently. Walter, also aged 16, said he tried being a builder's apprentice, but he didn't like the chap he was apprenticed to, so he left. Last week, John, aged 16, 'walked out' of the factory where he had been working for the last four months. I asked John to explain to me his reasons for doing this. He said he and some other chaps were on a job together. They had just finished the job and were clearing up. 'The boss put me on another job. I told him we weren't finished here yet. He said, "You heard me." I told him, "You know what to do then," and I walked out.' John objected to being put on to this other job for two reasons. One, it was near closing down time for the day, and John hoped to waste the time till then. Two, he objected to being separated from the chaps with whom he had been working.

Jean, aged 15, has left the sewing job she took on leaving school. She said, 'Me eyes are bad.' A few weeks later she took another sewing job with another firm.

(b) CLOTHES AND HAIR

During the last year or so at school the girl has experimented with make-up while both the boy and girl have become interested in their looks and clothes.

Margaret, aged 16, who used to be almost a daily picturegoer told me she has given up going to the pictures as she wants to save £14 to have a costume made to measure. (She was only able to sustain this effort for a few weeks and then gave up and bought a costume on the usual cheque system.)

Mr. A. told me that there is £16 owing to the Jew man for debts his three sons, aged 16, 18 and 20, have contracted on clothes. He is trying to pay it off in instalments. George, aged 16, is always buying new clothes. His mother never checked him but always gave in to his wishes. George has now become a Teddy Boy and has just bought a new Teddy Boy suit. Mr. A. detests the clothes. 'I've told him, now his mother's dead, if he brings any more drainpipes home, they go on to the fire.'

Adolescent boys become particularly interested in their hair and it is common to hear a young girl explain her attachment to a particular boy with the exclamation, 'Ah, he has lovely wavy hair.' One day while Roger, aged 20, was talking to me, he took out a comb from his shirt pocket, looked in the mirror over the mantelpiece and combed his hair. It seemed to me that it had almost become an automatic action.

Before going, both Stanley and Robert aged 16, borrowed my comb. They went to the kitchen sink and wetted their hair. Then they stood intently in front of the mirror setting a deep wave on their foreheads just as a hairdresser does.

This supports Betty Spinley's[1] observations of the preoccupation of the adolescent boy in her slum group.

The excerpt that follows shows the length adolescent girls are prepared to go to in order to improve their looks.

Both May and Ethel, aged 15, were wearing fancy earrings. They have both had their ears pierced. An Aunt did May's, Ethel did her own. She said that she had put the needle through her ears at work herself. She had difficulty in doing it and 'I had to put the needle through five times and hold it there before I could make the hole. The girls asked, "Isn't it hurting?" and I said, "No, it isn't," but I thought I would faint with the pain, but I held the needle there and I saw the blood dropping.' I said it was quite unnecessary to have their ears pierced, they could wear screw earrings just as well. Both May and Ethel disagreed that screw-on earrings look as nice. Thus in this case Ethel was prepared to go through all this pain for the sake of looks. Elsie, now aged 14, said she wants to have her ears pierced but her mother 'won't let me yet'.

With this awakened interest in clothes and looks, it is not uncommon to hear an adolescent express a wish for a wardrobe. In many homes, the girls complain that their best clothes have to hang on the back of the door with Dad's work clothes. One girl of 15 asked for a coat-hanger for her best dress as a present.

Both girls and boys start experimenting with smoking round about the age of 11. The experiment frequently starts in school lavatories. It is not unusual for children of 14 to have acquired the habit of smoking. While they do not smoke openly in front of their parents at this age, the parents know they smoke.

It has been interesting to watch the development of children who have visited us regularly over this period of five years. Up to the age of 14 or 15 their faces would light up when sweets were put on the table. Now when offered a sweet they ask for a cigarette.

(c) CLEANLINESS

In the same way we have had the opportunity of noting and recording many changes that have taken place in the developing

[1] Betty Spinley, *The Deprived and the Privileged*, Routledge & Kegan Paul, 1953.

adolescent both physically and mentally. During school age it is the exception rather than the rule for children to clean their teeth. An interview with three girls aged 13 drew the information from them that nothing would induce them to clean their teeth. 'It makes your gums bleed.' As these girls reached 15 and left school each shyly admitted that she had now started to clean her teeth. In each case this coincided with the acquisition of boy friends and kisses.

As soon as girls start going to public dances, great stress is placed upon cleanliness and personal hygiene. Two girls aged 16 used to visit us frequently on a Saturday night on their way to a dance-hall. They had both just had baths and washed and curled their hair. They had on clean underclothes and full skirts with elaborate blouses. They had washed their blouses the night before and had ironed them just before putting them on. Both girls work in factories. They had cleaned, manicured and painted their nails. Again, as in Spinley's[1] slum group, this exuberance and zest of the adolescent contrasts sadly with the apathy which later seems to set in. Both these girls said they cannot stand another adolescent, Ellen, 'because she does not change her sanitary towels often enough'.

Daisy, aged 15, was fiddling with her brassiére. I asked her if it was too tight. She asked me to feel the elastic at the back. It was much too tight. I asked her why she wears a brassiére as she is very slim. She replied simply, 'To flatten my breasts. You should see me in a swimming costume. I noticed them the other day.' Daisy, and Mary, aged 16, and Leila, aged 14, all three said that they disapprove of Louise, aged 15, who wears brassiéres to accentuate her breasts and which they think unbecomingly large. A year later Daisy was wearing an uplift brassiére. She had passed from the stage of aids to hide her figure to aids to reveal it. Audrey Hepburn, who had been her ideal, had been deposed; 'because she is flat up and down'. Marilyn Monroe and her curves had taken her place.

Adult dress is obtained in order to go to work. While the Mum still supervises the buying of most of the clothes, adolescents do at times break away and buy some of their own clothes with the money they earn. Generally they hand over a fixed sum each week to Mum, usually between 25s. to £2,

[1] Op. cit.

and keep the rest for themselves. They become very conscious of their status as workers and feel they should not be asked to help at home during the week. They feel that younger siblings should now be made to take over their jobs in the home. A long excerpt with three adolescent girls, quoted later in this chapter, illustrates these two latter points.

(D) SEX EDUCATION

The fact that both boys and girls receive no sex education from their parents has been discussed in the last chapter on 'Children'. Further details must now be considered owing to the important effect this lack of rapport has on the outlook of the adolescent girl in particular. The second of the following examples seems unbelievable in 1955.

Muriel, aged 13, screamed for her mother when she noticed a hair under her arm. She asked her mother for an explanation and her mother replied, 'Well haven't we all hair on our heads?' The child said, 'And wouldn't we look funny if we hadn't.' Some days later, when there were visitors present, Muriel came in with two hair-nets. They asked her what they were for. Her mother replied, 'One for her head and one for the hair under her arm.' Muriel left the room almost in tears.

As Mrs. T. herself told me, Maggie, aged 15, confirmed that she had learnt nothing whatever from her mother regarding menstruation. Her friend, two years older than herself, had told her about it. Yet when it appeared it was a shock. It first appeared one night. She awoke with a pain and found her clothes bloodstained. She got up and knocked at her parents' bedroom door. Her mother came to the door. When she saw her mother she was unable to say what she had come to say. She hesitated, then stuttered that she had got up for a drink of water. Her mother told her to go back to bed. She went back to bed and cried till she fell asleep. In the morning she had to go to school. So she went to her mother, turned her back on her and said, 'Look.' Her mother replied, 'That's nothing, give the clothes to me,' and handed her two pairs of knickers. One was a rubber pair. Maggie put that on with the other pair over it and went to school. When she got there she told the girls 'and they took me to a ladies' toilet and we put money in the machine and got three sanitary towels out and they showed me how to fix it.'

Mrs. J. said, 'In those days mothers were old-fashioned and thought it was not right to tell. It came on at school and I took fright and ran from school straight to the doctor and showed him. I thought something terrible had happened to me. I remember I was in such a state that he told me to sit down and then he told me and explained everything to me.' Nancy, this informant's daughter, is now 13. Mrs. J. said she thinks a girl should be told something about it before her first menstruation, 'But it is so hard to know what to tell. I've told her that if she sees anything to come straight home to me. If she sees it at school she's not to say anything to anybody but to come straight home to me. I've told her if she feels a slight tummy-ache she's not to be anxious. That's natural. I've told her to keep away from the boys.'

This mother has gone one step further than most in so much that she feels it is the mother's responsibility to tell her girls about menstruation and not the school's. Yet in spite of her own traumatic experience when a child, in spite of her statement that she thinks girls should be told before they start to menstruate, Nancy was left with this limited warning until after the event.

The second example illustrates the inability of the Mum to talk to her children. Even in cases where the woman has said that she believes in telling her children about sex the actual content of the instruction is, 'Keep away from the boys.'

The following comment from a mother with eleven children epitomizes what most of them think on this matter, and emphasizes yet again the statements made in this chapter and in the chapters on 'Children' and on 'Sex and Marriage'.

'I couldn't talk to me own children, I'd be too shy.'

Mothers do not feel that any responsibility rests with them over teaching about sex. The children may grow up with very inadequate knowledge. The following quotation is a typical one from the field notes.

Mrs. O. said that when the girls are $13\frac{1}{2}$ or 14 they are now told about menstruation in the schools. She thinks this is a very good thing and she is glad of it. She thinks schools should tell them and not the parents. She couldn't tell her own children. She has told Patricia, aged 13, nothing about menstruation. The school will tell her soon. Mrs. O. said in her days they knew nothing. 'I knew nothing till I had my first baby.'

Patricia did in fact start to menstruate before she had received any warning or instruction from the school. Her mother ran to the school to tell Pat's teacher and to ask her to speak to Pat. During this time Pat became extremely withdrawn and weepy. The interesting thing is that the mother-daughter tie in adult life is particularly strong in this family. All Mrs. O.'s married daughters, after an initial attempt at independence, have returned to their mother's home with their husbands and children.

(E) LOVE AFFAIRS

Although the tie to the mother remains during adolescence, this lack of contact has two results. The first is that the child is unable to speak to the parents about anything other than trivial matters, and therefore has a secret life of her own completely outside the parents' knowledge. The second is that for the first and last time, overt aggression is shown towards the Mum. The quotation that follows illustrates the lack of contact between parent and child and the beginning of conflict over mother and boy friend.

Mary told me today she is in love. His name is Ernest and his home is in the next street, but he is in an approved school. This does not prevent Mary from seeing him. She's going 'three Sundays from now' and expects to get in saying she's his cousin. 'Don't tell me mother, she doesn't know.' I asked what would happen if she did know and received the inevitable reply, 'She'd murder me.' Mary writes to him as his cousin but he can't write to her in case her mother should get hold of the letter. In reply to my question Mary said that even if Ernest were not in an approved school it would be quite impossible for her to bring him home. At $15\frac{1}{2}$ her mother considers her far too young to have boy friends and so she meets them surreptitiously and goes out with them. Today for the first time Mary expressed ambivalence in her feelings towards her mother and recognized that her attraction towards Ernest and

74

her love for her mother are in opposition to each other. Today, her 'I will not marry', recorded two years earlier, became 'I will not marry till I am 21. I won't leave me mother till I am 21.' When I asked her if she wants to leave her mother's home on her marriage, she replied, 'I don't know.'

(F) ADOLESCENT REBELLION

The next quotation is taken from a long interview with three adolescent girls, Lily, aged 14, Katie, aged 16, and Anne, aged 16½. It was a highly emotional outburst leaving the girls trembling and needing to run to the lavatory. We have known them for five years and this is the first time they have ever spoken against their mothers.

Katie and Anne started the outburst saying almost simultaneously that their mothers 'are for ever nagging'. Lily joined in.

Anne: 'Tomorrow me mother will murder me for something she went at me for last week.'

Katie: 'Me mother's just the same.'

Lily: 'So is mine.'

The main causes for 'nagging' at the moment appear to be, (a) that none of them do enough in their homes, (b) that they always want to go out in the evenings and stay out late, (c) that they don't give their mothers enough money for their keep.

Anne: 'If I sit down for a minute me mother says, "You do nothing in the home," and I've just scrubbed out the parlour. Mitzi,' [her younger sibling and illegitimate], 'mustn't rough her hands. She does nothing in the home to help. Me mother never asks her to do the dishes. Mitzi's being brought up all too much like a lady, I think.'

Katie: 'If you've been to work during the day, I think it is unfair to expect you to work in the house in the evening. Me mother expects me to do the dishes in the evening. I don't think it is fair.'

Lily, shouting: 'I have to do the dishes every night, me mother thinks I should never go out.'

Katie: 'That's true, Lily never goes out.'

Lily: 'Me mother doesn't come home from work till 8, and then she thinks I should stay at home.'

Both Katie and Anne said that their mothers had given them no birthday presents on their last birthdays and that this had made them feel unwanted and unloved. Anne reminded her mother of her birthday saying, 'Here, Mother, it's me birthday today, give us a present. Me mother gives us 2s. then, and the next day she borrowed 1s. back. She never gives us the bob back.'

Anne gives her mother 30s. a week for her keep. 'When I give it her she says, "The amount you give me wouldn't keep a cat." '

Katie gives her mother 25s. a week. 'When I give it her she throws it back at me and says, "Give it to the woman next door and ask her to keep you." '

Anne: 'Me mother says that too.'

Lily, shouting: 'Me mother wouldn't give me water.'

Katie: 'She'd give you water, Lily.'

All: 'Me mother's always saying, "Go and live with the people you stay out late with." '

Lily and Anne said this gibe has often driven them from their homes and they have gone and stayed with their aunts, 'who are awful nice and don't nag'.

Anne: 'If me aunt does not like something I've done she tells you straight.'

Katie: 'If I knew who to go to there's many a time I would have run away and stayed away.'

Here I managed to intervene and said, 'Whatever you all tell me I know perfectly well your mothers love you.'

Katie, quietly and bitterly: 'I don't think me mother knows what love is.'

I asked Katie if she could tell me. She replied in the same strain; 'I don't love anybody in our house', and repeated, 'If I knew who to go to there's many a time I'd have run away and stayed away. I think me mother's jealous of me and I tell her so.' I asked: 'What have you got for your mother to be jealous of?' Katie replied: 'I have nicer hair.' (There may be more truth in this than even Katie realizes. Katie is now 16, her mother 33 or at most 34. Katie is her mother's illegitimate child born before her marriage.) 'Sometimes I want to kill meself.'

These outbursts are of the greatest interest because they do only seem to appear during adolescence. It is the one time in a

Ship-Streeter's life that he rebels against the power of the Mum. It is particularly interesting to note that the rebellion takes place during the period when, for girls anyway, there is maximum contact with the outside world. From observation we have found that most married daughters do live with or near their mothers. The adolescent girl generally says she wants a home of her own, yet when she has been married a short time and babies arrive in quick succession, it seems inevitable that she will return to her Mum. Her husband becomes 'him' and the rebellion is over.

Spinley,[1] in her study of a slum community, comments on the rapid deterioration of the girls' looks, etc., after marriage and wonders why they bother to get married at all. She does not think from her work that they are particularly interested in sex. Ship Street girls on the other hand take a romantic and sentimental view of marriage and do appear to be interested in sex quite definitely. The boys too are not without a romantic view of marriage. For instance, in discussions with adolescent boys, most of them say they would not refuse to marry a girl if they are in love with her, just because she has an illegitimate baby by another man. They would want to know the exact circumstances. But the girls' interest in sex dies, with some exceptions, when the glamour of marriage wears off and they find that sex means babies. Then they are unable to cope with the responsibilities and give up and go back to Mum.

[1] Op. cit. page 70.

CHAPTER VII

SEX AND MARRIAGE

(A) LEARNING ABOUT SEX

THE attitude to sex in this group is a curiously mixed one. Prudery and crudeness are closely intermingled. In Chapters V and VI it was emphasized that no parent would ever speak of sex to a child and that definitely no sex instructions are given. One mother said she did speak to her daughters but in fact all she said was, 'Keep away from the boys.'

Because of this prohibition of speaking about sex, each age-group is left to discover the facts as best they can. Their knowledge is obtained from three main sources. Firstly, from the cinema, where they obtain some physical knowledge by watching the behaviour of courting couples.

Lizzie and her two friends, all aged 13, sat behind a man and woman at the cinema some nights ago. The man and woman 'were fooling about' and then said, 'Let's go to the back.' The children followed them. 'She had her things out'—Lizzie pointed to her chest—'and she was feeling him.'

The cinema, too, gives them a romantic model for sex behaviour, though, of course, an incomplete one. It is also a model of a life so obviously removed from their own. Probably the peak of picture-going occurs just before adolescence, and it is just after this that the only rebellion against the power of the Mum takes place.

Secondly, at times men attempt to lure the children into cars. A child is offered money to get in the car and direct the man to a non-existent street. No information has been given that the men technically seduce the child. Informants all say that the men ask them 'to feel them'. A fairly thorough check-up did indicate that these stories were based on fact and not on

78

phantasy. The Mums themselves have fears of a 'man' who might molest them in the street. The origin of these fears seems mainly phantasy; although there is frequent accosting in the neighbourhood it is generally of a verbal nature only. At times some real incident will light up the phantasy fears.

The third source of information arises from mutual sex play between boys and girls. For this again the word 'feeling' is used. This probably starts just before adolescence. Again the information is of a non-verbal nature. Girls say, 'but I don't open me coat', which is their synonym for sexual intercourse. The name the children give to sex activities—'dirty things'— has been learnt from adults and is to some extent indicative of the woman's attitude. One mother whose attitude differs, was faced with the following quandary. Both Mary, aged 9, and Sally, aged 10, have often asked her for a baby brother or sister. Sally said, 'But I suppose you can't have one now Daddy's away.' She was taken off her guard and replied, 'Well I could have one.' Sally asked, 'But you and Daddy have to do dirty things together before you can have one?' She said that if she and Daddy do them together and love each other it isn't dirty. Sally asserted, 'It's still dirty.'

At adolescence, when there is an increase in sexual interest, and when it has been shown there is a turning away from the Mum for the first and last time, there is a change in attitude towards sexual activities. The phrase 'dirty things' is dropped. One girl who at 11 had used that very term, when asked at 16 if she still felt the expression of love between the sexes is dirty, replied quite simply, 'Of course not.' It has already been stressed, that before marriage, both the boys and the girls in this group are interested in sex and in the expression of sex. But the effect of this early teaching, of course, persists in the unconscious if not in consciousness. For both the adolescent boy and girl, sex remains something secret and surreptitious and something of which to be slightly ashamed. Whether later in adult life the woman reverts overtly to the 'dirty things' attitude as a rationalization for her lack of interest in sexual intercourse, depends entirely upon the circumstances of her marriage. If a woman already has a large family and fears yet another pregnancy and contraceptives are not used, it is obvious that this acts as a deterrent to pleasure. Thus a woman

79

of 42, who married for love at the age of 24, said bitterly when she discovered her eleventh pregnancy,

'They say it takes two to make a baby, but it's not true. It takes one.'

The man's attitude is summed up by one Dad's comment on sexual abstinence, 'You can't go against nature.' The example that follows illustrates his point of view.

Mr. D. said his wife had been a good wife to him and their married life has been happy. She's had a lot of trouble over this last baby though and it has upset her. She had not been herself for some time, and he's sorry about it. She had not wanted another child and she blames him, 'But you know how it is between man and wife.'

(B) ATTITUDES TO MARRIAGE

A number of our families are happily married.[1] Some have their grumbles but have settled down to a 'give and take attitude'. Some are actively unhappy. There is vast material on this subject in the field notes, but the extracts that follow are a fair sample of both sides of the picture. Frequently, the relationship between the man and woman remains at an immature level because of the power of the Mum. As soon as aggression is felt it can be seen how it is at once expressed in violence.

Eileen, now aged 21, told me today—sixteen months after her marriage—that she is just as much in love with Peter as when she married him. 'He's the lad for me all right.' She expects to remain in love with him

Mrs. A., aged 30, with seven children, said how she met her husband was 'coincidental'. He was talking to her brother when she came up. Her brother introduced them. They 'fell for each other at once' and were married after an eight months courtship. She is happily married and her husband is good to her. Sometimes she grumbles at him about having so many children. He then goes out of the room and allows her to talk to herself. He never loses his temper.

Mr. S. summed up by saying, 'No man could have a happier home.' This is interesting since his wife goes out to work, and in theory, Mr. S. objects.

[1] 'Happy' is based on their own subjective statement.

Mrs. B., aged 31, with seven children summed up by saying, 'We are poor but very happy. I couldn't have a better husband.'

Mr. C., a widower of 40, left with nine children, told me three years after his wife's death, 'I will never put another in her place.' At a later visit his daughters told me that their father had asked them the other night, 'What would you give to have your mother back?' They tried to change the subject as they know how their father still grieves. He said, 'It would give me life.' The older children said their parents' marriage seemed an ideal one. Of course they had their tiffs, disagreements, but never rows or shouting. Their father never hit their mother.

Mrs. D. married at 23, her husband was 21. They have been married twenty-nine years and are happy. If she had her life again she'd marry the same man. She's enjoyed life. When the children were young and she was unable to accompany him, if her husband went out for a drink in the evening, he would hurry home and always creep in so as not to wake the children. Now the children are old they both go out together 'for a glass of ale' every Saturday night. They never go out without the other.

She had her last child at the age of 41. She found herself in hospital with 'all young girls'. They said, 'Oh, I hope I won't be having babies at 41. I hope I'll have finished with it by then.' 'I told them, "Don't throw your life away. Don't throw your life away before you're old."'

Mrs. E., aged 37, said of her husband from whom she is fortunately separated, 'I could feed him powdered glass.'

Mrs. F., aged 59, married at 21 and had seven children by her husband. 'Ten years ago me husband walked out on me and I have never heard of him since. I've had as much a penny off him as you have.' Her marriage had not been happy. 'He used to knock me about terrible,' but all the same at first she grieved over his loss and tried to find him. 'Now I wouldn't have him back.' Mrs. F. has four married daughters and twelve grandchildren living with her.

Mrs. I., aged 33, with four children, said, 'For every one he was making over here, he was making another over there.' Her husband has been unfaithful to her for the last five years, and she has known for the last four. Two years ago they separated and he went to live openly with the other woman.

Today, Mrs. I. had just returned from Court with her divorce. The case was undefended. 'It is better this way than the way we had been going on. I used to be frightened of bathing the children of an evening in case he should come in rolling drunk. He would use most awful language and swear horribly in front of the children. It's much better for them.'

Mr. J., aged 72, with no children, told me he had been married 22 years. After two years of married life he came home one evening to be told by his neighbours that his wife had had a soldier in the flat the whole afternoon and evening. He challenged her and she did not deny it. 'From that day I lay in a double bed beside her but I never touched her.' The failure of his marriage turned him into a rover. 'I was always off.' He did not lead a celibate life but he never thought of divorcing his wife. His reasons were not religious, 'But I had married her and therefore I felt she was my responsibility.'

Long before this, when I first met Mrs. J., she introduced herself to me by saying, 'Eh, I was a proper bugger.' After her death, I told her husband of this introduction. He grinned and said, 'She was that all right; but I was fond of her—I was fond of her till she died you know.' Her faults were faults of a generous nature. 'I expect we men would call her, just one of the girls.'

Mrs. X. said, 'He's trying to drive me to the lunatic asylum. He's always telling me I'm wrong in the head and that he's going to have me put away.' She grinned and continued emotionlessly, 'I've hit him many a time you know. I took the knife to him once and would have murdered him but Mrs. Z. next door stopped me. Ask Mrs. Z.' Mr. X. is now going into hospital for an operation. Mrs. X. said, 'Pray he'll die. God forgive me.'

Many women have told us of their sex ignorance when they first got married. The effect of this can be seen from the second quotation that follows.

Mrs. K. went into hospital to have her first child when she was 19. 'I had fits when I saw all the instruments lying about.' She asked the woman in the next bed, 'Here, where does the child come from?' The woman replied, 'Same place as it went in.' Mrs. K. said, 'Here, I'm going home. You see, I thought it came out of your navel.'

Mrs. U. said that her sister Mrs. V. got married when she was 21 but knew nothing at all about married life. It was a shock to her. Then she was in labour a whole day with her first child 'and she nearly cried her heart out'.

Mrs. V. said, while her husband 'is one of the best', and while she likes weddings, she doesn't like 'what comes after'. If she had her life over again she would not marry. If she had to marry, she would marry the same man.

(c) ATTITUDES TO SIZE OF FAMILY AND FREQUENCY OF INTERCOURSE

As most of our mothers are R.C., birth control, of course, is forbidden. But it must be pointed out, that in the few Protestant families in this group the families are just as large and none of our Protestant mothers have admitted to using contraceptives. This is due to the apathy and prudery that nearly all the women show towards sexual matters.

Mrs. Y. would not like to go to a clinic to learn how to use contraceptives herself. Her scruples are not religious but she'd be shy. So Mr. Y. is again practising withdrawal, although he is now married to her.

There are a number of Catholic mothers, however, with strong religious scruples about birth control. The exceedingly interesting ethical attitude expressed in the first quotation that follows is widespread in this group. Many mothers have admitted to taking pills and mixtures which purport to bring about a miscarriage; only one mother has admitted to using contraceptives. The second excerpt illustrates the extremely unhappy physical and mental states this ethical attitude can cause.

Mrs. L., a woman of 38 who has had six children, considers birth control wrong. It is definitely a sin. Yet under certain circumstances she appears to consider abortion permissible. She said, 'I mean to say I don't say I've never taken anything. We all do at times, don't we? You just say to yourself it is late. But after two months I wouldn't do anything, that would be wrong.'

Mrs. H. said that when she discovered her tenth pregnancy at the age of 41, 'I nearly went mental during the first three months. I thought I was going to end up mental but I'm better now. From the day me period was due but didn't come I started taking pills. I got them from the chemist. I took twenty-four in one day. I was very sick. I went on taking the pills regular for the first three months. I was very ill for the first three months. I couldn't eat anything. Lemonade was all I could take. I kept drinking lemonade and wanting more lemonade. I couldn't even drink tea.' The pills did not bring about a miscarriage and Mrs. H. stopped taking them after the first three months.

Today, during the fifth month of her pregnancy, Mrs. H. was eaten up with anxiety lest she had injured the baby in any way. She told me, 'I felt it kick in me stomach at $3\frac{1}{2}$ months,' and she still frequently feels movement, but she kept asking for and wanting my confirmation that she couldn't have injured the child. (Mrs. H. gave birth to a healthy child of 8 lb.)

The next two examples show the extremes of reaction of two Catholic mothers.

I asked Mrs. N. if she considers birth control wrong when a woman has perhaps twelve or thirteen children and really can't afford any more? She replied, 'If a woman is healthy I reckon she can have them.'

As soon as Mr. P. went out, Mrs. P., aged 38, with nine children, told me she does not want any more children. She said, 'If I have any more I'll put me head in the gas oven or throw meself in the canal,' and she sat silent, suddenly weeping. 'It wears you out: you don't know, it wears you out.' Muriel, aged 12, was present and sat watching her mother with alarm on her face. Mrs. P. said she does not now think birth control wrong. (Mrs. P., however, took no birth control measures and has since had another child.)

A Dad's disapproval of contraceptives, though not on religious grounds, was expressed in no uncertain terms.

'Not worth doing at all if you have to use one of those damn things.'

Frequency of intercourse varies greatly. Information was not asked on this subject but often it was volunteered. It must be stressed, however, that in this work there was no correlation whatever to be found between frequency of intercourse and the number of pregnancies. Again and again the women with

84

the largest number of children would tell us that they had rationed their husbands, while the husband and wife with the highest record of frequency, have three children. The wife added proudly, 'And a dose of syrup of figs every morning is my only birth control.' The extracts that follow record the two extremes volunteered. From the first excerpt it appears that there is some substance to the Saturday night of fiction.

Mrs. O. said that it is just her luck that she is pregnant again, because it is not as if they 'do it often. He's not one to bring it out every Sunday.' She does not allow it more than about once a month. If he wants it more she refuses him. (At 42, Mrs. O. has had thirteen children.)

Mrs. W. said it is a bit tough that there seems to be no correlation between frequency of sexual intercourse and the number of children a woman has. 'Me old man might go a fortnight to three weeks without, he's not like some, and yet those some have fewer children than I have.' Both Mrs. W., and Mrs. S. who was present, said this abstinence 'makes the seed grow stronger' and found the explanation of their large families in this fact. (At 41, Mrs. W. has had eleven children.)

I asked Mrs. Q. if her husband were permanently at home, if she thought she would have sexual intercourse with him so often. She replied, 'Oh yes, I can stand it at least eleven times a week.' In order to keep her on the subject I doubted it. She went on, 'Well at least seven times a week.' She does not like it more than once a night, but they often do it at night and then again in the morning when they wake up. 'I like it in the morning.' (At 39, Mrs. O. has had three children.)

In every case where the woman has admitted a pleasure in sexual intercourse, the number of her children has been small.

(D) ATTITUDE TO BARRENNESS

Yet as in Jamaica, to be barren is considered a far greater calamity than to have too many children. The married woman with no children is regarded with pity and sympathy, by children, adolescents and adults alike.

Flo, aged 11, said there's a woman who has a café, 'who's ever so nice and she's married but can't have children. Isn't that a shame?' She then asked me if it is true that you can be married and yet have no children, and you can have children without being married?

Bob and James, both aged 16, said there is a married woman who lives in their block of flats who has been married some time and has no children. She has been told that she can't have any. Both boys thought this 'tough, as everyone wants children, don't you think?' Bob asked me if there is really such a thing as 'barrenness'? He thought it a tragedy that there is.

From large families both Mrs. C. and Mrs. D. passed on to barrenness, and they both thought the former far preferable to the latter. A barren woman is regarded as unfortunate but with sympathy. Mrs. C. told me of a girl in the street who has been married three years but has never been pregnant. She has been to every doctor possible and has now been told finally she will never have children. 'Both she and her husband are very upset.'

(E) ATTITUDE TO ILLEGITIMACY

The attitude to illegitimacy in this group is very different from the English middle-class one. So far as we can see little shame or guilt is felt. Parents do not turn the girl out and generally accept the baby as another member of the family.

Beryl, Mrs. A.'s oldest child of 21, is illegitimate. She herself was 21 when Beryl was born. Beryl's father was 20. Mrs. A. said, 'It was my fault that I didn't marry him. He got into trouble with the police. He was had up for shop-lifting and was sent away for three years.' However, he only had to serve eighteen months and was then released. When he came home his stepmother told him that Mrs. A. was married and so he didn't come to see her at once. She hadn't married but married Mr. A. shortly after. Mrs. A. blamed the stepmother for this but said she did it 'because she thought he would be no use to me'. However, he has turned out well. He has only been married ten years. He and his wife have no children. He is R.C. He and his wife live quite near but she does not see him now. She married A. when she was 24. She never deceived him about Beryl and he married her knowing the full story. He has been a good husband except that his health isn't too good. She has had nine children by him.

Nelly, aged 20, has an illegitimate baby and both Nelly and the baby are members of Nelly's mother's household. When Nelly told Bill she was expecting his child he said he couldn't marry her as he was out of work then. Now he's got a job he wants to marry her, but Nelly now says, 'He kept her waiting so she's now going to keep him waiting.' Mrs. M., Nelly's mother, is glad really, because if two people are in love they can starve together. He ought to have married her whether he had a job or not. But Nelly still sees Bill and Mrs. M. thinks she will end by marrying him. Mrs. M. pulled a face as she said this. She meets him at the dance-hall and dances with him. When I asked, 'Supposing Nelly has another baby by him?' Mrs. M. replied, 'There's no question of that, she doesn't bring him home or go out with him alone really.' (Nelly married him when she was in fact expecting his second child.)

Mrs. D. said her mother never threw her out or even grumbled at her when she learnt she was going to have a baby, though unmarried. She helped her from the very beginning.

The next extract illustrates what a man thinks should be done if a girl is 'got into trouble'. Marriage is only one alternative.

While we had been talking about Mr. R.'s early marriage, his son Robert, aged 18, said that he has a pal who is only 18 who is getting married, and added, 'He has to.' I asked them both their opinion on this problem. Robert said that the boy was already engaged to the girl so it is only a question of getting married earlier. Mr. R. said that if a girl came and told him that one of his sons had 'got her into trouble', he would expect his son to do one of two things—either marry the girl or maintain the child till it is 15. He would make a very careful check up of facts first though. He would ask his son exactly what date he had been with the girl, and he would see on what date the child was born. Then if he was satisfied the girl was speaking the truth he feels his son must take one of the two courses mentioned, and he would encourage him to do so. Mr. R. then related an amusing story about one of his friends.

A girl is 'love lost' on this man but the man 'prefers his ale'. One Saturday night Mr. R., this chap and another man had a 'bit of a binge'. The other man had a car. On the way home this girl waylaid them and they stopped and gave her a lift. She got into the back with his friend. Mr. R. heard her going

87

all out for the man. Mr. R. told her to lay off because he knew his friend was rather tight. Whether his friend thought he had been rude to the girl or what, he told them to stop and he was seeing her home. Mr. R. tried to dissuade him but it was no use. The next morning his friend came round miserably and said, 'It had happened.' Three months later the girl told the man she was pregnant and he must marry her. He refused. The girl said she would take him to court if he didn't marry her and he said she could do so. She thought if she sued him for maintenance he would prefer to marry her, so she took him to court. She got a maintenance order but the man has never paid a penny. Every month he appears in court and says he won't pay so every month they pop him into jail for one week. This has been going on for $14\frac{1}{2}$ years. When the child is 15 he won't have to go to jail any more! Neither the man nor the woman has married. 'The woman is still hoping.' Mr. R. said in this case he really rather sympathizes with the man because there was no doubt the girl did the seducing. She was determined to get him.

(F) ATTITUDE TO PROSTITUTION

With one exception no member of this group has been a prostitute. This area contains many brothels and accosting is frequent in a variety of languages and with a diversity of approach. The Mums do not approve and complain about the badness of the neighbourhood.

Mrs. E. took me to her sitting-room windows, drew the curtains and pointed out two houses. They were bad houses. One was run especially for 'black men'. The girls are white. In reply to my question as to whether the girls are very young she said, 'I suppose so. They don't care how young they are so long as they get the money. I don't know much about the houses but me husband could tell you a thing or two.'

Perhaps two issues should be discussed shortly here. The first is that in a community where the woman is dominant the male clings to the vestige of power by refusing to allow his wife to be sterilized or to use birth-control methods. The religious aspect of this is, of course, manifest, but it is not impossible that this demonstration of power is possibly latent.

The other point is one that has arisen in previous chapters, that is the shyness shown in non-sexual relations between men and women. It does seem that in this community the only patterns of male–female relations are sexual; therefore the individual finds it impossible to take up a non-sexual role with a member of the opposite sex.

CHAPTER VIII

CLOTHES AND FOOD

(A) PRESENTS OF CLOTHES

FOOD and clothing for the large families which are prevalent in this group naturally present many problems. Although in some cases considerable sums of money come into the house as wages, clothes are expensive. In the better-off families the custom is to buy a lot of new clothes just before Christmas. These are handed out as Christmas presents. From the two examples below it will be seen that the older children too buy their parents and siblings clothes as presents.

Mrs. E., who had been untidy and unwashed, now went next door and started to get ready. Patsy, aged 18, had bought a button-up skirt at C. & A.'s. It was too large and she was moving the buttons back. I admired it and she fitted it on me. It cost 11s. 9d. She had bought it for Christmas. All new clothes bought for Christmas were then produced and shown to me. Patsy had bought herself a complete new outfit. The skirt for 11s. 9d.; a pink silk blouse for 8s. 11d.; a pinkish red cardigan for 16s. 11d., and a red gaberdine coat with a tartan lined hood for £7. Mrs. E. had bought Nancy, aged 16, a brown and white tweed coat which had cost £7 and Nancy was going to buy herself a skirt like Patsy's and a new blouse. Florrie and Ruth, aged 14 and 12, had both been bought new brown suède, fleece and lambskin lined boots. The price was still on them. They cost £2 17s. 11d. a pair. Florrie said she would rather have had a pair of shoes. All these new clothes would be worn on Christmas Day. Patsy explained that Florrie and Ruth had had new coats last Christmas and so they were not getting them this Christmas. They would have new ones again next Christmas. Patsy had bought her mother a gold brown woollen cardigan as her Christmas present to her. This was the only article of clothing which had not been bought from C. & A.'s.

It had cost 26*s*. and something. Mrs. E. came back into the room after washing and changing her dress. She brushed her hair hard. She had on a black silk dress which she had bought from C. & A.'s last year for her mother's funeral. She asked Patsy if she had better wear her cardigan under her coat. Patsy said 'yes' and told Florrie where it was and to fetch it. Florrie did so, Mrs. E. put it on and then put on a black coat which had just come back from the cleaners and which had cost £5 from C. & A.'s.

Mrs. E. told me they usually have their Christmas dinner midday on Christmas Eve.

David, aged 12, said he gets a new suit every Christmas. His mother takes him out and buys it. He told us of the presents the family have already bought for Christmas. 'Our Peter, aged 16, bought Dad a pullover and tie. Our Johnny, aged 22, bought Dad two pullovers, a shirt and two ties. Our Johnny bought our Peter a shirt and two ties.'

(B) BUYING CLOTHES

As already stated in the chapter on 'Children', Mums frequently go without in order to buy for their children. Sometimes they pay a price out of all proportion with their incomes for their children's clothes. A Mum who is separated from her husband and whose income is £3 10*s*. a week, bought her daughter a coat costing £8 last Christmas. She said, 'Maureen gets a new coat every year at Christmas. Oh, she expects one you know. And if I buy meself anything new at any time, she wants one just the same.'

(C) CHEQUES AND CLUBS

The larger families are unable to pay for all the new clothes which may be required simultaneously and so take out 'cheques' for them. Cheques are a hire-purchase system by which the shop allows the customer to have goods, well above their cash price, on credit. Cheques are taken out for round sums such as £5 or £10; i.e. credit is given up to that amount and only a small deposit has to be put down in cash. The customer is given a period of time in which to repay the cheque in instalments.

Vincent, aged 9, Teddy, aged 5, and Joseph, aged 3, were all in new suits, and I have never seen them all looking so clean. They all looked as though they had had a recent haircut too. The suits were dark Air Force blue serge and consisted of shorts and battle-dress with a zip. I said to Mrs. M., 'It looks as if you've won a pool.' She laughed and said, 'I wish I had. I took out a cheque.' She bought the suits on credit and so has to pay £6 for the lot instead of their cash price of £5. She is paying off in instalments and has so far paid something like £2 18s. She has not long in which to pay the balance. As soon as she's paid off this debt she intends to 'take out another cheque'. This time for herself. She told me she has no winter coat.

Mrs. J. said her husband makes her an allowance of £5 a week. When he's working overtime he gives her a little more. She has to pay all living expenses, including the rent and coal, out of this £5. It's a struggle. The only way she can manage is to buy all the children's clothes on 'cheques'. She knows it is a rotten system—'you're paying for the clothes after they're worn out'—but what else is she to do when five pairs of boots are all wanted at the same time?

Immediately children leave school they follow the Mum's example and buy on cheques. Here is an excerpt from the field notes of an interview with three children.

As soon as the children leave school and start earning and buying some of their own clothes, they fall into the habit of 'taking out cheques' and buying clothes at an exorbitant price 'from the Jew man' because they can pay in instalments and are not asked to pay cash down. Jane, aged 16, had on a grey costume which she got from 'the Jew man' and for which she has to pay £7 12s. and which she is paying off in weekly instalments. She herself told me she knows the costume would cost about £4 from C. & A.'s, 'but C. & A. don't let you take a cheque, you have to pay cash there, and where am I going to get £4?' It was quite useless trying to explain to her that if she eventually can find £7 12s., she could save £4 and it would be better to wait till she had £4 before she buys her costume. All three children shouted together that they would never have any clothes to wear that way.

Winnie, aged 16½, has nearly finished paying off a £5 cheque she told me about last time. 'As soon as I've paid it back I'm going to take out a £10 cheque this time.' Winnie said she'd paid 'the Jew man' £10 5s. for a green skirt and red coat she bought from him—rather she is still paying for it though she can no longer wear it—she has grown out of it. When I told her that I have seldom paid as much as that, she replied, 'Ah, you can pay cash.' I asked her why she doesn't try and sell the coat and skirt since she can no longer wear it, say, for about £5. She replied, 'Get away, I wouldn't get 5s. for it.' In reply to my question, she said that the first 'Jew man' they went to 'was a robber' but their present one 'is awful nice. Sometimes he lets you take away the things without putting any money down.'

Frequently, the 'taking out of a cheque' is celebrated by generosity towards one's family. Dora, aged 16, took out a £5 cheque last week and spent the whole amount the same week. It is worth noting that she bought some little present for almost every member of her household—certainly for all her younger siblings. She also bought her mother and her married sister Betty and Betty's young child who live with them, a present. The first thing she bought for herself was a home perm. The rest of the money went on clothes.

On the whole, possibly owing to the cheque system, members of this group generally have at least one good set of clothes. Children, for instance, have good clothes for school and ragged ones for playing in the street. Value is laid on having good clothes and especially on having something new each Christmas.

The latter is often achieved by 'joining clubs'. Months before Christmas every shop in the area displays notices such as, 'Xmas Club now Open.' This means that these shops will accept payments from customers which are credited to them and which enables them to do their Christmas shopping there later. Amounts varying from 3d. to a few shillings are paid in by every Mum in this group to some 'club'. The only variant is the amount paid and whether the Mum tries to make a regular weekly payment of 'I pay in a few coppers when I can spare them'. Mums tell you that this is the only way they can save, too, to buy extras for the Christmas dinner. No interest is paid on these credits and the Mums expect none. One Mum said, 'From about September I paid 2s. 6d. a week to me grocer, 2s. to me greengrocer and 1s. to the newsagent. I bought me Xmas presents from the newsagent and the other paid for all me Xmas shopping. Me mother joined the club for the butcher.'

Mrs. W. said she thinks clubs are such a good idea as 'one would never save enough money to buy big things otherwise. I always join a club and save 2s. 6d. a week when I want new curtains or the like, or when I want new clothes at Xmas.' When I asked if any interest is paid on the money Mrs. W. was most surprised and replied, 'Oh no, it wouldn't be fair to expect that. It helps you save money.'

The Ship-Streeter pays constant visits to pawnbrokers. The pawnbroker is another means of raising funds when one has failed to plan, when credit cannot be obtained and money has to be found.

Mr. H. said I would find a long queue of women outside X.'s in Y. Street every Monday morning. 'They have all spent all they had, over the week-end, and on Monday they are broke. The wages don't come in again till Friday so they go to the pawnbroker.' In answer to my question Mr. H. said some of them may redeem their things at the end of the week, 'But you'll see them queueing again on Monday.' He said he hates going past X.'s: it recalls his childhood.

Penny, aged 13, said her mother had bought a new coat. It had cost £12 and she had paid cash for it. But when she got home she found she had no money at all so she took the coat straight to the pawnbroker's. He gave her £3 for it. This was months ago. 'The coat's still there. Me mother never wore it.'

Pauline, aged 15, has always longed for a wrist-watch. Last Xmas her father gave her one. A few months later her mother pawned it. 'There was no bread in the house.' Her mother gave her 15s. of the pawn money. Pauline missed her wrist-watch, so she pawned her costume to redeem the watch. Her mother again pawned the watch. This time it was to send five of her children to the sea for one day. 'Me father says he won't take it out of pawn 'cos me mother'll only pawn it again. He says it's no use giving us an expensive present again: and it's true.' (Pauline's watch has since been returned to her. Her father took it out of pawn and presented it to her on a plate when he carried her up a cup of tea the morning after she returned from hospital after a very serious illness. It is also worth mentioning that he is only her stepfather, though Pauline herself does not yet know this. She was born before her mother's marriage and conceived by another man.)

(D) MONEYLENDERS

It is not surprising that this pattern has given rise to money-lenders from amongst the people themselves. There is a rich harvest to be gained, yet the moneylender is not regarded as an exploiter but rather as a saviour. The moneylender is usually a 'Gran', at any rate always an elderly woman. The usual rate of interest is 2s. in the pound per week. We have reports of 2s. 6d. in the pound being charged, but on the other hand a moneylender will lend a neighbour money in times of great distress and refuse interest.

Four children aged 15, 15, 14 and 13, said of Mrs. Z., 'She's always ready to help anyone if they are in trouble. She's a moneylender and she lends everyone in the street money, if they want it.' Both Daphne and Phoebe said their mothers have frequently borrowed from Mrs. Z. Daphne said Mrs. Z. usually charges her mother 2s. a week for £1, while Phoebe said she usually charges her mother 2s. 6d. a week for £1. 'But you can keep the money as long as you like. You have to tell her when you borrow.' Both children said they do not consider this a high rate of interest. Angela said Mrs. Z. has lent her mother money without charging any interest.

Mrs. Q. said, 'Mrs. Z. is a good woman. I have often bor-rowed from her and she has charged me no interest. She knew me mother and me aunty. When me baby died I had no money to bury her. I went to Mrs. Z. and told her, "I'm in awful trouble Mrs. Z." I told her I had no money to bury the baby. She told me to find out how much it would cost and to let her know. When I told her she give me the money. She took no interest. I gave her back so much a week. I will never forget that.'

(E) EATING HABITS

If the family is large and there is only a small kitchen with few chairs then it is apparent that all members of the family cannot sit down together to a meal. Frequently, the children are fed first before the adults; sometimes the family just stands around the table. One day it was close on 4 p.m. and Jim, aged 9, Bill, aged 7, Stan, aged 5, and Tommy, aged 3, were just about to have their tea. The boys called out to me but I was unable to recognize them as the room was in semi-darkness. Mr. D. lit the gas. There is no electric light in the house. The kitchen table in the centre of the room was laid with layer upon layer of clean newspaper. The boys stood around the table, no chairs were drawn up to the table. On each plate were two freshly cooked little rissoles. A plate of what looked and smelt like raw sliced onions, and a plate of freshly cut white bread, and a large brown china teapot stood in the middle of the table. A fire was burning in the black kitchen range and the room was warm and tidy. There was also a gas cooker in the room. A large frying-pan covered with a clean plate stood on it. Mrs. D. stood holding Maisie's illegitimate baby, her granddaughter, aged three months, while she supervised tea. Maisie goes out to work. The baby had a bad cold and its nose was running. Mr. D. was also standing. The boys proceeded to gobble their food. Mrs. D. poured out tea with one hand and fetched a milk bottle while she continued to hold her granddaughter in the other arm. I turned and talked to Mr. D. when conversation with Mrs. D became impossible owing to the noise the children were making.

It was the F.'s dinner-time and I had no intention of staying. The table was not even laid and Mrs. F. said she just snatched a piece of bread and marge when she makes tea for the children. They have school dinner but they always run home for a cup of tea after it. Sometimes she does not even sit down while she eats. Nina, aged 13, came in through the yard-gate for her tea while we were talking.

At Mrs. B.'s there was a white tablecloth on the kitchen table and such things as bread, milk, marge, sugar, etc., that were needed for the next meal, stood together in the middle of the table. The room was clean and warm.

(F) INDIVIDUAL TASTES

There are a large number of restrictions about food. It is doubtful if any are common to the group but are simply instances of individual taste. What is interesting is that even the children seem to choose what they want to eat. No attempt seems to be made to force them to eat anything they do not like.

Mrs. Q. mentioned that she hardly ever draws her full weekly ration of bacon or meat. They are none of them very fond of meat and except for her husband they are mostly fonder of sweet things. Tonight for supper they have sausages and potatoes, but Gerald, aged 16, only likes potatoes and sweet things. He won't eat meat or bacon.

Both Mr. T. and Vi, aged 14, said there are plenty of food fads in the house. Mr. T. said he has never eaten greens and never will. Potatoes are what he mostly eats. He hates onions. Because some of them like onions he allows a whole one in the cooking but this must be taken out before he is helped. Vi said he will not eat tomatoes or cheese. He never takes milk with his tea. 'Some of them won't touch eggs.'

In general, sweet cakes and chips and potato crisps seem favourite foods. A few families seem keen on curry and rice and on tripe.

For his midday meal, Mr. O., a bachelor son aged 48 who has gastric trouble, buys fish every day from 'the fish and chip shop just round the corner'. The cost of this meal varies with the price of fish, but it never exceeds 1s. 3d. a day. For his tea he usually buys three little cakes. He doesn't drink tea all day long but he likes one good strong cup with his meals. Fresh tea is made each time. He won't drink stewed tea like most of the people.

Cream slices are regarded as a special treat. The other morning her mother and Maggie, aged 19, bought four and had them with a cup of tea at 11 a.m. They cost 3d. each.

Eileen usually gets a meal in the evening at the restaurant where she works, before returning home; but last Wednesday Eileen came home to tea. 'Because do you know what we had? Curry and rice and chops.' Curry and rice is a prime favourite amongst the whole family. Meg, too, aged 13, loves it.

Nancy, aged 16, said, 'Me mother got me half a pound of tripe for me dinner today. She asked me what I'd like so I told her.' When I asked how her mother had cooked it, she replied, 'She didn't cook it. I like it just as she gets it from the fishmonger's. It slides down.'

When Mrs. F. and the boys came to tea with us she mentioned that she had been down to a big store in town to get a

quarter pound of boiled ham for her brother's tea. It had cost
2s. 6d. I remarked how expensive ham is. She said, 'Me mother
wanted it for Vic's tea.' Vic is a bachelor son aged 34.

Mrs. R. had ribs stewing in a saucepan on the gas cooker.
She took them out and put them on a plate just as I was going.
George, aged 8, came and stood by her and watched most
anxiously. They were having ribs, potatoes, cabbage and a
rice pudding for their tea today. Mrs. R. said she makes them
a rice pudding for their tea every day and turned to George
for confirmation, which he readily gave.

Where families have been influenced by the foreign population the cooking is quite exotic. The general rigidity towards
food seems to change into a more fluid attempt to give the man
the sort of food he is used to. Here is an account of a meal
shared by a visiting field worker.

During my stay this evening Mrs. S. made two pots of tea in
which we all joined. Suddenly, at about 10 p.m., she said, 'I'm
hungry and I'm going to eat and you're all going to eat with
me, but you'll have to eat the oriental way. I can't wash up a
lot of dishes at this time of night.' She heated up some rice and
soup which were already cooked and dished them up in two
large dishes which she placed in the middle of the table with a
bowl of home-made cheese chutney. I excused myself saying
I had had supper before I'd come. She replied, 'If you don't
eat with me you don't come to this house again.' I hastily
grabbed the proffered spoon and dug in! Mrs. Y., Mrs. S.'s
mother, was present on a visit, Behram the coloured lodger,
Mrs. S. and myself. As there were no plates and there was soup
we all ate with spoons. The procedure was to take a mouthful
of food from each dish in turn. Behram did not eat but watched
me very closely. The chutney was exceedingly hot. Unawares,
Mrs. Y. took a spoonful and passed out. Her lips were burnt,
her eyes streaming. It took some time to revive her, much to
Behram's amusement. Mrs. S., on the contrary, though English,
ate dessertspoons of the chutney neat. Her mother gasped. It
was made of pounded garlic, grated cheese and a large quantity
of cayenne pepper all mixed together with a little milk or
cream when possible. Mrs. S. uses butter in all her cooking.
The soup had been made in a pan in which butter and cloves
of garlic were first simmered, then sheep's heads and the

minimum amount of water were added and boiled. The rice had not been boiled in plain water but in a little of the soup, so it was saffron in colour and beautifully dry when served. The food was extremely tasty if a little overladen with garlic for English taste. I had intended to eat as sparingly as compatible with good manners. I ended by eating a large meal.

Quite often, when the family is large, and not too well off, discrimination is shown to the wage-earners.

Isobel, aged 12, looked in to see us on her way home. She had been doing her mother's shopping. She produced two chops, a large one and a smaller one, and said, 'This one' (the larger) 'is for me dad's tea, and this one' (the smaller) 'is for Margaret's.' Margaret is now 16 and earning. When I asked Isobel what she and her mother and her other siblings were having, she said, 'Vegetables and gravy. Dad and Margaret are earning.'

Just as new clothing is important at Christmas, so great stress is laid on the dinner itself.

Mrs. C. has bought two geese for their Christmas dinner—one for her own household, one for Sara's—her married daughter who lives next door. The geese are at present living in the back yard.

Mrs. E. told me she has bought two chicken and a piece of lamb for Christmas Day. It is all paid for already and the butcher is keeping it in his frig. for her. Her mother's sister has made her a Christmas pudding and they are going to have a good Christmas.

The poorer families will at least have a 'lump of pork'.

It appears that some of the Mums have a feeling against eating out. It seems to be connected with a dislike of strangers, especially of a strange man seeing you do anything important or intimate. Dads do not necessarily share this dislike and some adolescents go to cafés to do their picking up.

Milly's mother does not like eating out in restaurants. That's why she rushes home to midday dinner every day. She feels people may be watching her eat if she eats in public places.

Children too will often refuse to eat the school dinner, or if they do have it, they will come home to see Mum in the lunch-hour.

Although Hilda, aged 13, Barbara, aged 9, and Mike, aged 7, all have school lunches, they tear home after lunch for a cup of tea with their mother. They never miss a day.

Perhaps the most salient points in this chapter can be summarized as follows. Firstly, the lack of ability to live except for the moment unless drastic steps are taken is illustrated here by the club and cheque systems of saving for a specific object, and in other chapters by the taking out of insurance policies. If a payment has to be made on a cheque for some already bought article then it can be done. Though of course it might mean a visit to a moneylender or to a pawnbroker. It would not be possible to put money aside in the house for two or three weeks and pay cash. 'Don't be soft' is the answer if this alternative is suggested.

The following quotation by a 16-year-old child indicates how rarely anything is paid for on purchase.

'I often tell meself I'm going to find a £5 note today and as I walk along I'm planning how I'm going to spend the £5. Do you know what I'd do? I'd walk straight into C. & A.'s and pay cash.'

Secondly, from the section on food it can be seen that each child is catered for individually, literally as well as metaphorically. Thirdly, one aspect of the retreat from sociability is seen in the dislike of eating out. This starts with the child and continues into adult life, except for a break in some cases during adolescence. Drinks and snacks can be taken out but main meals should be had at home. People do in fact travel miles from places of work to a parent's house, rather than eat out. This makes yet another extension of the all-providing Mum.

CHAPTER IX

ASSOCIATIONS AND NEIGHBOURS

(A) LACK OF ASSOCIATIONS

PERHAPS the key to understanding the psychology of this group lies in the relation between the individual, his family and those people not in the family group. It might be said that in our culture pattern in general, as we grow up, family associations lose some of their importance while work, recreational or intellectual associations supplant them. With this group this does not seem to happen on the whole. The men have work associations but the women have nothing. It is interesting to note that many of the men are dockers and dockers just now are in a perpetual state of unrest. Undoubtedly the break-up of their traditional associations is a strong contributing cause. Most of these people are Catholic and therefore it might be thought that the associations centred round the Church would absorb what energy might be advantageously used in group life. However this is not the case. The majority of adults neither go to church nor take part in its social activities very often. The interesting thing is that the children are often ardent churchgoers, owing to the fact that they attend Catholic schools. Most of their parents also attended these same schools but the religious feelings generated in childhood do not seem to persist, in general, into adult life. From a practical point of view the busy mother will not have much time for church. All associations, except those concerned with the family, seem to drop away at marriage.

Mrs. A. mentioned that Mrs. M. and Mrs. N. both went to school with her and now are almost her neighbours; yet she emphasized that they are not on visiting terms.

Although Mrs. B. has lived in this neighbourhood all her life —she was born here—and although she went to school with

Mrs. F. who lives opposite, and although she has lived in this house fourteen years, she said she has no friends whom she visits. The only homes she visits are relatives' homes, and only relatives visit her. Mrs. T., a few doors down the road, runs in the back way sometimes and they may have a chat in the yard, or she may chat on her steps with neighbours, but they do not visit each other's homes. Mrs. B. keeps her front door closed.

Although Mr. L. has lived in this neighbourhood forty-six years and both he and his wife know everybody by sight, they both said they are not on visiting terms with anybody. They do not drop in at anybody's house and nobody drops in at theirs. 'We keep to ourselves.' I pressed: Mr. L. emphasized all the children know his wife, they call her 'Aunty Alice', but their parents and they are not on visiting terms.

(b) DUTIES OF NEIGHBOURS

Casual dropping in for a cup of tea in the afternoons, while husbands are at work and children are at school, does take place between some of the Mums, but this is the exception rather than the rule. The obvious facts that the size of many of the families and the lack of space in homes makes social intercourse very difficult, must not be overlooked; but the point remains that even where this visiting takes place, personal relations remain on a very superficial level. Yet the extent of neighbourliness, especially in times of adversity, cannot be overstressed.

One day I met Judy, aged 12, in the street, carrying a large basin full of coal. She told me her friend Teresa's people are without any coal and so she was taking them some so that they could have a fire. She was carrying the coal right across the street, up three flights of stairs to the tenement flats opposite.

While telling about the death of her baby one Mum said, 'I sat with my dead baby, alone, over the holidays, while no one came near me. The only person who came near me was the woman from next door, and she looked in and sat with me one night. She said, 'Ellen, you and I haven't always seen eye to eye, but you've got trouble now, so I've come to sit with you.'

During this investigation a fire broke out in one of our homes in the kitchen on Christmas Eve. The man next door was ill at the time, but he got up without hesitation to help his neighbour put out the fire. It might be argued that his concern was to stop the fire spreading to his own home. But the fire did in fact spread to his own home. He left his wife to deal with that! Both his and his wife's first thought was to get the baby next door to safety.

The kitchen was burnt down, the family was left without a Christmas dinner. The street saw to it that they had a Christmas dinner. Yet it is not without significance that the family, which was a small one, was not invited, nor even a single member of it, into neighbours' homes for Christmas. Rather, neighbours donated various items of cooked foods—including 'a lump of pork'—for the family's Christmas dinner.

Neighbours who are not on visiting terms hold keys of each other's homes. My house was stripped of lead and copper pipes after I had vacated it. I was telling one of our Mums of the burglary. She immediately asked, 'Whatever were your neighbours up to? A thing like that couldn't happen in our street. We hold the key to next door. If me mother hears the slightest noise next door, and she thinks they're out, she fetches a chair in the yard and looks over the wall. The coalman or the dustman couldn't call you know without me mother knowing.' (In case suspicion falls on any person in Ship Street, let me hasten to say that the burglars were caught and had no contact even with any members of our group.)

Again, Mums who are not on visiting terms will accompany each other to hospital. If a member of a family is ill in hospital and there is no relative available to accompany the Mum, a neighbouring Mum will frequently go with her and wait for her while she sees her sick relative. On the whole the Mums do not like visiting hospitals alone.

While Mrs. J.'s husband was ill in hospital Mrs. R. 'from opposite' frequently accompanied Mrs. J. on her visits there. Mrs. J. said, 'I don't like going alone.'

A young unmarried mother lost her illegitimate baby. A neighbour said:

'The baby was quite nicely laid out. The street gave her quite a good send-off.'

It is this strong feeling of neighbourliness in this group which makes most of its members prefer to give away second-hand articles rather than to sell them. Even in cases of known hardship, these are some of the replies we received when we asked, 'But why didn't you sell' this or that?

'Oh I prefer to give away Joyce's clothes. I don't know the woman very well, but she's a fellow victim, like meself. Her husband walked out on her. Her little girl is two years younger than Joyce.'

Another Mum said, 'I'll have to buy another cot this time. I gave John's to Mrs. O. She's very poor and she has a lot of children. I didn't think I'd be needing it again.'

The formal invitation to come for a meal between non-related people is almost missing from this group. A non-relative tends to go into the house (as differentiated from chatting on the doorstep) only when he has some definite purpose, such as serious courting, in view.

In reply to my question Helen, aged 19, told me that she does not often take her friends home 'because it's my grandmother's house really and it all makes work and my mother goes out to work'. On Helen's birthday Sid came to supper. Her family had pressed her to ask him and she did so, but warned them that they must not therefore jump to the conclusion that she is going to marry him.

Although there is as yet not enough evidence to be dogmatic it does seem that this pattern is limited to a definite type of family in this area. Reports from social workers and others suggest that in some districts frequent visiting is normal. Here is what one of our Mums says about her contact with this different pattern. She belongs, apparently, to a marginal group.

Mrs. P. said I would be surprised how the people from other flats in the building are always popping in to borrow 'a loaf of bread, or a bit of butter, or a bit of tea'. She doesn't like that and she doesn't do it. When she told me that they have little to do with the other tenants, she made one exception. 'The woman next door.' They have known her for a very long time. 'She used to live with us in X. street.' (The implication was that she was their tenant.) She moved with the P. family and took the flat next door. She gave them their turkey for Christmas. She is very good to them. When Mrs. I., Mrs. P.'s married daughter, came in, she said, 'My children would never want while she is there. She is always giving my children things.' Both Mrs. P. and Mrs. I. then explained that they had been good to this woman when she had lived with them. Their luck had been in then, and they were better off than she was, 'So we had been good to her then. She doesn't forget it. Now she's better off than we are, she's good to us.'

(c) FRIENDS AND LACK OF FRIENDS

Occasionally individuals have personal friends but this is not very common in adult life. Aunt Sara, who is unmarried, is an exception. Aunt Sara was sitting by the fire and was most hospitable to me. She is Mrs. E.'s father's sister. She started telling me at once of her old friend 'who lives up the road'. She is over 80 and lives all alone, and yet I would always find her room scrupulously clean and tidy. She has got no relations here but has got some in a nearby town. She would visit them sometimes but that would mean coming back to a cold room without a fire. When I said I thought I had heard about this friend and was she the one she takes coal to when she is in need, Aunt Sara replied, 'It is more often she brings me a bucket of coal.'

The nearest approach to social life that most of these families have is a visit to the pub. Even here sociability is somehow restricted. Here is one old lady's account of it.

Today Mrs. Y., aged 72, told me she goes to the pub every evening for a glass of mild. She goes alone and returns alone. She is quite unafraid to do so even when it is dark. At the pub she meets her 'old friend Mrs. X. whom you know. She's told me you've been to her house,' and they sit at the same table and have their mild together. Mrs. X. does not arrive till 9 p.m. Mrs. Y. goes earlier. These two old ladies have known each other for 40 years, yet they never make a change and have drinks in each other's homes for instance. They do not visit each other.

Aunt Sara's friend is probably a somewhat unusual extension of this type of relationship.

In some cases the pubs provide rudimentary associations. Even these, though, are associations which do not involve much personal contact. It is possible to gamble or go to football matches without making anything but superficial contact with the other people involved.

Every Saturday and Sunday Mr. and Mrs. D. go to the pub

together unless he's had a very bad week and has no money.
Between Saturday and Monday morning Mr. D. said he may
spend anything up to £5 on drinks and gambling. He backs
horses and goes in for football pools. A fortnight ago he won
£23 on a horse and he nearly made £60 on it. If he had backed
it for a win as he had wanted to do, and not only for a place, he
would have done. He gave his wife half this money. His wife
confirmed this.

Her husband is a member of the X. Rover's Club. The X. is
the pub just round the corner and every Saturday they play
football matches against other local clubs. Her husband is not
in the football team but he is very keen on football and he
watches every match on Saturday whatever the weather is like.
He takes Mike, aged 11, with him. Some of the wives accompany their husbands but she does not. She hasn't the time—and
again there is the baby.

One woman who is included in this group is of a very
different type. She is Protestant, an ardent Orangewoman, and
spends nearly all her free time in some association or other.

On Wednesday evening, Mrs. C.'s birthday, she went for a
charabanc drive with her club. They went to a pub a little way
out of the town where they had 'a chicken supper'. Then they
had beer and dancing. The club have been to this pub before.
They all like the licensee's wife very much 'because she joins in
with us'. Sometimes they go for mystery charry drives—that is,
the participants do not know where they are going. These are
extremely popular.

Mrs. C.'s main activities are to run an all-girl band which
marches in the Orangewomen's Procession, and to organize
Lodge teas and other entertainments. She raises money for the
Lodge by these activities which is frequently spent on the
children's section of the Lodge of which she is Honorary
Secretary.

(D) VISITING BY RELATIVES

In contradistinction to this lack of non-related visitors, members
of the family visit frequently and unusually regularly.

Mrs. Y. said that they are all on visiting terms, but her
husband's brothers and sisters visit the house much more

frequently as they live very near. 'They are here every day.' She often pops into their homes.

Dinah, aged 12, told me that her father has one brother and two sisters. She doesn't know where his brother is but his sisters live in the suburbs. She goes to visit these aunts, in turn, every Sunday.

Elsie and Bill said their married sisters Mary and Jane frequently visit them, bringing their babies. Their uncle and aunt frequently visit them. They live just opposite. Their mother and father frequently visit their uncle and aunt. Elsie, aged 11, said, 'Not every day because me mother's too busy. She hasn't time.'

This constant visiting does not, of course, apply to all members of the family. It has been pointed out before that families are on the whole pretty large. Equally obviously some members of the families must break away and live in other parts of the town, if not in other towns. The reason why one individual rather than another remains in the residual group round the Mum is not yet clear. In general, those who get away do so because of status. Our group is not very concerned with problems of status; in fact, in comparison with people living on a housing estate investigated by Mitchell and Lupton[1] they are conspicuously unconcerned. In the following two quotations our informants explain why social relations have been broken off with one or more members of the family.

Mrs. D. said that as children she and her sister were good friends. Her sister is 'comfortable' and so they now never visit each other. She used to go round to her sister's place but her sister was always out when she called. Her sister's husband would sit and put a newspaper in front of his face, so she never goes any more. She said of him, 'He's ignorant.' Her sister's children and her children never visit each other or play together. Her sister lives in another street. Her sister does not go out to work.

Mr. J. said his wife's mother and father are dead. Mr. J. told me that his wife never visits her brothers and sister. I asked Mrs. J. the reason for this. At first she said, 'I don't know.' Then she said, 'I'm not good enough for them,' and she looked

---

[1] *Neighbourhood and Community*, Section II, by D. Mitchell and T. Lupton, Liverpool University Press, 1955.

at her husband, who has been on sick benefit for years. The inference was clearly that they consider she has married beneath her. Mr. J. was listening. Then she added, 'They live in a better neighbourhood.' They never visit her. (This information was withheld on my first visit.)

In the next example the woman is married to a coloured man. At first she told me she has only one brother alive, then she said, 'Oh, I've another but I never see him.' Quite genuinely, I think, she was unable to give me any information of him. She does not know where he lives but feels he is in this town. She didn't mention the reason for the estrangement but dismissed the subject with, 'Oh, I don't bother with him.' Her other brother and she are on very friendly terms. He is married, has two children and lives near. He is a frequent visitor to the household. 'He was here at Christmas.' He and her husband work in the same firm.

The family residue sticks closely together and the main fear is of isolation. To be without family is terrible and loneliness greatly dreaded. This residual family is kept together by visits, letters and family 'dos'.

Sue, aged 11, says her family has a 'do' every year on the anniversary of the day her mother's father died. Sue got drunk last year as her uncle kept giving her beer and finally some whisky. They always drink at their 'dos'. On the other hand you do not have a 'do' at a funeral. You cry at weddings and funerals. May, aged 13, reported the death of an uncle and said 'don't be soft' when I asked if they would have a 'do'. Sue said she cried her heart out when a lodger who had lived with them got married last year. She wept all the time in the church when she was being a bridesmaid.

Christmas 'dos' are especially important and a variety of conventions prevail, depending on the numbers in the family. They all entail at least a visit to Mum on Christmas Day itself.

The fear of loneliness is an important factor in understanding this group. It is probable that their general lack of education and of opportunities to use their intellects, restrict quite drastically the number of roles individuals can play. The lack of integration implied by this faulty upbringing would be expected to produce fear, which is expressed in this case in dread of isolation. In our culture in general a person of not very high I.Q. and moderate education can often find plenty of satisfying roles to play in the complications of, say, suburban social life. With the exception of the Orangewoman this does not seem a possible outlet for this group. They need to form associations in order to attain adequate role-playing. They can only associate within the family group. The extra energy is therefore poured into this intensive association rather than spread over larger areas of behaviour.

CHAPTER X

STATUS

(A) SNOBBERY

IT has been implied that the people in this group, in general, are not particularly keen on improving their status. As some members of most of the families have drifted away into other social groups the Mums are aware that this may cause difficulties in family relations.

This time last year Ellen, aged 12, tried for the scholarship exam that Sybil is trying for this year. Mrs. H. said she was glad Ellen did not get it. She has seen too many children spoilt. It goes to their heads and they no longer know the children who were their friends and with whom they used to play. It makes them snobs.

Here is what a Mum says about a girl who is status conscious.

'Teresa (aged 14) is a snob. She never lifts a finger in the house. Every evening she goes straight out after tea. She goes to her friend Daphne's house. Daphne's parents are much better off than we are. They have a piano and a three-piece suite. When Teresa comes back she asks why we can't have a piano and three-piece suite. I tell her because "I bloody well can't afford it". I tell her, "Tersa, I'd like a piano and three-piece suite just as much as you, but I bloody well haven't the money." ' Teresa remains dissatisfied. Now that granny is ill she still never washes a dish or stays in five minutes. She just comes in to sleep and eat. All she does is to look at herself in the mirror and 'she's for ever brushing and combing her hair'. Mrs. W. has told her that all she'll see in the mirror one day is a 'Little man with horns'. Teresa retorts that she is only keeping herself tidy.

In the next instance the Mum seems rather ambivalent to the question of status.

Soon after Mrs. V.'s arrival she told me that she remembers her father always telling them, 'Never mix with people below yourself. Go with people as good as yourself or better than yourself so that in this way you will improve yourself.' Later in the evening when we talked of Esther's scholarship exam she said she would rather Esther does not get a scholarship to go to a better school if 'this goes to her head'. She has seen it go to the head of many a child who lives in their tenement flats. She has watched it happen. First the child does not know her neighbours then she gradually does not know her own parents and siblings. Mrs. V. would rather Esther stays at her present school than that this should happen.

(b) THOSE WHO LEAVE SHIP STREET

The next quotation illustrates the difficulties which arise when members of the family do move out of the group. It also shows the very firm reaction of the Mum to such behaviour. The twins' sister, Sue, said, 'The twins Billy and Willie have had a strange life. They are as like as two peas; they are of a clan.' Billy got engaged to a girl and when he broke it off Willie got engaged to her. She was a nice girl. When Willie learnt why Billy had broken his engagement, he did the same thing. Now they are both married to short-hand typists. Billy has married Muriel and Willie has married Eileen. They all live in suburbs just outside. 'They are all four as thick as thieves. They have lovely homes and yet the wives still go out to work.'

Three months ago Mrs. T., the boys' mother, had a row with them and has never seen them since. While she pretends not to care a hang Sue knows she is 'eating her heart out over it'. Mrs. T. went to visit Willie and Eileen in their home. While there, Billy and Muriel came. Eileen went to the door to let them in and Mrs. T. heard whispering at the door and then giggling. Billy came in, but Eileen and Muriel went straight to the kitchen where they continued to whisper and giggle. Muriel did not greet Mrs. T. as she passed. Mrs. T. waited a little while but when they did not come she got up and said, 'I'm going.' Her sons asked her why, what was up and she replied she knew that Muriel and Eileen were 'skitting' her. Her sons denied it, but the girls did not come in and so Mrs. T.

walked straight out. She was so upset she let three trams pass her before she trusted herself to board one. The next day Willie and Eileen came to see her, and Eileen assured her that they had not been 'skitting' her. Mrs. T. asked at what they had been laughing, but Eileen either would not or could not say. Mrs. T. refused to believe Eileen and told Willie and her to clear out and that they need not come to her house to see her again. She always knew that Eileen and Muriel had never thought her good enough for them and that when her sons married they tried to go as far away from home as possible. They were snobs and she would not embarrass them any more, and they could give the same message to Billy and Muriel. From that day none of the four has ever been to see her. Sue says she knows her mother was dreadfully hurt. For a month after this she often found her crying. But when Sue tries to say anything to her about it she always retorts, 'I'm not worrying, why are you?'

Sue does not know what to do. The family has always spent every Boxing Day together. They always come to them. If Billy and Willie and their wives don't come this year, her mother will break her heart, and yet she doesn't think they will come. 'It'll be an awful Christmas.' I suggested that Sue should ask them to come without letting her mother know. She replied quite firmly she could not do this. When I asked why, she hesitated, blushed and then said, 'I would never hear the last of it. I could never live it down.' I asked if she meant her brothers or their wives would tell her mother. She replied that she did not. They would not, if she asked them not to. No, she would never hear the last of it from the four of them. Reluctantly she admitted that they might be snobs. It's the girls really. Eileen and Willie are all right. 'They're solid, but not Billy and Muriel. They're flighty-tighty.' Muriel never even came to see Mrs. T. with any explanation of her behaviour. Sue always feels that if Billy died today, Muriel would marry again tomorrow. But not Eileen. 'She thinks the world of Willie.' Her mother often says to them all now that they are grown up, 'I married a rotter, but thank God none of you have turned out like him.' Sue hopes it is true: she hopes her brothers are all right. (Sue is 36 and married. Her mother is a member of her husband's household.)

The excerpt that follows gives the feelings of an unmarried girl of 24 towards status, and her reactions on coming into contact with people of a higher status. Maureen works in Woolworth's, she is attractive and intelligent. She does not feel that to be unmarried at 24 is to be on the shelf. In fact she has been courted for eight years by a boy who is anxious to marry her. She hesitates to do so, not because she is unwilling to leave her mother who died when Maureen was 8, but because she doubts if she loves the boy sufficiently. Maureen has no illegitimate baby and has not slept with this boy with whom she has been going for eight years. Thus it may be seen that in some respects she does not conform to the pattern of this group. Yet her views on class and status epitomizes those held by most of the group.

Aunt Lucy and Aunt Phoebe have climbed out of their class. Aunt Lucy by her own efforts: 'Aunt Phoebe has married money. Aunty Lucy took me younger sister Pauline, who was eighteen months when me mother died.' Pauline has remained with and been brought up by Aunt Lucy. Maureen's father married again later and has a second family. Maureen and another full sister are members of her father's and stepmother's household. Aunt Lucy and this household remain on visiting terms. Aunt Phoebe and this household do not. 'Aunt Phoebe is a snob, Aunt Lucy is not.' Aunt Phoebe has cut herself off from all members of the family except Aunt Lucy. Aunt Lucy and Aunt Phoebe visit each other. Maureen said that in spite of the fact that Aunt Lucy is not a snob, she feels ill at ease with Aunt Lucy. I asked Maureen to try and explain me her feelings. She replied, 'I like to mix with me own class. When I go to Aunty Lucy's, tea is brought in on a tray. I don't like that. I like it to be put on the table. Aunty Lucy is really awful nice but I feel she's looking round all the time in case you drop a crumb. All the rooms have carpets and everything is in order. There are only two of them there. Here there are all the kids, they make a mess and we clear up after. I prefer it like this.' I then asked Maureen how she feels when Aunt Lucy visits them in their own home here? She said, 'I feel I have to mind me P's and Q's. Perhaps the fault is me own, because I notice me father is just the same when Aunty Lucy comes. He behaves no differently, but I feel I have to behave differently and I don't like it. I feel Aunty Lucy's class sums you up by your H's.'

I asked Maureen of her younger sister Pauline who has been brought up by Aunty Lucy. I asked to which class Pauline now feels she belongs, if the difference in their upbringings has made any difficulties in their social relations. Maureen replied, 'She mixes with both classes. She has friends in both.' So far, Maureen feels that class differences have not made any appreciable difference in social relations between the sisters. 'To tell you the truth I think it is at granny's that Pauline feels most at home. Granny lives just around the corner and we all practically live there. Granny has a married daughter and her husband and child living with her and an unmarried son of 31. He's courting, but to tell you the truth I think he keeps postponing his marriage because he does not want to leave his mother. And me brother Pat lives with granny. He's 27 and his wife is expecting her first baby. They all get on well together. To tell you the truth I think it is at granny's we're all happiest. Aunty Lucy goes there too.' Granny is Maureen's dead mother's mother.

Maureen ended this subject by saying that if Aunt Phoebe now invited her to her home, she would not go.

When there is the attempt to alter status, it frequently seems to begin in childhood, and there is some indication that Dads are rather more status-conscious than Mums. Mrs. Q., in the third excerpt quoted, is atypical as she is very status conscious, although she lives in one of the dingiest houses of the lot, because she is tied to her mother who will not move.

Mr. N. compared his two boys, Stan, aged 14, and Robert, aged 12. He said that 'Stan is rough and ready whereas Robert has the manners of a gentleman'. (From what I have seen of the two boys I consider Stan has the better manners. One day fairly recently I saw Robert in the street with a whole crowd of other boys. He did not see me. Robert appeared to be the leader and was showing off. He is very large for his age. More than once he took a comb out of his pocket and combed his hair. I should sum him up as the spiv type.) So I now asked Mr. N. what he meant by the 'manners of a gentleman' and added that I often 'prefer them rough and ready'. Mrs. N., who was listening, nodded her head, but Mr. N. expressed great surprise. He said Robert is always combing his hair and looking at himself in the mirror while Stan does not care how he looks.

'Robert has the manners of a gentleman just as Miriam has the manners of a lady.' Mr. N. said he admires his daughter Miriam because 'she has improved her lot'.[1]

Veronica, aged 16, said, 'me father said he'd give me anything if I go to work at Wetherall's because Wetherall's posh, isn't it? But I don't like posh people or things, do you?'

Mrs. Q. and the boys came to tea on Saturday. Saturdays and Sundays are Mrs. Q.'s only possible days: she works until midday Saturday. They had gone into town shopping this afternoon and had to return home with ham for Mrs. Q.'s brother's tea before coming here, so they arrived late. They came incredibly grandly dressed. The boys had on suits of really good material. When I admired them Mrs. Q. said she always gets their suits at X.'s stores, and she never passes Alfred's clothes down to Bert. She gives them away to Alfred's friends. Mrs. Q. had on a black skirt with a white silk blouse and a black and white cardigan. Most of the Mums and children who have visited us have certainly felt most at home in our kitchen living-room where we have our meals. I felt Mrs. Q. was less at home in the kitchen than she had been in my room. They had come dressed for a 'front parlour' tea and were disappointed not to find one. They started by eating most gingerly. Mrs. Q. and Alfred, aged 14, kept this up. Bert, aged 12, soon gave in and called for a second helping of chips which I had to make. He said they were jolly good. Mrs. Q. immediately apologized for him and said he did not eat like this at home. I told Bert he was giving me great pleasure. Mrs. Q. said she was sure he would be sick when he got home.

While most of the group are tied to the neighbourhood, one or two people would like to move for reasons of status. The neighbourhood does contain a large number of coloured people, including half-castes who seem to be despised by both their white and coloured neighbours. 'Half-caste' is the name given to a locally born person whose mother is white and father either African or West Indian.

---

[1] An excerpt from the field notes four years later, reads, 'Robert, aged 16, has now become a Teddy Boy and has landed his parents in debt for Teddy Boy suits bought. His father has threatened to put the next pair of "drain-pipes" on the fire. Stan, aged 18, has not yet become a Teddy Boy and has just been called up.'

While talking of moving Mr. R. said, 'Another thing, it's not fair to the children now they are growing up, living in this neighbourhood.' I asked what he meant. He replied that there are a lot of 'half-castes' in the neighbourhood. I asked if unpleasant things happen or if his children had had any unpleasant experiences for this reason. Both Mr. and Mrs. R. promptly replied in the negative. They both went on to say that they thought coloured people are much maligned. If anything unpleasant happens, it is at once blamed on to a 'coloured man or a half-caste'. Actually they are no worse than the whites —'there's good and bad in every race'. Although Mr. and Mrs. R. hold this opinion they said there is undoubtedly a stigma attached to living in a half-caste area.

There is an isolated case reported in our field notes of a woman who had her husband's grave dug up years later and the coffin moved from the back of the cemetery, 'where nobody could see the grave', to the front. Here is what our informant thought of this and of the woman.

At one time Mrs. O. pushed a wheelbarrow selling vegetables. Now she has two greengrocery shops and she has bought her son and daughter one each. 'She has made pots of money and so she talks big. But she has nothing to talk big for, she's nobody. I must say if he'd been mine I would rather let him lie.'

(c) LACK OF COMPETITION

In general the competitive attitude of keeping up with other people is lacking in Ship Street. Not one television aerial has yet appeared amongst this group. Conduct such as cruelty to children or stealing from your mother may be heartily disapproved of but the people of Ship Street do not feel called upon to dictate to others what furniture they should have or what conduct they should pursue. Their family circles constitute their social background and so the wish and effort to be leaders in a non-related group are lacking. They would always like more money to spend but the desire is not strong enough to make them alter the pattern of their existence to get it. 'Getting on' would mean moving out of the warmth of their families and out of the familiar way of life of their streets. It would mean learning new modes of behaviour and having to

116

cope with situations for which they have no previously determined pattern. Therefore educational grants are turned down,
jobs and houses in new places refused. Heads will not then
'be turned' and the tie to the locality and so to the Mum
remains unbroken.

CHAPTER XI

CRIME

(A) IN GROUP AND OUT GROUP

'I PREFER to tell the truth though I know it never pays. Honesty doesn't pay, does it?'

This appears to be a prevailing belief in the district. The general feeling seems to be that it is a pity to be found out. The reasoning behind this behaviour is that the world is divided into the individual's own group, and the rest. The individual is loyal to members of his own group, but the rest of the world is fair game. Here is an example of a girl of 11 who was taking her turn of helping in a play centre canteen. June had been given Mary's place in the canteen. She had been working a racket. She had been giving her friends cocoa free and charging it up to the others.

In the next illustration this reasoning is extended to adult behaviour. The incident was not described as an anti-social act but as a permissible rather clever thing to do. Mrs. X. went to Z.'s January sales this year looking for a coat. She saw a brown one there which fitted her. It was marked £6 10s. There was another coat marked £3 6s.—an awful thing. She changed the two price tickets. Then when she went to pay for the coat she found she was 5s. short. She rushed home to get the 5s. She had the children with her. She dumped them at a neighbour's house. The whole time she was terrified somebody else would take the coat. She had thrown it on the floor in a corner hoping nobody would see it. It was there when she got back with the 5s.

(B) THEFT

Disloyalty to one's own group is regarded with strong disapproval. It has already been shown that for a child to steal from his mother is a cardinal sin. When a boy of 11 was caught for housebreaking and theft and the informer had been his sister, here is what the children's mother said.

'Fancy giving your own brother's name.' The girl, aged 12, replied, 'It was only when I was shaken and shaken and I was frightened they would take me away, as I had been playing outside, that I gave Frank's name.'

Two boys, aged 16, who live in tenement flats and who readily admitted that they have broken open and stolen from gas meters, hastily made this reservation. 'But never from our block.' The block has become the in-group, but not the building.

Stealing then is considered normal so long as it takes place outside the individual's group. Some children who often came to the field-workers' house sometimes took nuts or sweets but always managed it so that we saw what they had done before they went home. During a rather intensive period of the field work we had nearly become part of their individual group and therefore enough guilt was felt to make genuine theft impossible. Another group of children, who have visited us regularly over a period of five years and who have always been invited to join us in a meal when they have called, have come to accept us as members of their group. Nothing has ever been locked when these children have been in the house, purses have been in the room; nothing has ever been taken.

A boy of 12 when asked if he and his gang steal from a main street of shops near where they live, spontaneously replied, 'No, because we're nearly all on orders now' (i.e. deliver for the shops, out of school hours, on payment of a few pennies).

Although stealing from out groups is regarded as normal, the emotion generated over a false accusation can be most intense. One day Mandy, aged 13, and Marian, aged 11, were at the shop—a general stores. Mandy asked if it had ever been broken into. The shopkeeper told them not to be cheeky. That night the shop was raided. That evening Mandy was at the school concert and Marian was at the pictures. The shopkeeper went to their school and told Sister. Sister accused them. The Police Inspector also went there and accused them. Mandy 'was crying her heart out'. Marian started to bawl too. They went home to their mothers and told them. They were unable to eat their dinners that day. Mandy's mother went to the school and complained that they were blamed for everything. Later the man who robbed the shop was found and the Inspector and the shopkeeper came and said they were sorry. Sister never apologized. Marian's mother has threatened to go 'and break up Sister'. Marian hopes she will.

At times indignation is expressed over children's delinquent behaviour. However, this is generally because one of the children belonging to the indignant mother has been caught. The mother rationalizes either that it was not her child at all or that the others had led him astray. However, this attitude is very much a verbal one composed partly of fear of being found out, partly as an excuse that one of her children has been caught, and partly due to a rather vague perception that people in other social groups consider stealing wrong.

As this research was not essentially on crime, no attempt has been made to study criminal behaviour in the area as a whole. Anti-social acts have simply been recorded in the instances where they are part of the life of the group under observation. These people are not criminals in the accepted sense of the word; they are merely a group of people whose values are slightly different from those generally accepted in this country, or to be more accurate, those which sociologists think are more generally accepted. It would be likely for a group of people in this area to have some connection with more serious crime than that already described and ganga and Indian hemp can be bought. This is generally known to be available but there is no evidence that any member of this group uses it.

When her sister, Mrs. C., appeared this morning, Mrs. F. asked her if she'd heard the woman opposite last night. Mrs. C. said she had not. Mrs. F. said she had been unable to sleep a wink. 'It's disgraceful the way the woman carries on and her language'—Mrs. F. had to close her eyes at the recollection—'something ought to be done about it.' She's never heard such language in her life. 'The police ought to do something. She lives with a coloured man, not married to him. They smoke Indian hemp.' When I asked her how she knows she replied I ought to have heard her language. The woman is always shouting and fighting with everybody. 'She must smoke it.'

Various rackets are run in connection with ships. Here is a

description of one café. Rafi and Meg came here from another town about five years ago. They had been living together before this. 'Rafi has made a packet.' When I asked if he charges a great deal for meals then, Mrs. X. replied 'he only serves chips'. He has made a great amount of money through buying things cheap from coloured sailors and then selling them at retail price on shore. All the coloured sailors go to his café. Mrs. X. doesn't know if he does a traffic in Indian hemp—she has never come across it there—but he well might. I asked if the café is a brothel. Mrs. X. replied no, Rafi would never let a couple have a room there but it is a meeting place for all the prostitutes. He keeps open till all hours. It is here that the sailors pick up the prostitutes. 'The prostitutes owe their business to him.'

(c) BEING SENT AWAY

Owing to the general attitude described in the beginning of the chapter it would not be expected that parents feel much shame when their children get into trouble with the police. Again, it is just bad luck that our Johnny was caught and not the next door neighbour's Tommy.

One day in order to put Mrs. K. in a good mood I tried a topic to which she usually warms and asked, 'And how's Bill?' She replied, 'Bill's all right: it's Gregory now.' I asked what she meant and she told me that she had just come from the Juvenile Court and Gregory, aged 12, had got three years. He's in a remand home till a place is found for him. She saw him in court today and he was all right. He didn't even cry but he said he was not getting enough to eat at the remand home. He had stolen a bottle of lemonade and some bananas from a green-grocer's, that's all. Mrs. K. thought it most unfair putting the boy away for three years for this. She said the magistrate was all right, but what the probation officer said wasn't very good. She said the boy had already been given a caution and the boy's father was shortly going back to sea so there would be no one at home to exert any authority over the boy. Mrs. K. looked belligerently at Mr. K. as she said this and he remained silent. She went on, 'It's always our boys. Albert and Ronnie from round the corner were with him but they only got 28 days.' She thought this most unfair. They had done exactly the same as Gregory but they put all the blame on him. 'Why should Gregory get three years and they 28 days. It's not fair,' she flung at her husband, while he walked up and down but continued to remain silent.

Quite often it is the mother's favourite son who both becomes delinquent and gets caught. The custom is for her to go down to court to plead for him. Fathers do not go unless they are specifically sent for. Another interesting fact about these boys is that they are generally spoken of as being quiet and kind at home, very considerate to their younger siblings, and they pay great attention to their personal appearance. Here is what his father said of Tom, aged 18. He had been a good boy in every way but one vice had taken hold of him over which Tom had no control, and that was gambling. There wasn't a cleaner boy in this neighbourhood. There was never a day when he would miss cleaning his teeth first thing in the morning and before he went to bed. He would never wear a shirt more than two days. When he came home he would wash and iron his shirt himself. If he saw a line of washing hanging up waiting to be ironed he would quietly put on the iron and iron the whole lot for his mother. He would wash and iron his sister's clothes. 'He was the apple of his mother's eye.' For a long time she covered up his gambling and Mr. M. had no idea what was going on. Tom had a good job. Sometimes he wouldn't go to work but gambled all day. First he took the hinges off the wardrobe in this room and stole £12. Next time he did the same thing and stole £20. Mr. M. said he must have had more than this altogether. It was his grandfather's money. Then he broke open the gas meter and took the £4 15s. that was in it. That finished his mother. When he had stolen the other money they still had savings. When he took the £4 15s. they had none. His mother herself went to the Police Station. Tom was put in prison for five to six months. At the end of this time they were told that Tom was going to be sent to Borstal for three years. His mother went to the Police Station and said she did not want Tom sent there. She had wanted him sent to prison for a short sentence so that he could learn his lesson and then she wanted him home. The police told Mrs. M. that the case would come up on a Thursday and she had better come to court to plead for him on that day. She did so. She found the case had been heard on the Wednesday, the day before. The police had told her the wrong day purposely. Tom was sent to Borstal for three years. Mrs. M. always reproached herself that she 'had put him there'. They were her last thoughts before she died. Mr. M. said, 'It was his mother that spoilt him.' (This is the same informant who did not realize that pools are gambling.)

The following attitude on the mother's part is very typical. Mrs. B. laughed with affection and said Jimmy, aged 14, had always been a handful. 'Not bad, just devilment.' She couldn't get him to go to school. He would leave every morning, come home to dinner, leave at school time again, but he had never been near the school. When the master first came to her and said, 'Mrs. B. what about Jim?' she replied, 'What about him? He's at school.' The master said, 'Oh no, he isn't,' and produced the register which showed that Jim hadn't been to school for a week. After this Jimmy would go to school for a few days and then there would be a repetition of the same performance. He would go down to the docks 'to get the nuts. All the boys used to do this. How do you expect the boys to go to school when the nuts are in the docks?'

Girls do not seem to get into trouble with such frequency. As one granny says, 'boys give you trouble while they are at school and girls bring trouble home afterwards'. Anyhow the girls do not get caught so frequently! Only two girls in our 61 families are in institutions. Their offence was not stealing but in both cases consorting with men. A little while ago Flo, aged 15, got into trouble for sitting in cafés with Arabs. She didn't do anything wrong. The 'Welfare Officer' called on her and she had to go down to the Juvenile Court. They took Flo away and put her in a remand home. She was there for three weeks. From there she was sent on to a 'training school'. Mrs. D. has had a letter from Flo and she is all right. Flo has always given her a lot of trouble. As a child she had a lot of pain and vomiting and the doctor said it was a gastric ulcer. She was put into hospital and they were supposed to have 'drained it away' but Mrs. D. thinks it is still there. I asked if Flo is going to have a baby. Mrs. D. said, 'Oh no' and repeated that Flo did not do anything wrong only she would sit in cafés with Arabs. The 'Welfare Officer' had been very kind and told her not to worry but it was really the best thing for Flo to be sent to a 'training school' or else she would be sure to get into trouble. Flo gets a lot of pain when she menstruates. Mrs. D. said that when she had beaten Flo as a child she often had to take a good hold of herself as sometimes she had felt like murdering her, and then where would she be? Mrs. D. flushed and trembled as she said this. (Information was obtained at a later visit that Flo was found to be pregnant.)

Lately there have been many attempts made to explain the increase of juvenile delinquency. The main criticism that can be made is that delinquency so often appears to be treated as if it were the actual sickness itself and not merely one symptom of a much more fundamental social and personal disorganization. This group is not sick but socially immature. The in-individuals composing it have not been able, for reasons discussed elsewhere, to form an adequate number of associations. Their affections and loyalties are confined to the extended family unit and the rest of the world is regarded with fear and often hostility. An individual joining an association automatically generates some degree of loyalty to the association. In accordance with the development of sentiments this may, or at least have the potentiality, to spread to other situations. In the case of this group loyalty is only felt to the in group where it is inevitably accompanied by a rather primitive and very strong type of emotion. The possibility of feeling loyal to a group where strong emotion is not generated is outside the scope of Ship Street people.

Bowlby's[1] 'affectionless child' seems to have touched the heart of so many writers on delinquency so that they forget the early suggestion of Burt, that the over-indulged child could also become delinquent. There is enough evidence in this investigation to put forward the suggestion that it is frequently 'the apple of me eye' who gets into trouble. Most of the Mums who have a child 'put away' seem to yearn especially for him. They go to see him at his approved school whenever possible, sometimes spending the rent money on the visits. One Dad is frequently heard to say, 'Your mother's spent the rent money again, she's been to see Mike.' It is interesting to note that the presents they take are sometimes forbidden by the school. One Mum

[1] J. M. Bowlby, *Maternal Care and Mental Health*, W.H.O. Monograph, Series No. 2, Geneva, 1952.

frequently takes cigarettes for her son aged 14 because he particularly asks for them, although she knows he is not allowed them.

Here again, as in the case of gambling, words have different meanings or incomplete meanings for the Ship-Streeter. Doing the pools is not gambling, taking paint or spirits from the docks or other employer is not thieving. Employer here refers to some public employer such as the Dock Board or other similar anonymous body. Great loyalty may be shown to an individual private employer. The operative concept seems to be the amount stolen. It is not thieving for the cleaners to take paint in 1 lb. jars everyday from works or offices when those buildings are being repainted; taking away a drum of paint, even were it possible, probably would be thieving. On the whole there is a lot of 'obliging'. Our Bert has a job where he has access to some commodity someone wants. It's a waste to buy it in the shops where it is so expensive. He takes a small quantity and gives it. He in turn will then be obliged with something he wants. The situation is really very similar to the minor and amateur Black Markets which went on during the war where someone would give a few eggs and receive in exchange a bag of sugar. In neither of these instances is money used, and there is no consciousness of law-breaking.

The following quotations show the line drawn between private and public property. Mrs. A.'s children have been in trouble for theft before, a son is even now at an approved school. The fact that the theft was from a private person and it was found out pushed her into action. Gertie, aged 13, was walking down the next street with Rosie, aged 14, one evening. A woman's washing hung outside on a line. There were three nice, almost new dresses, on the line. Rosie whipped them off. The woman came round to see Mrs. A. and told her that she had seen Gertie and Rosie passing shortly before she noticed the disappearance of the dresses. She said that if the dresses were not handed back to her that evening she would report the matter to the police. Mrs. A. told the woman Gertie had not got the dresses as she had not taken them. The woman remained adamant. If the dresses were not returned to her that night she would go to the police. Mrs. A. went across to see Rosie, who was in bed. She said, 'Look, Rosie, if I have to stay here all night I am not going home till I have those dresses.' Rosie said, 'I've not got them.' Mrs. A. repeated that she was not budging till she had got the dresses and Rosie repeated that she had not got them. Rosie's elder sister May heard Mrs. A. and came in. She dragged Rosie out of bed and asked her where the dresses were. Rosie continued to deny all knowledge of them. May found two of the dresses in Rosie's bedroom. Rosie then admitted that the third was hidden in the basement amongst rubble and rubbish. Mrs. A. took the dresses back to the woman.

When Barbara, aged 16, was telling me of her first love, she mentioned that he is at present in an approved school for stealing. I expressed surprise. She promptly replied, 'Ah, only thieving from the big stores or the like, he wouldn't rob from you or me.'

It is interesting that Barbara emphasizes the distinction between stealing from public property and the individual by using different words for the two activities. It is 'thieving' to steal from the 'stores or the like' but it is 'robbing' to steal 'from you or me'.

(D) VIOLENCE

In Ship Street this general attitude of splitting what appears to be similar behaviour into quite differently evaluated sub-groups is general. Delinquent behaviour shades off in a graduated manner into genuine planned crime. The latter is rare in Ship Street as lack of ability to plan is a conspicuous part of the inhabitants' psychological make up. The crimes they do are generally impulsive. For example the switching of tickets on the coat was not previously planned but done under the stimulus of seeing the much nicer coat which was too expensive. The violence too is spasmodic and impulsive. Tempers get frayed and violence takes place. This ranges from a serious attack on someone which succeeds, to the throwing of household objects at members of the family. This is a general habit of all the Mums. We collected a list of objects thrown.

Stories of violence followed from all three children; violence on both the mothers' and the children's parts. It has already been recorded that pokers, shovels, forks, shoes and bowls of

water are used as missiles in times of stress. Tonight we heard
of knives. All three children stated that their mothers have
thrown knives at them. Sylvia, aged 15, demonstrated how her
mother coldly aims the knife and throws the blade at her. Sylvia
of course, has always dodged the knife, but she maintains, that
at the moment, her mother intends to hurt. One occasion after
her mother had thrown the knife at her, Sylvia picked it up and
ran upstairs crying. Upstairs she deliberately cut her finger
with the knife: 'I had to do something.' Her mother did not
yield when she saw the blood. Maggie, aged 13, said on one
occasion when her mother threw a knife at her she got so angry
she went to hit her mother with her fist. She put her fist right
through the window. Her mother tried to make her pay for the
broken window but she would not. On another occasion she,
too, picked up the knife her mother had thrown at her and cut
her hand with it. But her mother softened when she saw the
blood and put her to bed and waited on her. When she saw
however that Maggie was better the next day, 'she went for
me again'. Freda, aged 15, recounted an occasion when her
mother threw a knife at her and she got so angry 'that I kicked
me foot right through the panel of the door'. Another time 'me
mother threw the knife at me and I ducked and it went right
through the sideboard. Me mother was so pleased to have
missed me she made an awful fuss of me. Then she saw it
stuck in the sideboard and she begun to murder me all over
again.'

This is how this same mother behaved however when Mr.
X. opposite chased Freda out of his house with a poker. Freda
had gone home and told her mother. The next day Mrs. E.
passed Mr. X. in the street. 'As she went past him she hit him
on the face with the back of her hand like this.' Mr. X. did not
retaliate.

A woman of 50, who looks a more down-trodden Mum than
most, told us when she knew us well, while speaking of her
husband who gets drunk, 'Why I threw all the dinner plates at
him. I've hit him many a time you know. I took the knife to
him once and would have murdered him but Mrs. Y. next door
stopped me. Ask Mrs. Y.'

From these excerpts it can be seen that crime and violence in
Ship Street are seldom planned but happen impulsively. The

implications of this conclusion will be discussed fully in Chapter XVII. The other important point is that people in Ship Street define crime and delinquent behaviour rather differently from the middle-class usages of the words.

CHAPTER XII

SUPERSTITION AND RELIGION

IT is to be expected that this group, coming from a poverty-stricken area, would be prolific in the production of superstition and this has proved to be the case. Although these superstitions must originate in the same configuration of psychological needs they have been classified here into the following categories for convenience.

(A) LUCK

Luck is frequently mentioned, it was my lucky day or unlucky day, as the case may be. Colours such as green are considered unlucky. Objects may be felt to possess either lucky or unlucky qualities. One Mum said, 'My mother-in-law got off the bus the other day because a woman in green came and sat near her.'

Trudi found a little silver shoe on the road one day. She gave it to some girl who gave it to another and so on, and the shoe has now ended up with Maisie. Maisie rubbed it on her dress to bring her luck and then put it away. It did bring her luck. She found 11d. She gave 5½d. of this to her friend. Trudi said the shoe never brought her luck because she never found any money.

In another case a family moved from a house because the mother lost three children while living there.

'It was an unlucky house because very rich people lived there and me mother said very rich people are always unlucky.'

The next quotation, though concerned with luck, illustrates the making of a charm. This particular charm is common to other cultures.

Eileen was a cawl baby. Mrs. J. said she thought the reason

why the nurse was so rough and unpleasant was 'because she wanted the veil and we wouldn't give it to her'. (The nurse sat on the bed smoking though she knew Mrs. J. did not like smoke.) Mrs. J.'s mother, Mrs. B., dried the 'veil' in salt and then stretched it over cardboard. They gave a piece to Mrs. J.'s married sister Maggie and kept another piece for 'me cousin for her husband'. Both men were sailors. A sailor with a 'veil' in his possession will never drown. Unfortunately the cousin's husband never got home to collect his piece and was drowned. So they gave both bits to Maggie who still has them (12 years after). Shortly after the baby's birth a man came to the house and offered £25 for the 'veil'. Mrs. B. said, 'I reckon Maggie's husband is worth more than £25 to Maggie.'

(B) FATALISM

It is very common in Ship Street to find a feeling that things are 'meant'. It is, of course, an extension of the feeling of luck—that is, some external agency decides and the individual can only bow to this decision. Mrs. S. had just taken casual work and done two days before her mother's accident. On her accident she gave it up and hasn't gone out to work since. She said, 'So I wasn't meant to go out to work was I?' Mrs. Y. mentioned that both she and her husband were their parents' third child and there are seven children in both families. She felt there was an affinity between them because of the above fact.

(C) UNDIFFERENTIATED FEAR

Fear plays a very big part in the lives of this group. It is often disguised under the phrase, 'It's me nerves.' Even quite small children as well as adults say this. Exaggerated poses with the hand over the heart are common. When the children aged 11 and 12 visited us one day they asked to go to the lavatory. Once they asked they were unable to wait a moment and started dancing about. Yet they would not go across the yard in the dark by themselves, although a light shone across it. All three therefore went to the lavatory together. (This fear of darkness seems almost universal amongst children interviewed.) Another time other children were surprised that I have no fear at staying alone in a big house like this. They all said they would not do it. I asked them of what they would be frightened. They were unable or unwilling to say except Daisie, who said, 'I would be frightened that somebody would come in by the windows.' She had the most fears. She said openly, 'I would not sleep in a bed by myself.' During tea a friend came in unexpectedly by the back door. I was in the larder. When I came into the room they all told me she had appeared and they were all frightened out of their wits, despite the fact that they knew her. There was such an air of panic in the room that I was quite sure they were pulling my leg and said so. They assured me it was not so and that if I looked in the yard I would find her. I did. Daisie said, 'Oh, Miss, I nearly fainted.'

At times the undifferentiated fears are personified and ghosts are reported. One day during a visit of two girls, aged 12, the talk was about fears of the dark. Moira said her mother once sent her to the cellar for some coal. She screamed and ran back because she saw a man in a black cloak with a dagger. Her mother went down and said there was nothing, that she was soft and must get the coal. She went down again and a voice said, 'Come here.' She looked and saw the ghost of her Aunt Beatie. Aunt Beatie had lived and died in their house. She had been burned by a candle catching her hair. The family do not use her room and Moira would not even go in it. Both children agreed that they had heard a voice calling their names when they came out of the confession box in church. They had looked and saw no one. When we offered rational explanations, Joyce said she had seen her father. He appeared outside her window. He was not dressed as in a photo but in long robes. (We asked how she recognized him since he had died before her birth, and she replied, 'We have a photograph.')

These fears do seem to inhibit action through the imposition of restrictions on movement, etc. In contrast to this great fear of undifferentiated situations the children, anyhow, seem to deal adequately with concrete events which might well scare them. In the neighbourhood they are quite often accosted by men who try to lure them into cars. These attempts are usually foiled by the children with most apt rude remarks.

(D) INTUITION AND OMENS

Intuition sounds a long word to be used by members of this group but it is used quite often.

Mrs. D. said, 'I have intuition something awful.'

During the evening Mr. C. proclaimed that a 'woman's intuition goes far deeper than a man's'. When Jimmy went into hospital his wife said, 'He'll never come out.' He asked her what she was talking about; she repeated, 'He'll never come out.' He didn't.

Intuition frequently merges into a belief in omens and this is certainly the case with the Mums. When she entered her fiance's home, for the first time, after his death, a polo sweater that she had given him the Christmas before, fell off the line onto her. Her mother said, 'It was as if he did not wish me to enter the house.' Mrs. Y. had seen a spark lying on the grid this morning and had said, 'There is a stranger coming.' And I had come.

Another Mum announced: 'I notice it always goes dark when someone is hanged.'

(E) HEALTH

In a group of this type health and disease is an ever-present topic of conversation. As might be expected many magical beliefs exist. One Thursday when Cissy came to us her eyes were sore and she had styes. I asked her what she was doing about them. She replied that her Aunty Stella was going to pierce her ears on Sunday. When I asked what that had to do with her eyes, they all three told me that that was good for your eyes. Her Aunty Stella had pierced at least half a dozen people's ears in the family. When I asked if that had made their eyes any better Cissy said, 'Of course.' Mary said she ought to wear 'sleepers' after her ears are pierced. Cissy said she hasn't any but that won't matter so long as she has her ears pierced. Mary said she ought to wear 'sleepers' (little rings) to prevent the holes from closing up. On Tuesday when I saw Cissy her ears were pierced and she had on sleepers with a blue stone in them. Her Aunty Stella had done them. Her eyes were no better. (The belief that to have your ears pierced is good for your eyes is a common one in this group.)

A rather unusual remedy was suggested by Mrs. U. who said, 'Port wine is good for worms. It burns them out.'

As in Jamaica, there is a great fear of operations, and, as there, this fear seems to be expressed most often by the men. Mrs. R. said if she was told she needed an operation of any sort she would have it. She would not be frightened! Now her husband has very bad pain in his injured toe at times. The doctor says the toe should be removed but, in spite of the unnecessary pain he has, he will not agree to this. When she tries to encourage him to have it off he says, 'You want to be shut of me.'

Again, these women have much the same attitude to quack medical aid as the Jamaicans did to the balm yard healers. In this area there is a 'dispenser' to whom many of the Mums go. Molly goes to a '4d. Dispenser'. If there is anything wrong with either her or her children she goes to him much more than to her National Health doctor. She has more faith in him. She has introduced Elsa to the man and Elsa took her little girl who had not been at all well. He gave her some medicine. Everything he prescribes costs 4d. Molly showed me a bottle of mixture he prescribed for her children. She herself had been feeling utterly exhausted some little while ago. She did not know what was wrong. She was quite listless. He gave her some pills. He told her to take one first thing in the morning, before rising if possible, and another at midday. She never took the second dose. She does not know what is in the pills 'but blimey after one I felt I could get up on the roof and take the tiles off'. Molly showed me the pills; they were yellow and about the size of a Veganin. On the box was marked 'Caution'. She said the dispenser had told her that she must not exceed the dose nor leave the pills anywhere where the children could get hold of them. She hides them. She herself would very much like to know what is in them. She knows two other women whom the dispenser had put on the same pills, but they were only told to take one a day.

Mrs. C. said she felt very tempted to try the 4d. Dispenser. All the women round here go to him. He is just at the bottom of the hill by the main street. The only reason she has not been to him is because she has been with this doctor for so long. She thought she ought to give him a trial first. But if she does not feel better soon she thinks she'll pay the dispenser a visit.

Betty had been to the dispenser and he had said that she must go to bed and stay there a week. That was the only way to get rid of the pains in her legs. I asked if they had a National Health doctor and Mrs. W. said that they had, 'but to tell you the truth I have more faith in the dispenser'. Her grandmother, now aged 87, used to go to the same dispenser. At a later meeting I asked Betty about the dispenser. She said, 'He's much better than the doctor, Miss.' Whenever any of them have anything wrong they go to the dispenser.

As in Jamaica, and many other places there is the superstition that a lactating woman will be unable to conceive. One or two Mums seem to have breast-fed their children for an abnormally long time, but often, in spite of this belief, most put them on the bottle in about a month or two. Mrs. B. said that she had had her children in such quick succession because she had been unable to breast-feed any of them. She had no milk. The hospital 'reckoned it would have been better for me if I could have fed them'. When questioned she said that she believes a woman does not become pregnant while she has a baby at the breast.

(F) DREAMS

Dreams are considered important. The two quoted illustrate firstly a straightforward wish-fulfilment that one of the field-workers should quell a troublesome teacher, and secondly, a dream of the omen type. Violet asked if we knew Miss X., her teacher. She said she asked this becasue she dreamed that Miss J. went to the school with her. The teacher asked her name and Violet explained who she was. Miss J. hit the teacher for Violet. The teacher just stood.

Mrs. K. dreams frequently and she attaches significance to her dreams. She told me of two deaths at length. The first was her mother's death. She dreamt it the night before it happened and so was prepared for it. The other was her brother-in-law's, Fred's, death. He was torpedoed in 1941. In her dream she saw him drowning. He had an arm outstretched above the water calling, 'Katie, Katie, save me.' She tried to reach him but couldn't. His closed fist was the last she saw. That evening Mr. K.'s mother stood on their doorstep at 6.30. It was a bitter night and snowing hard. Mr. K. asked, 'What on earth has brought you out on a night like this?' as he opened the door to her. But Mrs. K. knew and asked, 'Is it Fred or Bill?' Her mother-in-law replied, 'Fred.' She had received a wire that evening telling her of his death. Mr. K. said that his wife had told him her dream that morning.

(G) RELIGION

The majority of the 61 families are Catholics. Where one parent is Catholic the children go to the Church Schools and are brought up in the Roman Catholic faith. There is only one exception to this.

In 34 cases both parents are Roman Catholic, in 6 cases the woman is Catholic the man Protestant, in 5 cases the woman is Protestant the man Catholic. In 8 cases both parents are Protestant. In 3 cases other religions are cited.

In 45 families, therefore, the Catholic religion is predominant. The children are ardently religious but the Mums do not belong to the various church associations. The following example illustrates the attitude of many of the Mums. Mrs. Z. said although they are all R.C.s religion is not of very much importance to her. Her children, of course, are being brought up as R.C.s but she herself doesn't go much to church. They hardly ever talk of religion in the house and she thinks fighting over religion is silly. Her father is C. of E., her mother R.C., but they never had any difficulty over this and certainly not fights. They never discussed religion in the home. She remembers, as children, it was their father who was always getting them ready for and hurrying them off to R.C. Sunday School. There used to be a lot of fights in the neighbourhood between Catholics and Protestants but people are more sensible about this now and don't take any notice. This street is very mixed but you never hear a fight over religion—or very, very seldom.

The next one starts from a slightly different assumption but really comes to the same conclusion in the end. Although Sheila, aged 19, thinks religious differences are at the root of her grandmother's, Mrs. E.'s, antagonism towards her father, she said, 'It's funny because none of us are really very religious —except Arthur, aged 10.' He's the only one who goes to church every Sunday 'and he really loves it'. He gets up early every Sunday, puts on his best clothes, and goes off to church by himself. On Ash Wednesday 'he went to get the ashes without saying a word to any of us'. No one suggests that he should go. While on this subject Sheila told me, too, that her Bert is not Catholic. Her family all know this but it doesn't seem to worry them in the slightest. They all like Bert and appear to want her to marry him—even Mrs. E. But she does not want to marry yet. Of course, if she did marry Bert they would 'have to come to an arrangement about the children'. And Sheila said—although she's not religious—the children would have to be brought up as Catholics 'because after all you can't get rid of your upbringing'.

As in Jamaica there is a very personal attitude to God among both Catholics and Protestants. There seems to be a belief in a deity who will intervene in the personal life of the individual.

'It was sad, but as I always say, God knows best.'

Emma told me she is Church of England. She said, 'I am a firm believer in God; in God mind you.' All her prayers have been answered. When she was injured in an air raid she prayed, 'God don't let me die, oh, God don't let me die'; and he didn't. She has always been lucky. It is better to be lucky than rich. The rich aren't always happy. I asked, tactfully, if she had considered herself lucky when she had got the bomb. She replied, 'Ah, that was for a purpose.' When I asked what purpose, she said, that we didn't know. We have to live to find out.

It has been stressed before that most of the Ship Street children are ardent church attenders. Sometimes the Mothers send them so as to get a little peace. They are questioned too in at least one school whether or not they have been. At adolescence this attendance seems to peter out gradually until marriage when it frequently ceases altogether. Here is what two recent school leavers say. Margaret and Rose who have left school now, say that they no longer go to church regularly every Sunday. They told me if they do go their mothers don't believe that they have been to church so there's no point in going. (Margaret once told me she wanted to be a nun.) Shirley, still at school, said if she goes to church her mother asks her which priest took the service. 'When I say Father X.

she says "No he did not", and he did and she says I haven't been to church so I am not going any more.'

The hold which the Catholic Church acquires over the children seems to persist, in this group, only in the form of prohibitions of conduct, and this not always very logically. For example, Ship Street regards birth control as a sin but abortion before the age of three months a perfectly legitimate measure. After three months it is not attempted for fear of maiming the child. The other contacts which the adults have with the church is through the taking of tickets in pools and sweeps, and in joining in processions which are extremely popular.

CHAPTER XIII

FEUDS

(A) EXAMPLES OF FEUDS

FEUDS are fairly common and range from simple quarrels, which are not made up, to the most complicated vendettas which produce a series of lawsuits. The topics over which feuds begin are numerous, money and abuse being perhaps the most common. Mrs. L.'s mother's sister and her siblings all live in Liverpool near her. She never visits them; they never visit her. The reason for this estrangement is her marriage. Her aunt opposed her marrying a R.C. and 'she has set them all against me'. Even her young brother, whom she looked after for eighteen months when he was six months old and who is now 17, never comes to see her. But then, of course, he still lives with his aunt. None of her family came to her wedding. A little while ago she met her aunt in the street and 'we had words over the children'. Mrs. P. had Florrie with her and the inference was that the row was over her children being brought up as R.C.s. Her aunt struck her. Mrs. L. was so ashamed that this should happen in the street that she did not strike her back but hurried home. She said she feels sure that if her mother were alive today her mother's attitude would not be so uncharitable.

Betty went on to say that they would not have been so poor if her mother had got any of the money that her mother left her. 'But Aunty Aggie pinched it all.' Aunty Aggie lives in London and is married to a rich man but her mother and Aunty Aggie don't speak any more.

Mr. P. fell out with them all over his mother's death. When his mother died they all agreed that they wanted her buried decently and that she should have a headstone. Mr. P. made the necessary enquiries and found it would cost between £30

138

and £35. He reckoned if they all six shared expenses it would work out at a fiver each. They agreed. When it came to paying up his eldest sister gave £1—she was the eldest of the family—his other two sisters paid £2 each, his youngest sister Eileen, who was ill, paid £4 and his younger brother £2 10s. He was disgusted with the lot of them, except Eileen, and he told them what he thought of them. He told them that they need never put their feet inside his house. So he is not on visiting terms with his brothers and sisters. (Eileen has since died.) In fact, he and his eldest sister are not on speaking terms. He was also disgusted with the way they all behaved after their mother died. His sisters did not wash his mother's body after her death and left her lying in a dirty kitchen living-room. He asked them if they were going to scrub the floor and they said they were not. They had to go out to buy black. He asked his brother if he would help and he found something else to do.

On her way back home Mrs. B. went to her friend's shop to fetch the children. While there a 'jack' (C.I.D. man) came up to her and asked, 'Mrs. B?' The woman opposite who had slept with her husband before his marriage, and whom she wanted to flatten, had set the 'jack' on her. He had come to warn her to leave the woman alone. In reply to my question Mrs. B. said she had been 'phoning the woman from the office where she cleans and abusing her. The other day her husband answered the 'phone and Mrs. B. put on an awful refined voice and asked if she could speak to Mrs. R., the husband was duly impressed and put on a refined voice back, asking who was speaking please as his wife was in bed, not very well. She replied that it was an old friend, she wouldn't remember the name. The husband was just going to fetch his wife when she heard the child Tina say, 'Daddy, I believe it is Mrs. B.' She shouted down the 'phone that it bloody well was Mrs. B. The jack said he had come to advise her to stop this kind of thing. Mrs. B. let fly. She told him she knows the law and that he shouldn't accost her like that in a shop in front of other people. Everybody knows he is a jack. If he wants to issue her with a summons let him bring it to her house and then they can go to court. She told him to go back and tell the woman that 'she could come kiss her arse'. During this Mrs. B. mentioned that she had seen the jack on her doorstep three times but she wouldn't open the door to him. Mrs. B. was boiling and continued to boil. That evening she went over to the woman's house and put her finger on the bell and kept it there until the door was opened. The woman opened the door. Mrs. B. 'hit her for four'; she 'flattened' her. The woman fell in her hall and Mrs. B. would have 'pulverized her' if only she had known that the woman's husband was away in Manchester that night. But she was afraid the 'whiskers' would come out any moment and hit her in his wife's defence and then her husband would be involved in the fight. He was away at the time and doesn't yet know anything of all this. The woman has never said a word to her since and Mrs. B. feels much better.

(B) PRIVATE JUSTICE

We were fortunately able to get both sides of one feud and both versions are reproduced below.

Mrs. O. is unable to talk of the T.'s without flushing. She said, 'I don't know why you go to see them but of course you can please yourself.' I don't know them as she does. She lived below them once. Molly and that eldest girl are the worst. Everybody in the street dislikes them. Only this morning the butcher began talking about the family. She said, 'Don't talk to me about them.' Mrs. O. said I didn't know, but one day when her little Alice was a baby and she was expecting her son, Alice got drenched through early in the morning when she was in bed. 'The filthy woman.' When I could get a word in I said, 'Accidents do happen you know, Mrs. O.' 'Accident my foot,' she replied, 'the bucket was full. She never empties it, the filthy woman.' I asked what Mr. T. is like. She replied, 'A little red-faced man.' The children 'pinch anything'. From time to time Mrs. O. appealed to her husband for confirmation of her opinion of the T.'s. He said nothing but nodded his head and blinked his eyes when she waited for a response.

The people on the other side, the T.'s, said that at one time they had a flat above the O.'s. Mrs. O. used to entice Donald T., aged 5, to her flat and teach him bad words. After much blushing they decided they could not tell us the words but they were f f f. One day Bill missed his pot in the dark. Mr. O.

came upstairs and complained that his baby down below was wet through. He is a mild man and didn't say much. Mrs. T. said she couldn't help it and shut the door and went back to bed. Mrs. O. came upstairs and started to curse. She made a terrific row so that the neighbours heard. She asked one woman to be a witness but this woman was a friend of Mrs. T.'s and in the court spoke against Mrs. O. Mrs. O. was fined £5. The families are not now on speaking terms. Mrs. O. has tried to speak to Molly T., but Molly won't answer her.

Feuds are thus settled at a rather primitive level. Direct action is taken against the offender or else the police are utilized for reasons of private vengeance. When the police represent public order then every attempt is made to hoodwink them. The police[1] are generally regarded with suspicion and it is believed that they will frame you for something you haven't done and anyhow are natural enemies.

[1] It must of course be stressed that this group attitude may have little to do with reality.

CHAPTER XIV

PROJECTION TESTS

I. THE RORSCHACH

IT would be neither possible nor desirable to give a full account of the Rorschach Technique. The range and development of modern Rorschach testing can be appreciated by the size of Klopfer's *Developments in the Rorschach Technique* and the bibliographies included in these two monumental volumes. The following brief and very inadequate description is included for readers who may never have heard of the test.

The test was invented by Hermann Rorschach in 1922. It consists of ten symmetrical ink blots printed on cards. Cards I, IV, V, VI, and VII are in achromatic colour only; cards II and III achromatic plus red; cards VIII, IX and X in various chromatic shades. Each card is presented in turn to the subject who is asked to say what it looks like. The scoring and interpretation is extremely intricate and cannot be explained here. A simple description of some of the main categories only will be attempted so as to make the tables comprehensible.

Location is the term given to that category of response which indicates whether the subject used the whole blot, part of the blot, etc., in his answer. It is concerned with the area of the blot which he uses to form his concept. The Determinant categories are concerned with the way in which the subject forms his concept from the blot. This will be clearer when the major determinants are outlined. In the case of Form (F) it is the shape of the area used which determines what the subject sees. In the case of Movement (M) the subject projects some sort of action into the blot. M is used for human-beings in action, e.g. a man running; FM is used for animals in action, e.g. a horse jumping; m is for inanimate movement such as a wind swirling.

In the case of colour responses it is the colour of the blot which suggests the concept to the subject. There are three main types. C is used where the subject mentions colour only; CF where form is mentioned too but colour is the more important element in determination. FC is used where form is more important than colour though colour is mentioned. The achromatic colour responses are similarly coded with C' as the correct symbol.

Where the shading in the blot is seen as diffusion k, K and KF are used. FK is reserved for cases where perspective is mentioned. When the texture of the blot is more important than the diffusion in the shading, c, cF and Fc are used. The content of the blot is not neglected, and it is recorded whether the answer is human, animal, plant, etc. The symbolical aspects of the content are also taken into account.

The uses to which this technique can be put are many. The following are the most important. Firstly it can be used to distinguish between the different types of emotional disturbance; secondly between functional and organic mental disorders, and thirdly to differentiate between various normal personality types. The first and third categories are the ones with which this account is mainly concerned. A fourth, and rather newer usage, is the attempt to utilize the test as a tool for cross cultural analysis.

(A) THE ADVANTAGE OF THE RORSCHACH

The reasons for the choice of the Rorschach and the Lowenfeld Mosaic Test in this investigation have been mentioned already. The L.M.T. was used because it had been found to be particularly useful in Jamaica in picking out non-integrated children, while the Rorschach was used for its great value both in the cataloguing and analysis of depth material, and for its utility in cross cultural comparisons.

By 1945 Hallowell was able to say: 'The value of the Rorschach technique as a tool in the investigation of problems of personality and culture in non-literate societies seems unquestionable. It is not a substitute for other methods of approach but it nicely supplements them.'[1]

[1] A. I. Hallowell, 'Rorschach Technique in the Study of Personality and Culture', *American Anthropologist*, 1945, Vol. 47, No. 2, p 208.

Since this time much material has been collected from different cultural groups and some projection test or other has become almost standard equipment for the social anthropologist in the U.S.A. To the social psychologist the main value of projection techniques lies in their use in conjunction with field work. Hallowell's point that they can never be substitutes for field work must be strongly emphasized. They are, however, invaluable as subsidiary means of getting to know about the people under observation. The experienced field-worker knows how very easy it is to make a slip in the interpretation of observed behaviour or custom. The analysis of the projection tests should help him in his estimate of the function of the custom to the people concerned.

The advantages of including projection techniques in field work are as follows:

1. To gain access to deeper levels of the personality than can be reached through conversation without using psychoanalytic techniques.
2. To act as a check on deductions made about personality from data obtained in the field.
3. To obtain norms where possible for comparison with similar studies made on other culture patterns.
4. To get some idea of the development of thought and emotion with special reference to areas of strain and tension in the society under observation.
5. To be able to compare situations in different culture patterns. This would be a preliminary attempt to estimate just how a sociological process such as role deprivation affects the psychological structure of the personality. This can only be done through comparative studies based on both field observations and projection tests.

In this research the projection tests have been used mainly to throw light on the following questions which have emerged from the field work.

(a) Whether role deprivation may impair intellectual development and keep latent much undeveloped ability. Practically, this can be examined under the heading of whether there is more immaturity than might be expected in Ship Street. The tie to the Mum would lead one to anticipate that this might be so.

(b) Whether emotional disturbance is an inevitable concomitant of role deprivation. Is there evidence of emotional breakdown and lapses into violence? Can violence be correlated generally with non-integration?

(c) Whether difficulties in social relations are almost bound to arise among people who are role deprived. Do Ship Street people have difficulties in forming associations or making human contacts? Does this form constriction?

The results of these tests will be analysed under the headings of the impairment of intellectual ability, and emotional disturbance. This is for convenience in handling the material as, of course, the categories are bound to overlap. The division is, therefore, artificial but convenient.

(B) THE IMPAIRMENT OF INTELLECTUAL ABILITY

Perhaps the most appropriate way to start this section is by a quotation from Klopfer.[1]

'. . . There is a gradual accumulation of clinical evidence that early deprivation or serious emotional disturbances may prevent the individual from manifesting more than a fraction of his capacity either in general intelligence tests or in his general adjustment to life.'

The section on the field work has demonstrated that some deprivation is present. The function of this section is to show how this is reflected in the results of the projection tests and to relate these to observed behaviour in the field. The first question to arise is whether the tie to the Mum gives rise to a high incidence of immaturity. This is a big claim to make, so perhaps it is safer to rephrase the question and ask whether the children in Ship Street show a high incidence of immaturity. That they are tied to their Mums has been demonstrated already. In the case of the Rorschach the age of the subjects presents some difficulties. If an adult shows an excess of FM over M, then immaturity might be deduced, other things

[1] Bruno Klopfer, *Developments in the Rorschach Technique*, Vol. 1, George C. Harrap & Co. Ltd., London, 1954, p. 355.

being equal. In this case all the subjects are children. However, the figures work out as follows: Out of 47 cases where M, FM, or m, is given 32 show more (FM + m) than M. In percentages this is 62·74%. Figures are:

Out of 51 children, 11 give more M than FM + m, 32 give more FM + m than M. In 4 cases M is equal to FM + m, in 4 cases no M, FM or m score is given.

Klopfer says: 'If fewer than 30% of the total responses are given to the last three cards, the hypothesis is that the individual is either inhibited in his productiveness under conditions of strong environmental impact or basically lacking in responsiveness to such impact.'

'If more than 40% of the responses are given to the last three cards the hypothesis is that the productiveness of the individual is stimulated by environmental impact, whether he gives overt expression to his emotional response or not.'

The distribution of Ship Street children giving under 30% or more than 40% of answers to the last three cards is as follows:

Sixteen children give under 30%, 21 children between 30 to 40%, and 14 children over 40%.

Nothing of value to the analysis of the group results can be found in these figures taken on their own. This finding is again reinforced by the figures indicating succession.

Out of the 51 children, 1 gives Rigid Succession, 6 give Orderly, 11, Loose, 7 Confused and 26 No Succession.

Loose plus confused come to 35·3% of the total. To give loose or confused answers indicates a weakening of control because of I.Q., emotional, or pathological condition.

So far I have rather taken it for granted that intellectual factors have been impaired by emotional disturbance rather than that the children had low I.Q.'s anyhow. Undoubtedly some children are not too bright but this is not the case with the majority. The W : M ratio seems relevant here. If the means only are taken the optimum relationship prevails, that is roughly 2 : 1, the figures are W : M = 5·1 : 2·7. However, when the number of children in three categories are calculated a rather different picture results.

In 9 cases the proportion is 2W to 1M, in 24 cases W is greater than 2M, in 9 cases W is less than 2M.

When W is less than twice the number of M the interpretation is that the subject possesses creative potentialities for which he has been unable to find an outlet. Nine children come into this category while another nine show the optimum relationship. Twenty-four of the children had W greater than 2M. The interpretation of this is that the level of aspiration is too high. This seems unlikely for this group and therefore this category has to be broken up and re-examined. When form level is high then the person is not using his creative potential enough to achieve anything. When the form level is low then—
'. . . the hypothesis is that there is a general interference with the use of intellectual capacity (or low capacity itself) so that efforts to gain an integrated view of the world will be ineffective and there will be disappointment in the gap between aspiration and the ability to achieve.'

While the detailed form level ranking was not done on this group, it is true that form was not particularly good. Therefore, it can be said that this last statement is likely to hold good for these children.

In order to make a rough quantitative estimate of intelligence the following procedure was used. Each W, M, F%, A% and O response was classified as either good, fair or poor; succession was not used as so many children showed no succession at all and this might have invalidated the rating. The number of goods, fairs and poors are then counted up for each child. Table 1 shows the results of two children as an example.

TABLE 1

	Good	Fair	Poor	Weighted Total
Child No. 1	1	3	2	$5\frac{1}{2}$
Child No. 19	4	1	1	$7\frac{1}{2}$

The weighted total was obtained in the following way. Each good answer was counted as $1\frac{1}{2}$, each fair as 1, and each poor as $\frac{1}{2}$. Table 2 shows the number of children who gave each weighted total.

No claim is, of course, made that this rating scale is an accurate measure of intelligence. Its value lies in the fact that

TABLE 2

Weighted Total	$8\frac{1}{2}$	8	$7\frac{1}{2}$	7	$6\frac{1}{2}$	6	$5\frac{1}{2}$	5	$4\frac{1}{2}$	4	$3\frac{1}{2}$	3	$2\frac{1}{2}$
No. of children	0	3	2	0	8	5	5	8	3	7	9	1	0

in this piece of research it enables us to sort out the children who are not very intelligent from those who are intelligent enough but who may not be able to utilize their gifts for emotional reasons.

(c) EMOTIONAL DISTURBANCE

The second question is concerned with the frequency of signs of emotional disturbance in the Ship Street results. This category must overlap with the previous section. The divisions are for convenience in handling the material only. The determinant to be studied first is, of course, the FC ratio. The well adjusted individual should have FC greater than CF + C. Numerically the ratio of the means of this group was FC : CF + C equals 0·92 : 0·98. The difference shown is very slight. However, when the number of children who give each of four categories are counted then the picture becomes clearer.

Thirteen children give more FC than CF + C, while 18 children give more CF + C than FC. In 5 cases FC equals CF + C, and in 15 cases no colour response was given at all.

The interpretation for the largest category, that is, where FC is less than CF + C, is that the subjects have poor social contact and that their emotions have not been canalized into the modes of expression provided by the environment. People giving this ratio too are prone to outbursts of violence. This is certainly true for Ship Street people. Out of the 51 children 28 gave no FC at all. The second largest group is the 15 children giving no coloured responses at all. Klopfer points out that 'colour reactions are related to emotional integration' . . . 'the colour reactions indicate what the individual is actually doing with his integrative capacity in various life situations'. He goes on to say that disturbances in the production of this determinant 'appear to point towards disturbances in the mechanics of interpersonal relations'. This would tie in with the observed difficulties which Ship Street people have in playing roles other than rather simple and rigid ones.

One of the marked features of Ship Street life is the inability to think ahead. This shows up in the test results. Klopfer says where FM is greater than 2M 'the individual is ruled by immediate needs for gratification rather than by long range goals'.

Out of the 51 children, 29, that is 56·8%, give more FM than M, while 18 children, that is 35·3%, have an FM score which exceeds 2M.

The excess of FM over M means that 'impulses to gratification come fairly readily to awareness'.

F% is one of the major determinants. Three main values are important for this work. They are as follows. An F% over 80 is pathological, F% between 50 and 80 shows neurotic constriction, and F% under 20 indicates an inadequate response to reality. Of the Ship Street results 62·78% gave responses of over 50%, 13·7% of over 80% and 7·84% under 20%. The following table shows the distribution of F% responses.

TABLE 3

	0–10	11–20	21–30	31–40	41–50	51–60	61–70	71–80	81–90	91–100
No. of children	1	3	2	7	6	8	9	8	1	6

From these figures it can be seen that restriction is very high. An F% of over 80 means that an individual has a very poorly integrated personality structure. If the F% is between 50 and 80 it means that the person is intellectually capable of more differentiated responses but is inhibited from producing them.

The relative insensitivity to the outer world is again seen in the balance between F and C' and c. Klopfer says: that in cases where F predominates at the expense of C' and c 're-striction seems to apply to a relative insensitivity to the emotional impact of the outer world, while the person remains aware of his inner values, needs, and impulses'.

The fact that F is high at the expense of Fc is rather important. Only 49% of the Ship Street children show any Fc. The frequencies are as follows:

Out of 51 children, 26 give no Fc, 15 give 1, 6 give 2, 2 give 3, 1 gives 4 and 1 gives 6.

The lack of Fc suggests that the infantile craving for contact still exists at the expense of more controlled manifestations of affection. Klopfer says:

'It is believed that this is a development essential for the establishment of deep and meaningful object relations and that it occurs only where the basic security needs have been reasonably well satisfied.'

These people without Fc have the need for affection but do not realize they have more than a desire for physical contact. This can be linked with the observed fact that the Ship Street person, adult or child, cannot sleep alone, and with the theoretical side of role deprivation.

The ratio between the chromatic and achromatic colours can be taken in conjunction with the last paragraph.

Twenty-one children have achromatic scores greater than chromatic, in 11 cases the scores are equal, and in 19 cases the achromatic is less than the chromatic. In 15 cases the achromatic exceeds the chromatic by 2 to 1. In 7 cases the chromatic exceeds the achromatic by 2 to 1.

Where the achromatic exceeds the chromatic by 2 : 1 the indication is that the person's responsiveness to the outer world has been inhibited by some kind of traumatic experience and withdrawal has resulted.

'The implication is that the need for an affectional response from others is so great that the person is inhibited and toned down in his overt reactions to others for fear of being hurt or repulsed.'

In the other case where the chromatic is twice as big as the achromatic—'the individual tends to act out his emotions . . . he feels relatively little need for approval and affection and is not held back by related anxieties which might serve as a brake for his strongly developed reactivity to emotional stimuli from the environment'.

The lack of creative expression and the turning in of emotion can be seen in the proportion of Flexor and Extensor scores.

Thirty-two of the fifty-one subjects gave some M response. Of these 28·1% gave predominantly Extensor M, while 53·1% gave mainly Flexor M. The interpretation is that passivity and submission would be expected. This will be dealt with later in the comparison with Kardiner's work. For the 19 who give no M the interpretation is 'that emotional factors may interfere with the empathy with other people and the utilization of imaginal resources necessary to see live human figures in the blot material'.

It is possible too that these children have poor relations with their parents.

It would seem reasonable to state that the two questions put at the beginning of this chapter have been answered. In Ship Street, intellectual ability has been impaired and emotional disturbance has been frequently demonstrated. This disturbance most often takes the form of an immature clinging to what appears to be security. Because of it the individual is unable to develop a more mature personality and tends to remain non-integrated.

(D) COMPARISON WITH OTHER RORSCHACH INVESTIGATIONS

In *The Deprived and the Privileged* Betty Spinley described a London slum area which has much in common with Ship Street. The way in which the child is raised, indulged, cared for by siblings, is never alone, homesick when away from home, is violent, suspicious, has food fads, etc., all could be written about Ship Street children. The major difference, of course, is that the power of the Mum in Ship Street is so great that it is the over-ruling factor in the psychological make-up of the people.

It would be expected, therefore, that considerable agreement would be found between Ship Street Rorschachs and those of Spinley's slum group. On the whole this proved to be the case. It will perhaps be most profitable to take the figures which show close correspondence for granted and to examine those which show differences between the two groups. This will be done under three main headings chosen entirely for convenience.

(1) *Rejections*

Only 23·5% of Ship Street children rejected one or more cards as against Spinley's 43·3%. The main differences between the two groups in this respect is that more of Spinley's group rejected one card out of the ten, whereas when Ship Street children rejected it was usually more than one card.

The cards most frequently rejected in Ship Street were IX, IV and VI, and VII, in that order. Spinley's were IX and II, and VII. More children in Spinley's group rejected I than in Ship Street. It looks as if the highly shaded cards presented more difficulty to Ship Street children. There may, too, be significance in the fact that the Ship Street children rejected IV and VI rather often, as recently IV has been alleged to reveal attitudes to the father, and VI to have sexual implications. VII has been called the 'mother' card and the incidence of rejection in both groups may be due to ambivalent feelings towards the powerful Mum. Rejection of IX is said to occur most frequently among emotionally disturbed people. It is significant that it is the most frequently rejected by Ship Street and Spinley's subjects.

(2) *Introversiveness and Extratensiveness*

Quite large differences can be seen between the two groups if the M is greater than the sum of C figures are compared. More children in Ship Street are introversive than in Spinley's group. The figures are 41·2% in Ship Street and 23·3% of children in Spinley's London group. The stable nature of Ship Street introversiveness is shown by the fact that 66·6% of the children have FM + m is greater than Fc + c + C'. Spinley's group on the other hand did not come out as stable extratensives, in fact the reverse. Whether they are in the process of becoming less extratensive or whether their introversiveness has been repressed is not possible to deduce. It might be suggested tentatively that this difference can be accounted for by the great strength of Ship Street home life and the tie to the Mum. Ship Street Mums would not, for example, go out dancing as Spinley reports. It is possible that Spinley's group are forced into more extratensive behaviour.

(3) *Emotional Balance*

A considerable difference between Ship Street and Spinley's group can be seen in the table showing emotional balance. In Ship Street only 25·5% of children have FC > CF + C. In Spinley's area the figure is 53·2%. In Ship Street, too, the percentage of children giving no colour is higher, 29·4%, as against 15%. From the F% table it can be seen that in Ship Street 62·7% and in Spinley's group 64·9% come in the categories of over 51%. In the over 70% category Ship Street has 29·4% as against Spinley's 23.3%. In both groups, however, constriction is very high.

Two other differences should be noted, those between Fc in the two groups and those between C'. The percentage of children giving Fc in Spinley's group is higher than in Ship Street. It is not particularly high in either. Fc is the score that indicates tact. Now to have tact means to be aware and responsive to other people's roles and this is very difficult for people who are role deprived. The low Fc score does give some support to this conclusion.

Ship Street gives more C' than Spinley's though again neither give very many of these responses. This determinant indicates immature phantasy caused by emotional repression.

Comparison shows that the Ship Street A% is consistently lower than Spinley's. This may be due to a consistently higher I.Q. among the Ship Street children or to more leanings to stereotype among Spinley's group. It would not be possible to say for certain which factor was operative or in what proportions.

Another comparable piece of research in which the Rorschach was used is that of Kardiner and Ovesey on American Negroes.[1] I attempted to compare their results with those of the Jamaican and Ship Street work in a recent number of the West Indian *Social and Economic Studies*.[2] Kardiner and Ovesey too found that their subjects did not utilize fully their potential intellectual capacity; showed signs of difficulty in adjustment

---

[1] Abram Kardiner and Lionel Ovesey, *The Mark of Oppression*, W. W. Norton & Co., New York, 1951.

[2] Madeline Kerr, 'The Study of Personality Deprivation through Projection Tests', *Social and Economic Studies*, University College of the West Indies, Vol. IV, No. 1, March 1955, p. 83.

to other people; found life dangerous and hostile; were profoundly anxious and spent much energy coping with their own hostile impulses. Many of the Rorschach scoring categories were similar to those of the Jamaican, and at times even to those of the Ship Street children. For example, the percentages of Extensor and Flexor M are: Jamaican children, 28·0% and 61·6%; Kardiner's and Ovesey's American Negroes, 29·0% and 63·0%; Ship Street children, 28·1% and 53·1%.

In view of this agreement it seems justifiable to assume that deprivation, whether in London, Ship Street, Jamaica or New York, produces very similar personality configurations, both as regards structure and as expressed in behaviour.

CHAPTER XV

PROJECTION TESTS

2. THE LOWENFELD MOSAIC TEST

THE Lowenfeld Mosaic Test was invented by Margaret Lowenfeld and has been used continuously at the Institute of Child Psychology for the last twenty-five years. As in the case of the Rorschach it is possible only to give an inadequate description for the benefit of non-psychological readers. A complete account of the test and an appraisal of the work, both here and in other countries, is given in *The Lowenfeld Mosaic Test* by Margaret Lowenfeld.

The test consists of a box of five types of shapes made in plastic. These consist of a square, a half square, equilateral and scalene triangles, and a diamond. The colours are red, blue, green, yellow, black and white. A tray, fitted with a piece of white paper on which the design can be recorded, is given to the subject. He is then presented with the box of mosaics and given the following instructions. 'Use the pieces in any way you like on the tray.'

Again, it is possible only to outline briefly some of the more important classifications. The first is between Abstract and Representational patterns. Some people use the material to make an abstract design of either a simple or very intricate nature. Others do not even think of doing this but make a representation of some person, animal or object. Another important classification is concerned with whether the patterns are compact or spaced. The description of these terms is given below:

'The pieces can either be laid together so that their geometric properties are exploited and each piece fits closely to its neighbour, or they can be laid separately on the paper or touch only at the points so that the spaces between the pieces are an essential element in the final Pattern.'[1]

[1] Margaret Lowenfeld, *The Lowenfeld Mosaic Test*, Newman Neame, London, 1954.

Recently[1] I have suggested that another relevant classification, especially in areas where deprivation is rife, is that of Whole or Broken. Whole does not need explaining, it simply means that the subject organizes his mosaics into one pattern, either Abstract or Representational. Under the heading Broken I have included all patterns which do not constitute one unit, whether Compact or Spaced, Abstract or Representational. In this paper I have suggested that Broken mosaics indicate non-integration both in Jamaica and Ship Street.

Non-integration in this context means that the individual has not managed to organize the roles of which his personality is composed into a persistent and consistent pattern. The non-integrated person will appear immature. The high incidence of immaturity, shown by the Rorschach, will support this hypothesis. An analysis of the Ship Street mosaics produces the following figures:

TABLE 4

Showing the proportion of types of pattern made by Ship Street children

Types of Pattern	No. of children	%
Broken	26	47·27
Very disturbed	15	27·27
Slightly disturbed	7	12·73
Normal	7	12·73
Total	55	

It is indeed obvious from these figures that Ship Street does seem conducive to emotional upheavals. A striking contrast was obtained from children belonging to a housing estate and attending school on the outskirts of the city. The ideational behavioural norms of these people are nearer those of the conventional English middle class. However, this has not been achieved without strain. This shows in the high incidence of neurotic disturbance among the children. They have lost the simplicity of Ship Street, which, though immature, is fairly happy, but have not yet achieved enough educational and emotional sophistication to make them properly functioning

[1] Madeline Kerr, op. cit., 153.

individuals. Table 5 shows the incidence of Broken mosaics compared with the incidence of those showing anxiety. The combined anxiety category was based on mosaic types which each indicate some degree of anxiety. Those included under this heading were, edge, slab, frame and item, empty frames, and filled or partially filled trays.

TABLE 5

Showing the comparison between Jamaican, Ship Street, and housing estate children's patterns with reference to non-maturation and emotional disturbance

	No. of children	Broken patterns expressed in percentages	Combined anxiety type patterns expressed in percentages
Jamaican	179	70·4	3·4
Ship Street	55	47·27	39·99
Junior School	44	25·0	38·2
Junior School (C. of E.)	29	20·6	51·7
Secondary School	25	12·0	44·0
Grammar School[1]	22	0	50·0

The most interesting fact which emerges from this table is the steady decrease of the 'broken' type. Among the estate and grammar school children social immaturity has been overcome, though at the rather high price of anxiety. In Ship Street, although the ages of the children ranged from 8 to 13, this was not apparent. The high incidence of emotional disturbance in all the groups perhaps suggests that all is not well with our social and educational systems.

The next problem is concerned with the meaning of these figures. The most obvious conclusion is that conditions in Jamaica and to a slightly lesser extent in Ship Street are conducive to lack of maturity. On the other hand those on the housing estate lead to anxiety and general feelings of insecurity and worry. Jung and others have pointed out that non-integration makes for a type of person who is at times subject to outbreaks of violence. This was noted in the Rorschach results and appears again in the mosaics. It has been recorded already in the field notes.

[1] These children did not come from the estate. If estate children had got to grammar school this is the school to which they would have gone.

Again the lack of complexity of the Ship Street mosaics is an indicator that this sub-culture pattern is a very simple one. This would be expected from people suffering from a blockage of maturation.[1] There would be defective control of emotion. This lack of organization would be reflected in the simple form of the culture pattern. The objection that, as these mosaics were done by children, more integrated results might be obtained later, and that they were retarded rather than non-integrated, can, I think, be met by the fact that the older children in the Ship Street group do no better than the younger. The same observation was made in Jamaica.

In the case of the housing estate[2] children something quite different has happened. Literally and metaphorically they can perceive overall order but they are too anxious to achieve it successfully. The main problems on the estate are concerned with status. This implies that people are anxious and worried, negatively that they may be thought to belong to lower status groups, and positively that their children may not achieve high enough status. This indicates, of course, uncertainty and often a grasping of external forms of behaviour without understand-the function of that behaviour.

The L.M.T. has been of the greatest value in this work. Firstly, it was the diagnostic tool by which this group was found. Secondly, it was possible through the test to make clear the differences between two groups of these Northern city children and to relate these divergencies to their social background.

(A) RELATION BETWEEN THE RORSCHACH AND THE L.M.T.

It is commonly thought that tests of projection should correlate highly. This is not necessarily true. We know as yet little of the mechanics of projection though, oddly enough, quite a lot is known about why people do it. It seems highly probable that the different types of projection test will prove sensitive to different facets of the personality.

---

[1] (a) *Personality and Conflict in Jamaica*, p. 177.
[2] This estate was studied by Duncan Mitchell and Tom Lupton—a report published by Liverpool University Press.

In analysing the results of this investigation the interaction of several factors causes considerable overlap and sometimes confusion. These factors are chronological age, I.Q., emotional disturbance, and immaturity caused by social and emotional factors rather than low intelligence.

In *Personality and Conflict in Jamaica* and previously in this book I have postulated that a 'broken' type of mosaic indicates a non-integrated personality. The term 'broken' was defined on page 156. Dr. Lowenfeld has shown that collective patterns occur frequently among children up to the age of about eight years, but that after that tend to disappear unless some form of immaturity persists. Pieces distributed on the tray in ones and twos generally disappear by the age of six years in normal English children. The ages of the Ship Street children ranged from 8 to 13 years. In order to see if the usual relation between chronological age and broken mosaics was present the Yule Co-efficient of Association was worked out between these two factors. The children were divided into two groups, the first aged 8 to 10, the second 11 to 13. Fifty-five children did a mosaic. $Q = 0.05$. This shows clearly that in the Ship Street group no relation exists between chronological age and the tendency to do broken mosaics. As this tendency has been shown to exist among normal children the conclusion must be drawn that the immaturity demonstrated in these results is due to emotional causes rather than lack of intellectual ability.

Another co-efficient was worked out between broken mosaics and a low score on the Rorschach intelligence rating scale. Forty-four children did both the tests. The co-efficient was found to be -0.09. If I.Q. were the main factor here some positive relation should be present. As this is not the case the conclusion can be drawn again that the immaturity is due to emotional disturbance rather than to lack of intellectual ability. The full table of the relation between the Rorschach intelligence rating and mosaics categorized under the headings of normal, immature, immature and disturbed, and disturbed must now be discussed. It should be emphasized here that the Rorschach scale is only operative on the intellectual side. A child could, for example, have a score of 8 but still show disturbance in his emotional life.

The conclusions to be drawn from Table 6 can be expressed

TABLE 6

Rorschach Intelligence Ranks compared with Mosaics

Rorschach Ranks	Mosaic Categories			
	Normal	Immature	Immature and Emotionally Disturbed	Emotionally Disturbed
8 to 6	3	4	7	2
6 to 5½	5	2	3	1
4½ or under	1	6	7	1

as follows. Firstly, of the most intelligent children only three do mosaics which could be considered normal for their ages. The rest show immaturity with or without emotional disturbance. In the cases where emotional disturbance is shown separately from immaturity the implication is that the disturbance does not appear to have affected intellectual development. In the immaturity only column the implication is that the lack of maturation may or may not be caused by emotional disturbance. When the child has a high rating score on intelligence the likelihood is that immaturity is emotionally caused.

The second point which emerges clearly is the high percentage of children showing immaturity and the low percentage of children whose disturbance does not appear to affect their intellectual performance. This makes an interesting contrast to the results obtained from the schools on the housing estate where emotional disturbance is expressed much more in worry and insecurity feelings rather than in immaturity.

The next question is whether both tests show the same children as being emotionally disturbed, or whether there is any diagnostic conflict. This is not an easy task as the interpretations of both tests is exceedingly intricate and dependent on a series of gestalten rather than on discrete scores. However, if the material be analysed in the following manner some idea of the way in which these two techniques support each other can be seen. The four categories used in the previous table are again utilized to show the agreement between the tests. The category immature is taken to mean that immaturity is the major aspect of the personality. Similarly, disturbed means that the disturbance outweighs other factors present. Disturbed plus immature means that both factors are present.

TABLE 7

Mosaics	Rorschach			
	Normal	Immature	Disturbed and Immature	Disturbed
Normal	7	—	2	—
Immature	—	12	—	—
Disturbed and Immature	—	—	17	—
Disturbed	—	—	—	6

This table shows a most striking correlation between the two tests. Only two boys upset the symmetry of the table. Both did a normal mosaics but slightly disturbed Rorschachs. One of them is a highly individualistic child. Some years ago his mother gave him something which he did not like for dinner. He walked away to his aunt's rooms, where he has lived ever since.

These results show a most satisfactory relationship between the tests. They also serve to strengthen the evidence about the extremely high incidence of emotional disturbance in this group of children. Perhaps it is relevant here to mention that a few of the children did drawings of people. In all cases the arms were truncated in the manner that Machover[1] suggests indicates immaturity and over-dependence.

(B) SUMMARY OF PROJECTION TEST RESULTS

At the beginning of the chapter three main problems were posed and answers sought for them in the test results. Each of these will now be discussed.

The first question is whether role deprivation impaired intellectual development. The answer is that it does. Evidence first discovered in Jamaica has been substantiated by this work and some support has been found in Kardiner's study of the

[1] Karen Machover, *Personality Projection in the Drawing of the Human Figure*, Thomas, Springfield, Ill., 1949.

American Negro and Grygier's[1] of Displaced People. The next problem to consider is the cause of this relation. The answer seems to be that people are kept immature because they are unable to develop adequate role configurations so as to produce flexible personalities able to cope with complex situations, especially those complex situations involving change or choice. The personality is non-integrated and therefore unable to achieve consistency of purpose or unity of effort. The major cause for this non-integration seems to be the crippling strength of the tie to the mother.

The second problem is whether emotional disturbance is an inevitable concomitant of non-integration, and again the answer is yes. This may seem slightly paradoxical after the discussion on Table 5. However in non-technical terms it means that while the housing estate children express their disturbance in anxiety, the Ship Street children express theirs in hysterical fears, violence and what Spinley termed 'the textbook signs of maladjustment'.

The third problem is best taken in conjunction with the second because the emotional disturbance expresses itself in terms of human relations. The situation in Ship Street resembles that in Jamaica because in both cases there is culture conflict. The Ship Street person gets on all right within his own group; outside it he shows signs of culture conflict. His simple and non-integrated role constellations are not capable of coping with a more complicated world.

The next major question to be answered is the relation between non-integration and I.Q. One possible criticism might be that Ship Street people had low I.Q.s. Another is that the samples tested were all children. However, no relation was found between chronological age and the tendency to produce Broken mosaics. In other samples of the population this relationship is present. Again, no relation was found between the tendency to produce Broken mosaics and a low rating on intelligence on the Rorschach.

Fortunately, two other researches have been published lately containing comparable test material. The first is Spinley's work done on a London slum group. A close similarity can be

[1] Tadesz Grygier, *Oppression*, Routledge & Kegan Paul Ltd., London, 1954.

observed due no doubt to the fact that the environmental conditions seem very alike. The second, Kardiner's work, corresponds closely with the Jamaican results as again the social conditions are similar. The four researches taken together —Spinley's, Kardiner's and my own on Jamaica and on Ship Street—do present, through the media of projection tests, very strong evidence for the relation of non-integration to deprivation.

CHAPTER XVI

SHIP STREET BASIC PERSONALITY

THE concept of a basic personality is a valuable and useful tool in the case of the Ship Street people. Although to the investigators they stand out as unmistakable individuals, as soon as they become abstracted and recorded in field notes, a general pattern emerges with clarity.

In describing the structure of a specific basic personality it is customary to describe the nature of the social disciplines to which the children of this culture or sub-culture are subjected. It is hoped that the following summary of these will bring into focus this aspect of the field work.

While the first baby is generally born in hospital, subsequent ones are often had at home with the maternal grandmother in attendance. The baby is breast-fed for a short time though this is seldom prolonged. Feeding is not a time for affection and seems generally to be considered as just another job to be done. After what has been said about lack of pleasure it is hardly surprising to note that this is extended to the baby's meal times. Babies are fed when they cry. This habit is continued as the child grows up. In most homes bread and marge are always on the table, or in some other accessible place, from which children are allowed to help themselves. As there are seldom enough chairs for the whole family to sit at once, meals can hardly be of a formal nature. Again, if more than one member of the family is at work he or she will want food immediately on arriving home. Food, therefore, is taken on a sort of running buffet system. It is used, too, as a reward in childhood when favourite foods are given as treats, and in adulthood when those working are given more or better food than the others.

Food, too, is used as an almost aggressive assertion of choice. From early childhood individuals tend to have innumerable food fads which are catered for as a matter of course by the Mum. Maybe the great importance attached to having what you like is concerned with the fact that in a group where so many roles are rather rigidly determined, this is a chance of individual choice, even if only on a limited scale.

Weaning appears to be done by an early supplementation by bottle feeding of milk or soup. Only one mother reported any difficulty. Possibly the lack of affection shown to the child during breast-feeding makes it less interested in resisting weaning.

Although feeding is unaccompanied by caresses much physical affection is shown to the child. Cots and prams are bought for the new baby but it only has to open its mouth and Mum hauls it into the parents' bed. This habit persists so that adults are often frightened to sleep in a room by themselves. Children are often frightened to sleep in a bed by themselves, even though there are others in the room. This extremely close physical intimacy with a few people helps cement the group family tie of adulthood. It is possible, too, that the authority figure has to be physically close to be recognized. Anyhow, Ship Street people only feel secure within their own group of blood relatives under the dominance of some Mum.

The Mum maintains her authority by a mixture of indulgence and threats. Shouting and violence are frequent and occasionally a Dad is brought in to back her up. However, most children do not worry over the threat that 'your Dad will bash you when he comes in' because they know Mum will not let him hit them hard. Whatever the child does the Mum will always defend him against other people. He is never to blame but has always been led astray, or just been mischievous and blamed for other children's faults.

The two main topics about which Mums are severe are bad language and speaking about sex. Children consider it daring to write swear words on the school blackboard or chalk them on fences. They all exclaim with horror at the idea of saying them before their mothers. The mothers themselves use the same words in their quarrels. Probably the prohibition is explained by the fact that these forbidden words are sexual in meaning and therefore must not be mentioned by or to children.

The absolute prohibition about speaking to children on sex

matters is extremely interesting. The older generation of Mums think the topic should never be mentioned at all, except perhaps by the teacher at school. The younger Mums feel they have some responsibility, but the content of their instruction is to warn the girls to keep away from the boys. Sex is referred to as 'dirty things' by the children, presumably under the influence of this ban. At adolescence and in adult life sex is considered natural and desirable. The turning away from it seems to occur mainly when the woman has got too many children. Great modesty is shown over such things as changing clothes, but jokes are exchanged, especially those of an anal character. It is likely, therefore, that there is some fixation in an anal stage. This would agree with the general level of immaturity.

Children, therefore, learn to be furtive about something which later it is permissible to enjoy. This emphasizes the split between the family and the contact with non-relatives. It takes a generation for the man to belong to the family, so in all difficulties the young married woman goes home to Mum.

The most salient feature which all Ship Street people have, whether male or female, is this incredibly strong tie to their mothers. In every chapter describing the field work results it can be seen that the Mum is the central figure and that the household revolves round her. One of the psychological results of this tie is to be seen in the immaturity of adult relationships. It should perhaps be stressed here that in calling the results of this tie immature a perhaps unjustifiable value judgment is being made. There is most definitely no intention in this work to advise or alter people. The term is simply being used as a word which describes the results of certain eventualities. This tie is so strong and so prevalent throughout the group that it must be considered normal for Ship Street. With this warning in mind a non-emotive classification of the results of the tie can be made in the following way.

(a) The tie tends to be stronger than other love relations, e.g. than the tie to the husband or wife. This leads to insecurity and loss of ego strength.

(b) It generates an attitude of reliance and lack of independence. Also a lack of ability to take responsibility.

(c) The immaturity set up by the tie results in non-integra-

tion of the personality. The results of this behaviour are
violence and piecemeal reactions, and inability to plan.

(d) The resulting institution is a matrilocal mother domin-
ated culture.

The pattern of male response in this group is a rather complex one. England is generally considered patriarchal and a
man likes to be considered 'master in his own home'. Possibly
even among the middle classes 'considered' is the operative
word here. In Ship Street the Mum will attain the most amaz-
ing ends through her power over the man. The males stand a
very greal deal of pushing around and it appears that only
when they have been made to do something very much too
often against their wishes that even a Dad will turn. The field
notes extract in Chapter IV dealing with the way a woman
manipulated a job in the docks has an unbelievable conclusion.
The story was repeated identically on different occasions as we
found it difficult to believe.

A day came when Mr. R. turned, when he couldn't stand it
any more. One day when she was an old lady, he set fire to her
clothes; he put a match to her clothes and said, 'Burn, you old
bugger, burn.' Her son came and put the flames out. When he
asked his father about it, the old man told him she was evil,
she'd done wicked all her life. We treated this story as a joke.
Our informant said, 'It's as true as I am standing here, Mr. R.
put a match to his wife's clothes.'

Even here the Mum was rescued by one of her family. At
times when the man is drunk he may try to get his own way by
violence. However, in most cases the woman can be equally
violent in return with the aid of pokers, crockery and other
throwable weapons. If she is getting the worst of the battle
there is usually a big son or daughter to come to her aid.

One very interesting fact we noticed is that many of the boys
who have committed most crimes are rather effeminate looking,
or at least take great care of their appearance. They tend to be
perhaps fussily clean, keen on hair-do's and deceptively gentle
in manner. This year (Spring, 1955) the Teddy Boy movement has reached Ship Street boys of the type just mentioned,
whom we noticed were always combing their hair, and who
have taken up the fashion with avidity. This type of boy is
generally favoured by the Mums. It is a possibility that these

boys have identified themselves with their mothers, or even re-identified themselves in order to solve their difficulties in male role playing, in a dominantly female society. A Mum does as she wishes from the child's point of view, therefore if he identified with her he should be able to do the same. He puts this into action and gets into trouble with the police. This would account for the inability in some cases of an intelligent boy to stop thieving even when he knows he is being watched and is bound to be found out.

It seems likely too that the very strong sibling affection may arise from this identification with the Mum. This tie may also account for the inability to leave this most unsalubrious neighbourhood of damp, tumbledown houses. The personal space of the Mum becomes that of her children. Outside the radius of her influence they feel afraid and insecure. Security to them means being with other people and in Ship Street these people must be relatives.

Perhaps a more vivid idea of the child's picture of the world can be grasped from the following story made up by a girl of 15 years while staying at a convalescent home. The matron there encouraged the children to write and act their own plays. While much of the manifest content of the play is derived from pantomime, the child's own views about human relations transforms the conventional story she was trying to produce. The story is told in note form as the speed of telling was too great to reproduce the dialect.

'I was the mother, Aladdin was my son. I sent him on a message and when he was out he met the wicked uncle, who said: "Ask your Mum if I can take you out." Aladdin brought him home. I said, "Come in as you are there. Who are you?" ' (At this point it was explained that Aladdin's father was dead.) 'The wicked uncle said, "Can I take your son out?" I said, "He is useful to me for messages." The wicked uncle gave some money. He then takes Aladdin to a cave full of jewels. Aladdin is in a "daze". The wicked uncle tells him to fetch the lamp and shuts him in. Aladdin rubs a ring and a genie comes. Aladdin asks for jewels and then comes home to me.' (From now on 'I' became 'Mum'. The identification is complete.)

'Mum asks where he has been. He tells her and Mum rubs the ring. She is scared of the genie. She asks for lovely food to eat and crockery and gold plates. Meanwhile Aladdin has peeped over a wall and seen the Princess having a bath and decides he wants to marry her. He tells Mum and asks her to ask the Emperor for his daughter. Mum says: "I'll do anything for you." She goes to the palace and forces her way in to the Emperor. The Emperor is greedy and asks for more jewels. The wicked uncle has disguised himself as an old man and goes round saying, "New lamps for old." Mum hands over Aladdin's lamp. The wicked uncle asks for lots of jewels and chases after the Princess. The Emperor says she is to marry him. She prefers Aladdin and marries Aladdin.' The story ends here, though the informant said she had difficulty in ending it.

Six main points emerge out of the story. Firstly, the father is dead. Mum is in charge and he would just be irrelevant. Mum is not pleased to see a visitor but accepts him when she hears he is a relative and he gives money. The children all make pocket money by running errands. The second point is Mum's choice of wish, food and crockery. This fits in with the claim that the Mums want more of what they know and not different things. The gold plate was added as an afterthought and I think belongs to the manifest pantomime theme. Food, too, is sometimes scarce in this family. Thirdly, Mum is scared of the genie. There is a lot of fear of the supernatural. Most redoubtable Mums are nervous of the dark, going out alone, etc. Fourthly, Mum says, 'I'll do anything for you.' This epitomizes the culturally approved attitude of a Mum to her child. Whatever he has done she will be there to defend him and make excuses. The fifth point is that Aladdin sees the Princess in the bath. This story was told just before the romantic adolescent period. Sex knowledge is acquired frequently by these children by climbing and peeping. The sixth point is that even the Emperor has to give in to the female.

In the world picture the average Ship Street person carries, determinism and luck appear as contradictory elements. They are not really contradictory. While things are fated you rather hopelessly try to influence fate by charms. People really do believe in the effects of dried cawl in the preservation of seamen's lives. This fundamental outlook of things being predetermined ties in with the rigidity and lack of ambition. To live in a different world is not within their field of aspiration.

What they want is more spending money in the world they have. To save money to live a different sort of life just does not make sense. They do not like leaking houses, lack of coal, food shortages, etc., any more than anyone else, but they do not see any way of avoiding them. More money so that these trials do not exist is all they ask.

Life for them is lived in their kitchens, which are the centres of family ritual, and around the streets. There is never a dull moment, what with boys being caught by the police and 'sent away', girls having illegitimate babies, feuds among the adults, skirmishes with the police, violence at home and outside, and the constant toll of death from disease and accident. To be moved out of this to a housing estate on the outskirts of the city, or sent to the country to convalesce is intolerable. During this last year (1955) a notice has been put up in one of the streets that demolition will be taking place shortly. Faced with this one or two families who previously said they would never go, now say they would like to move. But they have most carefully specified the only place to which they would go. On investigation this place is much the same as their own street except that the houses are not quite so dilapidated. They have not yet, however, been put to the test of being offered houses or flats anywhere except in the Ship Street area.

The home with the comings and goings of relatives and the nearby streets seem to form the only picture they have which can be said to be structured or to have any form about it. Because of the failure in integration and the consequent lack of structure in the ego the rest of the world is an unstructurated area in which it is dangerous to venture. This is intensified by their general lack of cognitive knowledge and the failure of the schools to interest them. It is interesting to note that women will seldom go out of the area except in twos and children in raiding expeditions go in gangs.

The Catholic Church probably retains the hold it has because it is a highly structured institution. There are ritual and therefore invariable things to do and say. Just as in family life, roles are simple and rigid. Outside again would be danger. The Ship Street people are quite unable to force a new order onto events. This is illustrated very clearly in the children's mosaics where broken rather than unified patterns are in the majority.

The next point to be considered is the structure of the human relations in this world picture. In other words what are the stereotypes which act as guides to these relationships. The main stereotype is that there is someone who is responsible for you and to whom you are responsible for your actions. It is hardly necessary to say that the responsible person is the Mum. The feeling of responsibility to her alone means that she sets the moral code. Individuals do not feel it incumbent on them to accept the general legal code of the country unless the Mum has made it her code too.

Perhaps it is reasonable to say that because the Mum's social contacts are limited the content of the child's super ego is more restricted than it would be if the Mum were more influenced by the society in general. As the Mum's world is limited what the children introject through her as the content of their super egos is limited too. This means that areas which should be organized are left without structure. This lack of ego development leads to a corresponding limitation of cognitive abilities. Action thus tends to be motivated by effect rather than organized thought, by the super ego[1] rather than the ego.

This lack of cognitive control appears in the projection tests. In the L.M.T. by the inability to bring the pieces together into a whole pattern. In the Rorschach by the large numbers of children giving loose or confused succession for one thing.

Some support for the theory that the ego of Ship Street people is comparatively unorganized and that this results in non-integration can be found in Leopold Bellak's[2] book *Manic Depressive Psychosis*. He outlines his theory of ego strength as follows.

'It seems to me that the outstanding factor in manic depressive psychosis, as in schizophrenia, is, as Federn pointed out long ago, a weakness of the ego, that is, the constellation of those forces of personality which are concerned with reality testing, mediating between the basic drives (id) on the one hand, and the commands of reason (one of the functions of the ego), the internalized rules of society, (the super ego) and the externalized rules on the other hand. The degree of frustration

[1] Original meaning of the term.
[2] Leopold Bellak, *Manic Depressive Psychosis*, Grune & Stratton, New York, 1952.

tolerance and the ability to engage in detour behaviour for the long-range achievement of pleasure are some aspects of the ego's strength.

'Ego strength can be principally defined by the effectiveness with which the ego discharges its functions, namely, of coping with the id, the super-ego and reality, and of intergrating (as described earlier), and by the energy remaining to permit self-exclusion of the ego for purposes of creativity and *ad hoc* needs. This latter one might call flexibility, (in distinction to rigidity of the personality when the ego is very capable of mediating between the id, super-ego and reality, but only at the cost of utter impoverishment of its resources).'

It is not suggested that Ship Street people are latent psychotics. What is put forward tentatively is that the social psychological conditions under which these people live do not allow them to develop sufficient ego strength to cope with anything other than the very limited situations in which they live.

A developed ego, too, enables a person to plan for the future, even to the extent of enduring temporary discomfort. This is not possible for a Ship Street person. Saving for something you want, cleaning your teeth so as not to lose them, in fact thinking out any non-immediate action is unheard of. Support for these field observations comes from the Rorschach. Violence too will be connected with lack of ego development. It is interesting to note that outbursts resulting in the throwing of crockery, knives, etc., are referred to almost with pride.

Further support for the hypothesis that deprivation engenders immaturity which in turn results in non-integration can be found in Grygier's book *Oppression* in which he claims that oppression results in egocentricity, isolation and delinquency.

Some hints about the mechanics of how the parents retain their hold on the children in the face of contact with the more ordinary English urban waves of life can be deduced from a paper by Bettelheim and Sylvester on *Delinquency and Morality*. They say that in many cases delinquency results when children find that the code of the society taught to them by parents and teachers differs from the parents' own code.

'While their own actions are motivated by "what will get by" (which the child observes), they demand that he himself be guided by "what is right". Later this requirement is officially endorsed by school and church, and unofficially supported by reading matter, the radio, and movies. The child who tries to internalize these discrepant demands is confronted by a seemingly insoluble conflict. As he realizes that parents do not live by their moral teachings, he is faced with two contradictory desires. On the one hand he really wants to identify with his parents; on the other, he must have the security of social conformity. In many such cases, delinquent action represents the child's attempts to stress his loyalty to a parent of whose actions he is intensely critical.'[1]

They suggest too that the involvement of the parents with the child's delinquency '. . . is incompatible with distance. Therefore the parent has to counteract any emancipation. In this respect the child entering adolescence becomes a particular challenge since the adolescent's assertive independence is felt as a threat by the parents, while his greater need for identification is misused by the parents to cement closeness through seduction.'

If the child gives in he regresses. 'In return, he may give up all desire for emotional gratification, even those which are legitimate.'

Factually, in Ship Street the return of the daughter to the mother after the birth of one or more children is rather similar to this situation. The daughter gives up the pleasures or gratification of a home of her own with her husband to return to her Mum and so lose responsibility. Her husband's chief social role in many of our houses then reverts to being a sort of brother or uncle to his wife's younger siblings. He is useful for taking them to the pictures and giving them pocket money.

Again the attitude to outgroups is rather like that of delinquents. On the one hand there is the view that so long as one is loyal to the in-group, theft, violence, etc. directed towards others is all right. On the other hand all the Catholic children are subjected to the strict teaching of the Catholic schools in the week and the church which they attend on Sundays. Attempts to ask questions about this code do not seem to be favourably received by the teachers.

[1] B. Bettelheim and E. Sylvester, 'Delinquency and Morality,' *The Psychoanalytic Study of the Child*, Imago Publishing Co. Ltd., London, 1950, Vol. 5, p. 330.

The suggestion of Bettelheim and Sylvester that when the parents are involved in the child's actions they dare not let the child become emancipated is very important. We have seen how the Ship Street Mum loses contact with the external world on marriage, so her teachings will be somewhat outdated and her feelings immature. The child is therefore brought up by someone whose thoughts and feelings are not mature. This and the isolation of the family tends to tie the child. So the added involvement in the child's conflicts with the outer world would help to explain the strength of the bond. The last sentence of the quotation is certainly true for Ship Street. The attempt at separation from the Mum on marriage nearly always fails. Faced by adult responsibilities the woman gives up the emotional gratification of the tie to her husband and homes to Mum.

Two main and somewhat contradictory factors determine the Ship Street people's attitude towards social institutions. The first is the attitude of withdrawal from contact with the unknown world outside the street; the second that the church regulates the individual's attitudes to institutions formally and clearly. For example how a person should act and think about marriage and the church itself.

In practice this results in the withdrawal of the individual from institutions for which he has not got readily available roles. Alternatively, he may be confused. Ship Street people know what they should think and do about marriage. Only in one case do we know of a divorce and where there is a hope for a consequent civil remarriage. In all but one of our Catholic families the church's decrees about contraceptives are strictly kept. An illustration of the confusion of thought caused by rigid and restricted role playing can be given by the fact that though so few of the Mums use contraceptives the majority have at some time or other tried to bring on an abortion. Pills, jumping down the stairs, etc. are perfectly legitimate up to the end of the third month, after which the woman stops in case she hurts the baby. This is not thought to be illogical behaviour at all.

The generalization can be made that where role behaviour is clearly and rigidly laid down the Ship-Streeter finds it easy to acquiesce in the institutionalized playing out of the roles.

At times he will show by his evasion of an inconvenient one that he has not grasped the principle behind the roles. His attitude belongs therefore to the super-ego rather than the ego and is yet another proof of ego weakness.

In general the basic personality of a Ship Street inhabitant is composed of rather rigid constellations of roles. He can function adequately within his own world but not out of it. When his emotional control breaks down he is often violent, sometimes the violence being greatly in excess of the frustrating agent. Within his own sphere he is happy, generous and care-free. He does not worry especially, as he is not interested in improving his status or putting on a show for the neighbours. He spends what he has freely because there is always some Mum figure who will help him out. Economically the woman's custom of taking a job for a few weeks to 'tide over' is connected with this. He learned this dependence when a child and his Mum was always there to get him out of scrapes. He gambles steadily both for the fun of it and in the hope of a windfall to get something he wants or needs. He is intensely loyal to his group but does not care much about those who do not belong. He would be incapable of stealing from his in-group but would happily do so from public property such as docks or railway yards.

One final but rather important point remains to be discussed. How does the dependent girl, afraid of responsibility and indissolubly tied to her mother, develop into the dominant responsible Mum? At first it appears as if on the death of Mum some complete rebirth of character structure occurs in one of the female members of the family. This, of course, is not the case. Perhaps the situation will seem clearer after two conditions of a Mum's behaviour have been outlined. The first is that there has to be a Mum as she is the central figure in the social organization of this group. Her roles are socially approved, rigid and limited. Therefore the second condition is that she will not be asked to produce new behaviour patterns but only continue the old. She will already have helped her Mum in most of the old roles.

The fact is that the Mum's authority is vested in her as the centre of an institution, not as a specifically dominating and efficient individual. The husband who calls his wife 'mother' implicitly acknowledges this and when she becomes Mum she automatically carries out her roles just as the chairman of a committee carries out the duties of his office. She does not have to fight for her authority, it is given to her because of her status.

The more difficult question to answer is why one daughter becomes the Mum rather than another. We had not formulated this until nearly the end of the field work so the evidence is somewhat scanty. The answer seems a mixture of practical consideration, individual temperament and, in general, opportunity. The same problem occurred in Jamaica and the answer seemed much the same. The Mum has generally stayed at home with her Mum, bringing her husband with her and thus is in possession of the house. In Jamaica this generally involved some land as well. This house thus becomes the extended family centre. In Chapter III it was mentioned that a Mum will 'leave' her house to her successor, although, in fact, the house is only rented. Therefore she merely takes over a series of well-established and smoothly running roles. How much temperament is involved is not known. It is possible that the Mum keeps nearest to her the daughter most like herself. On the other hand the succeeding Mum may be, in fact, rather more efficient than her sisters. It must be emphasized most strongly that efficiency and the ability to take responsibility in the Mum roles does not imply that this behaviour will carry over into other situations. The authority is in the institutionalized role complexes which make up a Mum's behaviour, not in the Mum herself.

CHAPTER XVII

ORGANIZATION AND PERSONALITY

In the previous chapter the suggestion was put forward that the social conditions prevailing in Ship Street have resulted in ego weakness or insufficiently structurated egos in the inhabitants. A further assumption was made that any individual who is going to function adequately in whatever society to which he happens to belong must learn a minimum number of roles. Now constellations of roles can only be learned by people whose egos are reasonably well developed. This implies a definite relationship between the psychological state of the individual and the social conditions of the society in which he lives. That this relation exists is not, of course, a new assumption; it is the basic one of both Mead and Kardiner. However, this chapter is an attempt to tackle the problem of this interaction from a rather different angle. The basic assumptions developed in this research and in my previous work in Jamaica are as follows:

The first is that any individual has an optimum number of roles he can play. These roles are like the parts an actor plays on the stage. They are internally consistent and linked into configurations. Being asked to play either too few or too many roles may be disastrous for the individual's mental security and balance.

The second assumption is a new one and arises out of the first. It is that structuration of the ego is accomplished through the learning of roles. Perhaps a statement from Hartmann, Kris and Loewenstein on the nature of the ego may help to clarify this.

'—Freud speaks of a gradual differentiation of the ego from the id.—We suggest a different assumption, namely that of an undifferentiated phase during which both the id and the ego gradually are formed. The difference is not merely one of words. The new formulation permits a better explanation of some of the basic properties of both id and ego. During the undifferentiated phase there is maturation of apparatuses that later will come under the control of the ego, and that serve motility, perception and certain thought processes. Maturation in these areas proceeds without the total organization we call ego; only after ego formation will these functions be fully integrated. To the degree to which differentiation takes place man is equipped with a specialized organ of adaptation i.e. the ego.' [1]

Ideally as the child grows the 'undifferentiated phase' should shrink. Every role the child learns means a more structurated ego. This process seems somewhat similar to the Jungian concept of individuation. In order to play any role, perception of a situation and some relation to reality, however tenuous, must be present. These of course are ego functions. As the aim of this chapter is to attempt to clarify the relation between the individual and the social forces influencing him the following statement of Hartmann, Kris and Loewenstein concerning the relation between mother and child reformulates the Freudian position regarding ego development.

'The mother's role is a double one. She sets the premium on learning; in order to retain her love the child has to comply. Secondly, once the ego organization is established, by the consistency of her requests the mother supports the child's ego in his struggle against his impulses.'

Little work has been done on the development of the ego on 'normal' populations. Most of the assumptions arise from work on ego weakness. Kate Friedlander's work on delinquency is an example of this. She says:

'If we are right in regarding the failure of the ego to develop towards the reality principle as the key to the disturbance, it becomes clear that an early environment that fails to exert consistent pressure on the expression of those instinctual urges, which, because they are of an antisocial nature must eventually be modified, tends to predispose an individual towards this character disturbance.'

Again she says:

'For delinquents, satisfaction of the instinctual desires is

[1] Hartmann, Kris and Loewenstein, 'Comments on the Formation of Psychic Structure', *Psychoanalytic Study of the Child*, Vol. 2, 1946, pp. 19 and 24.

invariably more important than satisfactions gained from an object relationship; their impulses demand immediate gratification; postponement is impossible, and their regard for right and wrong is wholly subordinated to instinctual satisfactions' (p. 190).[1]

This type of attitude towards immediate gratification which she describes could well have been written of the Ship Street people. More confirmation that lack of development of the ego is related to the desire for immediate gratification has recently come from Hoffer.[2] Roles then are taught to the child from birth on, for all learning is really a changed or more formulated type of role playing. As a role is concrete and often dramatic it tends to be more easily assimilated than formal abstract teachings. For example a child will learn the expected roles to play to different people more easily and quickly than acquiring the twice two table. Concrete dramatizations are after all the language of the unconscious.

Organization of the ego translated into role theory implies the imposition of order into the available roles the individual can play. The more he learns from his society the more roles fall into ordered configurations. Becoming acculturated simply means the process involved in getting a number of roles into an ordered and workable configuration acceptable to his social group.

The next assumption is the necessity for some degree of organization whether in the individual's ego or in the social structure within which he lives. It is indeed very obvious that any society has to have some organization. However, the operative word is some. How much is entirely unknown.

Again when we think of organization either of the ego, or of the perceptual field we have to remember that there is both a structural and a functional aspect. Krech and Crutchfield say:[3]

'By structural factors are meant those factors deriving solely

[1] Kate Friedlander, 'Formation of the Antisocial Character', *The Psychoanalytic Study of the Child*, Imago Publishing Co., London, Vol. I, 1945, p. 201.
[2] Willi Hoffer, *Psychoanalysis*, Abraham Flexner Lectures, Williams and Wilkins Co., Baltimore, 1955.
[3] Krech and Crutchfield, *Theory and Practice of Social Psychology*, McGraw Hill, 1948, pp. 81, 82, 83.

from the nature of the physical stimuli and the neural effects they evoke in the nervous system of the individual.

'The functional factors of perceptual organization on the other hand, are those which derive primarily from the needs, moods, past experience, and memory of the individual.

'Neither set operates alone; every perception involves both kinds of factors.'

That is to say that although much of what we perceive is functionally determined it would be foolish to neglect the structural aspect.

The question arises next, therefore, whether anything analogous to the structural factors of individual perception can be found in group relations. The early work of Moreno[1] on the relation of size of group to segregation seems to give some support to this possibility; while it is likely that in the case of groups, as well as in the case of individual perception, structure and function cannot be dissociated, yet it might be possible through careful analysis to dissect away the functions leaving the bones of structure.

Again we are faced by the fact that more attention has been paid to groups showing some aspect of disorder rather than to the normally functioning group. It seems possible that one of the difficulties in making democracy work is that it presupposes that a given group will be able to function well enough in an unstructurated form to meet the demands of the group. Within the last twenty years we have seen many large social groups turning to authoritarian types of leadership. It might be possible that in group relations we are still in the stage that the free discipline schools were in the nineteen twenties—that is if we hope that people who have previously lived undemocratically will suddenly turn into experienced democrats. Susan Isaacs[2] pointed out that the extreme free discipline school put too much strain on the immature ego. We know that the individual must have some organization in order to maintain adequate contact with the perceptual world. If for some reason he was in a state of disorganization his very perception of the world around him

[1] J. L. Moreno, *Who Shall Survive*, New Nervous and Mental Disease Monographs, No. 58, Washington, 1934.

[2] Susan Isaacs, *Social Development in Young Children*. Routledge & Kegan Paul Ltd., 1950, p. 206 (abridged edition).

would be impaired, not to mention his emotional relations with it. In fact he would be unable to make either adequate perceptual or emotional contact.

It might follow, too, that a group in an unformulated situation, helplessly looking round for some organized structure through which to work, falls an easy prey for the authoritarian mode of behaviour. Possibly one of the mistakes of our time is to confuse order and authority. If this were true then it should be possible to demonstrate that a minimum amount of structure is necessary for any group to continue on a satisfactory basis. Now groups are composed of individuals and it is certainly not proposed to introduce any superorganic element or explanation. The personality of the individual is composed of a series of role constellations and it was suggested earlier in this book that each person has a minimum and maximum number of roles which they must play if they are to remain stable members of their culture pattern.

In the case of a group in an unstructurated situation the following analysis could be made. Each individual brings to the group his own constellations of possible roles; they are co-ordinated enough for him to be able to co-operate. (Margaret Lowenfeld,[1] in *Play in Childhood*, has pointed out that the neurotic child cannot co-operate in play.) If the situation is fairly structurated he will probably be able to adjust his role patterns while fulfilling the group requirements. But if there appears to be no order in what the group requires he will be faced with the paradoxical situation of having to break up order to achieve disorder. The authoritarian with his unquestionable and rigid order thus appears to offer refuge from disorder.

The next step is to put forward the hypothesis that a culture pattern is the best 'good form' for the particular group of people of which it is composed. The best good form will of course be modified to follow changes in institutions. Cultural lag can then be seen as the time taken to perceive the new form of the culture pattern. One might deduce from this that cultural change would be difficult, especially in cases where behaviour is highly organized and roles clearly and rigidly defined. This would be supported by the statements made earlier on about role uncertainty.

[1] Margaret Lowenfeld, *Play in Childhood*, Gollancz, London, 1935.

This is not an easy hypothesis to prove as there is so little evidence about the history of primitive cultures. So much of the evidence of what they were like in the past arises from sources which would be highly suspect in modern anthropology. However, Elliott and Merrill are able to say:

'Social disorganization is part of the price of social change.' [1]

Herskovits[2] too recognizes the organizational aspect of cultures.

'It is apparent that every normal culture is an integral whole, possessing a stability which causes its patterns to continue in a recognizable form despite the changing personnel of its carriers in successive generations . . . every society that is a going concern has a culture tightly enough knit so that only under conditions of the greatest stress does it yield sufficiently to blur its identity . . .'

From these statements taken at random from a great volume of literature on culture and personality it can be seen that some social scientists at least are stressing the ideas of pattern and organization in group activities much as the Gestalt psychologists did for individuals.

Again Elliott and Merrill say:

'Social organization is a state of being, a condition in which the various institutions in a society are functioning in accordance with their recognized or implied purpose.'

In my book on Jamaica I tried to put forward a rather similar viewpoint to Elliott and Merrill and said:

'Configurations of behaviour can only be said to be pathological when they hinder the normal growth and development of people within that specific culture pattern.'

This hindrance can mainly be said to take place when elements are introduced which are destructive to the economic and ideational continuance of the culture pattern.

The implications which arise from these ideas are threefold. The first is that any group of people have to organize their responses to both the internal and external world in some sort of order. The second is that if the pattern gets blurred, or the

[1] Elliott and Merrill, *Social Disorganization*, Harper, New York, 3rd edition, 1950, p. 25.

[2] M. Herskovits, 'The Process of Cultural Change', *The Science of Man in the World Crisis* (ed. Linton), Columbia, 1945.

order turns into disorder, then this is reflected in the behaviour of the individuals composing the group. The third is that some degree of order is essential both for the individual and for the group. These statements put in this way and devoid of jargon appear self-evident. The difficulty becomes apparent when we try to determine the nature of order. So often in social science we equivocate order with convenience. For example we say that a man orders his responses to the external world because of cultural prohibitions with which it is easier to acquiese. We neglect the possibility that there may be internal strivings towards some structural pattern. The functional aspect would be mainly concerned with the content of the pattern. Perhaps the suggestion of an archetype of 'wholeness' may be stating this in a different terminology.

If this assumption about some degree of order being a requisite both for the development of the individual and for the continuation of society be accepted, then the next step is to apply it to Ship Street. In the last chapter an analysis was made of the results of social conditions on the personality of Ship Street people. An attempt must now be made to assess the sociological aspect of this sub-culture.

One of the main difficulties in making a social analysis of a complicated society such as that of Britain, is that it is composed of so many sub-groups. The fact that there are differences between Welsh, Scottish and English patterns of life, and also differences between Northern and Southern England are generally recognized. This recognition is popular and probably mainly composed of stereotypes. What is not generally realized, however, is that in any one town there can be sub-groups whose differences can be identified through complete inability to appreciate each other's ethos. It seems justifiable to claim that the Ship Street people form just such a sub-group. These particular people coming from the nexus of streets that have been called Ship Street are not of course unique in this town. Other nuclei of streets housing people with similar backgrounds and outlook may well behave in much the same way although the environment would have to approximate to Ship Street for this to take place. In fact it seems likely that the power of the Mum extends beyond this group and is fairly typical of lower working class groups. Whether a similar lack of personality integration exists in other similar groups cannot, of course, be claimed without further research.

The reasons for the assumption that the Ship Street people form a specific sub-cultural group are as follows.

Firstly, the historical origin of the group which was discussed in Chapter I gave them a different provenance from other people within the city. The feeling of being Irish has been kept alive by the somewhat self-conscious Irishness of the Roman Catholic Church in this town to which they mostly belong.

Secondly, being Catholic in England implied belonging to a strong minority group. In fact the town in which Ship Street is situated seems to be the last one in England where feuds based on religious differences exist. Either Catholic or Protestant processions are very important to the participants whose numbers are quite considerable. The police have the processions well regulated and the danger of a physical clash is probably not very great these days. However, strong fears and beliefs of what 'the other side may do', appear to exist in the people's mind. These phantasies thus give a reality to the belonging to one or other group.

Thirdly, as early as 1914 Hobhouse, Wheeler and Ginsburg pointed out that one of the marks of what they termed 'the simpler peoples' was their tendency to engage in private justice, or at the most for the individual and not the society to take action over a wrong or in a dispute. Feuds in Ship Street fall into this category of private justice. At times direct action is taken and people have fights both physical and verbal. At others a little judiciously given information may reach the police over illegal activities. Revenge or getting even is considered perfectly legitimate. A person who did not himself retaliate in some way if hurt would be considered 'soft'.[1]

This preference for private justice presupposes a somewhat different set of ethical ideas from those generally supposed to be operative in England. The word supposed is used deliberately as there is no evidence to use comparatively as this type of work has not so far been done on other social groups. It may well be

---

[1] 'Soft' approximates in meaning to the American use of the word, 'sissy' as defined by Geoffrey Gorer in *The American Child*, Pilot Papers, Vol. II, No. 2, June 1947.

that Ship Street people are honest about desiring revenge, while other people do so but are ashamed to admit it.

Stealing from big stores or from people not belonging to the related in group is common and seems to indicate a splitting of ethical code. It is considered wrong to steal from relatives but perfectly legitimate to take from big stores—some distinction is made about the small shopkeeper, many people say that it is not fair to take from him. Coronation decorations in Ship Street were carried out in paint stolen from the docks. It is interesting too, in this connection, that decorations were on individual houses only and not combined efforts as in many other streets.

Similar processes were noticed at work in Jamaica where theft at times was used as a legitimate way for the underpaid worker to get what he considered a fair wage. Traditional customs of land inheritance too were adhered to in spite of the dominance of the ordinary English traditions. These two phenomena of private justice and the retaining of customs not in accordance with the dominant culture pattern and often in spite of it, both appear to be characteristic of simpler or at times subordinate sub-cultural groups.

These arguments are given as a justification for the theory that Ship Street is a sub-cultural group existing within the wider English society. Probably no one of these social processes would be powerful enough acting alone to produce this effect. However, acting together they produce this rather far-reaching differentiation of customs and personality.

It is possible to say, therefore, that Ship Street forms a simple sub-culture within the more complex and complicated English culture pattern.

Social life in a complicated community such as those of modern England or the U.S.A. implies that the individual has to learn many more ways of response to more and more complicated situations. In Chapter I, I suggested that in the simpler communities roles are more rigidly and clearly defined. In complicated societies roles may be less easy to perceive as they may be amalgamations of simpler roles built up from divergent or even antagonistic ideologies. For example, the Christian parson's role in the army.

As the roles become more complex so it needs greater powers

of discrimination for the individual to respond with exactly the correctly constituted action. For example, the almost imperceptible differences in behaviour of an old-fashioned diplomat saying yes or no without either side losing face. This subtlety will be missing from simpler communities where the rigidity of role makes it unnecessary. Both the complexity of role and the discriminatory powers of the individual appear to develop with the increasing number of associations which people have to make. This, in turn, leads to a more flexible and complex personality. Role restriction in Ship Street appears to prevent association and this in its turn prevents the individual from widening his horizon. Social mobility is restricted and people wish to stay put and cling to their traditions. If, however, social mobility is thrust upon them, then the price paid is a high degree of anxiety.

Owing to the possibility of complex and simple roles co-existing, which they almost certainly will do if the argument in the preceding paragraph is correct, the individual may become involved in what is essentially cultural misunderstanding. Many years ago Celia Fremlin[1] pointed out that difficulties between domestic servants and their employers arose because of verbal misunderstandings, for example, over what is rude. Similarly in Ship Street incomprehension is shown over more complex roles. The inhabitants tend to preserve their simple roles. Those people who through other associations develop more complex attitudes will be those who leave the area.

The personalities of Ship Street people consist of simple role constellations. These tend to be rigid and few, resulting in the sort of behaviour discussed throughout this book. Given his circumstances this is the 'good form' which enables the Ship Street person to discharge his available energy along the socially accepted patterns of his group. Outside his group, roles are either too complex to be comprehended adequately or his own role restrictions are too great for him to be able to respond even if he can comprehend the situation.

In other terms this means that firstly he may not be able to apprehend the order or form of a situation. Secondly as the situation has a different form from the one he would normally

---

[1] Paper read to the Department of Psychology, Bedford College, London. The writer, regrettably, cannot remember the date.

expect he is unable to adjust to it. Results from the projection tests would substantiate this suggestion.

Throughout this book as well as recently in the Press the word immaturity has been extensively used. The Report of the Commissioners of Prisons for 1954 has stated that many young criminals are immature. In Chapter XIV the results of the projection tests again showed immaturity. In lay terms immaturity is correlated with childish behaviour. For example it is generally considered childish not to be able to postpone gratification or to insist on 'getting my own back'. The operative question is the cause of this immaturity. From this research and that on Jamaica, I should suggest role deprivation or restriction. That is viewing the problem from the psychological angle. From the sociological angle it can be said that role deprivation sets in where people are prevented from acquiring an adequate number of roles. When their roles are restricted or they are presented with alternatives between which they are not equipped to discriminate. Obviously where culture conflict is operative there role disturbances are bound to appear. It can be seen that conditions in Ship Street do in fact cause a type of culture conflict. It is not so obvious as in countries where the dividing line is colour, but it is insiduously present. The social effect is to put the individual in a vicious circle.

Because he is role-deprived he is unable to acquire adequate roles to become an integrated and mature person. The following quotation from Nadel's new book seems to give support to my ideas on role deprivation.

'The advantages of role summation lie in the strengthening of social integration and of social control. For the more roles an individual combines in his person, the more he is linked by relationships with persons in other roles and in diverse areas of social life. Equally any additional role assumed by an individual ties him more firmly to the norms of his society.' [1]

He is restricted, liable to outbursts of primitive violence, unable to plan and tied emotionally to the only person who gives him security, his Mum. The poverty of associations resulting in little contact with people outside his group again reinforces his isolation within the confines of his family group. As models of

[1] S. F. Nadel, *The Theory of Social Structure*, Cohen and West Ltd., London, 1957.

other behaviour are lacking, or, if available, incomprehensible, then the pattern is self-perpetuated. Some individuals escape, of course. They do, however, have some unusual factor in their lives, or have undergone change owing to pressure of external forces. For example at times a man after doing his national service refuses to come back.

In general it can be said that if a culture deprives people of roles then consequences will follow which will be deleterious to the growth and continuity both of the individual and of his culture. On the other hand the culture pattern must be reasonably clear for people to discern it and must contain within it reasonable opportunity for the expression of basic drives. In the individual social weakness is expressed by lack of ego growth. If enough individuals show ego weakness in a persistent form then the culture pattern too remains oversimplified, contradictory and undeveloped.

CHAPTER XVIII

CONCLUSIONS

I N a book of this sort it is inevitable that there are two major themes. The first is a descriptive account of the people studied, followed by an attempt to explain the structure of their personalities, and their relation to the society in which they live. The second theme is theoretical and concerned with what generalizations we can draw from the material presented to further our knowledge of social processes, both in the specific society under observation and in general. Gradually, as more sub-cultures are studied in depth, it should be possible to make predictions that specific groupings of social forces should, other things being equal, result in certain types of social organizations. The chances of doing this in our present state of knowledge are about those of an outsider winning the Derby. It is possible to bring off a gamble so long as it is borne in mind that it is still a gamble.

Several conclusions arise out of the descriptive analysis. The first is the rather obvious recording that a sub-culture pattern of the type described in this book does exist within the complex of patterns which constitutes English society. Geoffrey Gorer, in *Exploring English Character*, mentions the lowest 10% of the population with whom he was not in contact and therefore excluded from his analysis. It looks as if the Ship Street people belong to this group. It is also interesting that he refers to 'survivals', which is what Ship Street people are to a great extent.

This brings me to the second point, which is the rather astonishing persistence of the past when conditions are favourable for its retention. Roles are rigid and simple, and the rate of change, whether of habitat or ideas, is slow in Ship Street. The past persists, therefore, in this group to a much greater extent than is generally realized.

189

The third point is that the Ship Street people who remain in the locality and carry on the tradition do so because owing to the role restrictions caused by the rigidity of their group customs, they are unable to reach emotional maturity. Ego development is impaired, with a consequent wealth of what, to a non-Ship Street resident, appears to be behaviour difficulties. The people themselves view these divergencies as normal behaviour.

Since the bulk of this research was done general sociological studies have been made of working-class areas in which the importance of the Mum is stressed yet again. Although Ship Street, by virtue of the origin of the people, is rather a specific case, it seems as if poor working-class conditions do tend to result in a dominant female. As these groups have not been studied psychologically it is not possible to say whether they fulfil the other requirements for a sub-culture pattern which fosters ego weakness with its resultant social consequences. Certainly immature behaviour seems highly prevalent in industrial disputes, apathy, the high incidence of crimes of violence, and religious revivals of a hysterical type. It may be that people who will not undergo technical education, or any education except the most elementary, are lost in a culture based on a highly skilled and intricate technology. They cannot, by their own choice, learn the roles which must be played, if they are to cope successfully with a modern technological civilization.

Some of the general conclusions can be summarized as follows. The first is that in this work more evidence has been obtained for one of the assumptions made in the previous but linked work in Jamaica. That is, that non-integration is not unique to Jamaica but can occur in any society where people are deprived of adequate role playing. Certain personality configurations familiar in Jamaica are apparent too in Ship Street. It is possible, therefore, to begin to predict very tentatively that if role deprivation, restriction or impairment are present then non-integrated personalities would be expected to exist.

The second general conclusion is closely linked with the last. It is that any culture pattern must have a minimum amount of form, just as an individual has to have figure and ground in order to perceive. Form is communicated to the individual in the guise of roles. A role gives form to the behaviour expected of him. He thus learns what the society wants through the roles he has to play. Being asked to play too few or too many can have equally unfortunate effects. Form therefore is apprehended as role configurations which can then be translated into action.

The next point is that the individual's perception of the demands of the external world are closely linked with the development of the ego. In cases where there is impairment or deprivation of roles, ego development is retarded, resulting in non-integration. The situation is a vicious circle. A person must have role demands made on him in order to develop. If this does not happen he will be unable to perceive the possibility of other roles or even variants on the ones he knows. This state can be demonstrated by projection techniques such as the Rorschach and the L.M.T.

The last point is whether there are, so to speak, simpler societies corresponding to the simpler, non-integrated individuals, and in which these very individuals would be normal and happy. The answer seems to be that there have been, and probably still are, simple societies where roles are somewhat rigid but clear, with deviation unheard of. But when such behaviour is produced as normal in either a West Indian island or a North Country English industrial town then the results may be somewhat unhappy. Both in Jamaica and in Ship Street people try to live out their lives surrounded by restrictions both of their own and other people's making. The simpler society with non-integrated members cannot meet the demands made on it by the modern industrial world. They are prevented from developing their own pattern and yet, at the same time, this prevention stops them from assimilation with the major complex societies. Whether in Jamaica or Ship Street culture contact of this type has led to a narrowing of interest rather than to a re-creation of a new pattern of cultural contact and development.

APPENDIX I

FAMILY ROUTINE

THE reason for the inclusion of this appendix is as follows. In doing field work the value of a daily routine file is enormous. Isolated items jotted down as the field worker is visiting or observing in his village or area may prove to be of great value when he achieves a total picture of the community. The keeping of this file in fact helps to achieve this total picture, as constant reference to it enables the investigator to check whether he has managed to visit his area at all possible times of the twenty-four hours and has not fallen into a routine time for visiting which might mean the neglect of large periods of time in which interesting things may happen.

The aim of this appendix is to give to the reader the advantage that the daily routine file gives to the field-worker. It is an attempt, through quotations from informants and more particularly from the field-workers' own observations, to show the daily life of Ship Street. This file, then, serves two purposes. It gives a picture of the Ship-Streeter's life and it also acts as a check on the veracity of information obtained from the field.

This appendix is designed more especially for other workers in the field. As it is at times repetitive it has to be taken out of the main body of the book so as not to break up the continuity.

(A) GETTING UP

The Ship Street day starts with the getting of breakfast and with lighting the fire. Some variations both of procedure and persons occur even in these somewhat inevitable actions.

Mr. P. leaves the house at 7.30 in the morning and does not return till 7 p.m. He always gets his own breakfast and Mrs. P. does not get up to see him off.

192

Mrs. F.'s husband goes to work at 7.30 each morning. Mrs. F. always gets up to get him his breakfast.

Her father or Uncle Pat light the kitchen range each morning—'whoever's down first'. If her mother or she tries to light it, it doesn't burn. Her grandmother can light it with the minimum amount of sticks.

(B) MIDDAY MEAL

The midday meal is eaten at home by anyone who can manage to get there. Children will sometimes have dinner at school but come home for a cup of tea afterwards.

On one occasion I looked in at the Y.'s living-room window as I passed it, before knocking at their front door at midday. The table was laid for their midday meal so I thought it wiser to disappear till I knew the family better. A child saw me and was sent to fetch me back. I explained that I had gone as I had seen they were about to have their dinner. Mrs. Y. was most friendly and introduced me to her husband. Today I met and identified all the children. They were all there except Bob, aged 9, who had gone to fetch some bambies. He returned with one for each member of the family. A pile of sliced bread had been taken out of its packet and placed straight on the table which had a plastic cover on it. A piece of dried salt fish had been unwrapped and lay in its newspaper on the table. The table was laid with plates, cups and saucers, a bottle of milk, sugar and marge.

Sarah, aged 15 months, was again sucking her dummy. Again she cried from time to time and held out her arms to be lifted. Each time her mother did so. Rather like the Jamaicans, Mrs. Y. asked me if I would take the three youngest children.

I called on the T.'s immediately after lunch at 2 p.m. today. Mrs. T. had made four jam tarts and cooked a midday dinner of meat, dumplings, boiled carrots, onions, potatoes and gravy for the household. Mr. T.'s dinner was waiting for him in the oven. The plate was overflowing. There was meat, gravy, three vegetables and two dumplings on it. Mrs. T. said that John, aged 7, had eaten just as much for his dinner. When he got up from the table he said his tummy ached. One and

three-quarter tarts the size of dinner plates had been con-
sumed at lunch by the two women and John. I was made to
sample a piece of tart. It really was excellent. It was a covered
tart with a thick layer of jam between two layers of pastry.
The pastry was light and beautifully cooked.

Today was his half-day and David, aged 16, came in just
before 2.30 p.m. David is working for his Uncle Maurice who
has a grocer's shop. He has been with him for the past year
and is now earning £2 8s. a week. David hands his pay-packet
to his mother who gives him 10s. back each week. He keeps
his tips. His mother had been keeping his midday dinner hot
in the oven. She brought it in and put it before him. It consisted of a small helping of cooked dried beans—about three
tablespoonsful—with gravy poured over them. As she put
the plate in front of David, she said 'I'm sorry, son, that's all
I have for you today.' She turned to me and explained that
the family had struck a bad patch as her husband had been
off work with a broken leg for some little while. David made
no complaint. He ate his beans good humouredly. In spite of
this Mrs. K. insisted that I had a cup of tea and a fresh pot
was made for me. Nobody else had a cup. Mrs. K. was anxious
lest her daughter Angela, aged 20, had made the tea too weak.
Before I realized what Angela was doing she cut me three
slices of bread and marge, taking a fresh loaf. As she put them
before me Mrs. K. said simply, 'I'm sorry there's no butter in
the house.'

(c) TEA

Bread and jam and marge are nearly always on the table and
a pot of tea stewing in the oven. In record after record the
only variant on this is whether this food is on a clean table with
cloth, cups and saucers, etc., or whether it is on the bare table
with the sliced bread taken from its cover. Tea is the next
main meal. Most households have a cooked hot meal. The
better off will have meat or sausages and vegetables, or less
frequently fish. Often it is dried fish. The poorer will have
chips or boiled potatoes and gravy. Frequently the chips are
bought. Where a child is indulged he will have sticky cakes
and tea, while the rest of the family have the cooked hot meal.

In spite of the fact that Mrs. J. had previously told me that her housekeeping money varies from week to week as her husband is a builder working on his own, she today told me that her meat bill is approximately 30s. a week. This is for a family of five—two adults and three children. They have meat at least once a day. Today they are having sausages and beans for their tea. 'I gave them chips for their dinner today so I can't give them chips again tonight. I want something to go with the sausages.' Mrs. J. and I went into X. stores together and she bought and paid for a large tin of baked beans.

We invited the children to tea one Friday and I had told them they could choose what they would like for tea. Some were coming straight on from work so they all arrived together at 7 p.m. They 'phoned me and asked if they could have chips —'Home-made chips please, miss, and ice-cream.' I told them they must have something to go with the chips and they could choose meat or sausages. They chose sausages. It was the chips that were most appreciated. They all called for a second helping and I made a fresh pan. Maggie, aged 15, told me that I would make a lot of money if I set up a fish and chip shop. Joan, aged 15, refused ice-cream saying quite straight-forwardly, 'I have me period, miss, and me mother says it gives you a stomach-ache if you eat ice-cream.'

It was 4.45 p.m. and I had been there since 2.45 p.m. When I tried to leave Mrs. R. said, 'You're going to have tea with us. Do you know what we've got for tea today? A little bit of boiled ham.' Mrs. R. proceeded to marge the slices of cut bread and Miss S. produced the bag of ham which contained four thin slices. Mrs. R. was in a dilemma as to how to make a pile of sandwiches with the bread already cut and marged, and four thin slices of ham. When I saw this I tried to beat a hasty retreat but it was no use. She said, 'You must have a sandwich first.' In desperation I said, 'I mustn't eat ham', and I helped myself to a piece of bread and marge which I doubled and started eating. Mrs. R. sanguinely replied, 'I don't believe you. Lucy, pass the apples and custard. If you won't eat ham you must have some apples and custard. The custard is lovely.' There was a long white hair in my custard which I tried to get rid of unnoticed.

I went to fetch Mrs. B. in the car today at 4. She was coming to tea with me. There was a plate of quite expensive-looking cakes on the table. They were for Peter's tea when he comes in from work. Peter is just 17 and doesn't like meat. 'He prefers cakes' so his mother had bought them for him.

Just as the cleanliness of the table varies, so does the general ability of the Mum to cope. Mrs. U. in the first excerpt is one who obviously has difficulty in managing whilst Mrs. T. in the second excerpt has not. It should be noted, however, that the youngest child in Mrs. T.'s household is 8.

Mrs. U. opened the door in answer to my knock, just after 11 this morning. She is 33 but looked haggard with dark shadows round her eyes. She is fairly tall and slim. Her trunk bent backwards from the waist. Her fire was lit, the chimney smoking. As she talked to me she went round compulsively with a duster saying, 'The dust, the dust.' Her straight bobbed hair was plastered down off her face and behind her ears. Joseph, aged 3½, and Ella, aged 14 months, were at home. There had obviously been recent puddles on the floor. They had been mopped up. Ella was sucking a dummy. Joseph tried to go out in the rain more than once during my visit. Each time his mother called him back. He said the rain had stopped. It hadn't. Once he went to the door with a lighted piece of paper and held it outside the front door. Mrs. U. told him to stop playing with fire. When I handed Mrs. U. a small packet of sweets for the children, she thanked me, opened the packet and half the sweets fell on the floor. I picked them up. When she gave Ella sweets, Ella put them in her mouth and the discarded dummy fell on the floor, where it remained. Again, I picked it up. From time to time Ella whimpered and held out her arms to be lifted. Mrs. U. picked her up, sometimes held her with one arm, and went round with the duster with the other. While she did this she said it was no use dusting as it was the fire. Yet she had only had the chimney swept two months ago. The wind was blowing the smoke back into the room. The kitchen living-room, into which the front door opens, contained a large scrubbed table, a sideboard with a wireless set on it, and some chairs. The fire was a black kitchen range on which Mrs. U. does all her cooking. She has no other means of cooking. A line of washing hung above the smoking fire. A canary hung in a cage by the window. The floor was obviously frequently scrubbed; most of the lino worn. A pram stood in the corner of the room. Ella, aged 14 months, sleeps in it both during the day and at night.

(D) HOUSEWORK

Mrs. T. has been in this house eleven years. What I saw of the house couldn't have been cleaner or tidier and the house smelt clean. Even the paint, though it was the inevitable chocolate brown and dark green, looked newly washed. Mrs. T. herself goes out to two hours' work each morning. When I arrived at 2.30 this afternoon she said she had just finished the beds and was emptying the slops. She put the slops down in the backyard before opening the front door to me, then excused herself and emptied them before she started talking to me. I peeped in the backyard. It couldn't have been closer swept or tidier. Mrs. T. said when they moved into the house 'it was crawling. Three families lived here. When it was quiet at nights it was like sand dropping down the walls. You could hear them crawl. There was coal dropped all over the place. I stripped every bit of the paper off the walls myself. There was layer upon layer. Then I painted the walls myself. I wouldn't have paper or distemper on any of the bedroom walls. You must have paint in an old house like this. There's disinfectant in paint. I mean to say, I think paint washes the walls. There's an old lady next door who's bedridden. I don't think she's any too clean and then there's two other families living in the same house as her.'

When children come in from school they are made to change into old clothes at once. As soon as Stan, aged 5, came in from school his mother made him get out of his school clothes. He had on a pair of grey flannel shorts, a sleeveless grey woollen pullover and a clean white shirt. A pair of old shorts with no buttons and which had to be kept up with three large safety pins was substituted for his school shorts. The shorts and pullover were all his mother was able to get off him. Stan ran out to play in the streets in his clean shirt and neither admonishes nor bribes of sweets would induce him to come and change his shirt.

At 7 this evening Sue, aged 9, was still in her school clothes.

Her mother said, 'Just because I was out when Sue returned from school this evening she couldn't do what she knows I make her do every evening. Why even her naughty sister has changed her clothes. You can please yourself, Sue, if you want to go to school in dirty clothes and hear the other children say, "Dirty little pig." '

(E) WASHING AND BATHS

Certain parts of family routine take place once a week. On most Mondays the Mums go to the washhouse to do the week's washing. They usually transport the linen in an old pram. This is one of the few public appearances they make. Some seize the opportunity for a gossip and a bit of fun. However, like the man's ritual Saturday football, there is no need to be social or to enter into any intimate human relation.

Mrs. O. said they play cards every Sunday evening and invited me to join them next Sunday. 'We're always so lonely on Sundays.' Her husband, who is now old, always goes to bed after tea. 'This makes the evenings so long and lonely.' They said they would teach me and I accepted. I was invited at 6 p.m. and asked to stay the evening. I was told, 'If you'd like to stay the night, there's a bed for you any time.'

Mrs. N. goes to the cemetery every Sunday morning to put flowers on her stepfather's grave. He died three years ago. Her daughter Brenda, aged 12, usually accompanies her.

Most houses have not got baths and water has to be heated. For instance, Mrs. A. gives all the young children baths at least three times a week—sometimes four times. She has to boil water for this and lights the kitchen fire and gives them their baths in front of it. The house has no bathroom. Joyce, Eunice's illegitimate baby, gets a bath every day.

While passing the G. household on my way home from the field at 1 p.m. today I was asked in and kept. . . . A child's white enamel bath with hot water in it—which had been heated on the kitchen gas cooker—stood on the kitchen table in the middle of the room. Mrs. G. threw a cake of toilet soap into it, whisked off Anastasia's clothes, and stood her in the bath. She beat up the water and made it quite soapy just as if there were soap-flakes in it. Then she washed Anastasia all over.

There were white scratches on A.'s back which looked as if they were newly made. I remarked on them. Mrs. G. said that A. has had these marks for years and nobody thinks they are of any importance. 'I once took her to a skin specialist who said, "Anastasia, now isn't that a pretty name. And are you happily married Mrs. G.?" And that's all I got my dear for taking her to a skin specialist.' Mrs. G. placed a towel on the kitchen table while she went on talking and lifted Anastasia out of the bath and stood her on the towel. With another she started drying Anastasia vigorously. Then the hunt for clean clothes began. They were airing on a clothes-rack that hangs in the kitchen. The only vest that could be found had a huge patch. Mrs. G. said she had better wear one belonging to her sister Bella, aged 10, and 14 months older than Anastasia. Anastasia said 'no', her sister Bella who had come in shouted 'no'. Mrs. G. flung the patched vest over Anastasia's head and tucked it into a pair of clean warm panties. Over these she put on a woollen skirt and jumper and then put Anastasia's legs into long warm socks. Her shoes, coat and hat had to be fetched from the wardrobe upstairs. Bella and I fetched them. Mrs. G. asked Bella if she could use her hair-slides for her sister. Bella said 'no'; Mrs. G. used them. I put on Anastasia's shoes for her and Mrs. G., A. and I went out together. It should be noted that I have on other occasions seen A. dress herself. Mrs. G. dressed her today only because she was in a great hurry.

Adults either wash in the same way or go to the public baths. In general the man washes in the scullery after work in the traditional manner.

When I arrived Dennis, aged 17, was in the scullery washing. I could see him through the open adjoining door. He was stripped to the waist. Later he appeared in the kitchen doorway as he was drying himself. Mr. F. introduced him as 'this is our Dennis'. When I asked if he was his eldest son he replied that he was not, 'But we don't bother with him, do we, Dennis?' Dennis laughed and they explained that Sam, the eldest, 'is courting.' He's out most of the time and does not help Mr. F. at all with the housework while Mrs. F. is in hospital. Dennis does help. He helps with the cooking and the cleaning. He'll help Mr. F. tomorrow, Sunday, to clean out the whole house, for Mrs. F.'s return from hospital on Monday. When Dennis was dry he ran upstairs. Soon he came down in a brown suit and clean white shirt, with his hair carefully greased and brushed down. He was very pimply and adolescent looking. At about 2.30 he left to go to the pictures with his 'mate'— another boy.

Once a week her mother tries to have a bath in the cellar, but it's not so easy as 'we have to boil all our water you know'. They used to have a large tin bath in which they bathed but the bath leaks now and it's not possible to mend it, so Moira, aged 13, usually goes to the public baths or to her married sister's once a week for a bath. If she goes to the public baths she goes with another girl from school.

Children, too, have routine jobs of cleaning and errand-running. A large proportion of their weekly income is earned on Saturdays by running errands for those unable to go to the shops. Every Saturday Amy, aged 13, scrubs their front-door steps. When Maggie once suggested that Amy and she should come to tea on a Saturday, Amy said simply, 'No, I have too much to do on a Saturday; I have to scrub the steps on Saturday.'

(F) SUNDAYS

On Sundays, routine will probably be upset. The following graphic account by some children illustrates why.

'On Sundays we have our breakfast at dinner-time, our dinner at tea-time, our tea at supper-time, and supper I don't know at what time.' This is because they always go to morning mass on Sundays and they mustn't touch a thing before they go to mass.

The excerpts that follow give further glimpses of the Ship-Streeter's life both on informal and formal occasions.

(G) HOSPITALS

I accompanied Mrs. Z. and Rosie, aged 8, to the Children's Hospital where Mrs. Z. had an appointment at 1.40 p.m. today for Rosie to see the specialist. Rosie is jumpy, nervy, underweight and sleep-walks and talks. As soon as we got to the hospital Mrs. Z. was told to strip Rosie but for her vest and pants. A nurse then weighed Rosie and took and recorded her pulse and temperature. There were many children in the room and the same procedure was adopted with them all. Some were diffident and nervous, but Rosie on the contrary smiled serenely and enjoyed being the centre of attraction. Mrs. Z. dumped Rosie's clothes on my lap, and presently she dumped Rosie with me too while she went outside to have a cigarette. A nurse called Mrs. Z.'s name. I fetched her and she and Rosie went into an inner room where a young doctor took Rosie's history which he later passed on to the specialist. A nurse went in and out of the room constantly and each time the door opened Rosie turned and gave me a gracious smile. She was enjoying herself immensely.

When Mrs. Z. and Rosie went in to see the specialist he examined Rosie thoroughly but could find nothing wrong. He said, 'She is just terribly under weight and must be a highly strung child.' He asked Mrs. Z. if there is anything in the child's home conditions that could cause anxiety but Mrs. Z. said she could think of nothing. (There is plenty.) On the contrary, she held up her other child, who is healthy, strong, and very big for her age, as proof of good home conditions.

An incident occurred while we were in the hospital which well illustrates that delinquency is not just an expression of adolescence but is carried on into adult life. Mrs. Z. knows me well and has accepted me. She saw no need to change the routine of her life in my presence.

While the nurse was taking Rosie's temperature, Mrs. Z. leant over to me and whispered to me, 'Shall I pinch it?' I asked, 'What?' She repeated, 'Shall I pinch it for Bert?' and waved her nose at the thermometer. I was unable to retain the role of a participant observer and said 'no'. When the nurse had gone, she laughed and said, 'It would have been fun to have pinched it just for a joke for Bert and so easy.' Bert is her husband who was ill in bed at home.

One day I called on the R. household at about 7 p.m. Mr. R. and Tom, aged 6, were alone together in the kitchen. Mr. R. was sitting by the fire smoking his pipe, while Tom was having his supper before going to bed. It consisted of tea, bread and marge and chocolate biscuits. Tom immediately offered me a chocolate biscuit. Mrs. R. was upstairs in bed as she had a bad cough. As soon as she heard me she called to me to come upstairs. The stairs were dark and unlit. Mrs. R. was in bed in a vest. A burning candle was stuck to a plate and gave the only light in the room. The plate was on a painted chest of drawers that stood beside her double bed. A packet of cigarettes and a saucerless cup with dregs of tea left in it lay on the chest of drawers. An empty bucket stood in the middle of the room. Mr. R. brought me up a cup of tea which I couldn't drink as I had been visiting since 3 o'clock. Mrs. R. readily drank it.

Tom came up to bed. I undressed him, taking off his shorts and pullover only, as instructed. He went to bed in the rest of his clothes. He put his arms tightly round Mrs. R. and me in turn and hugged us good-night. Tom calls me Aunty. Then he jumped into a single bed in the same room. He lay on his right side and drew his knees right up to his chin. I asked him if he was cold but he said he wasn't. Mrs. R. asked me to tuck him well in and to cover him with an old mackintosh which hung on the door as there were only two blankets on the bed.

It was four days before Christmas. I was invited to spend Christmas with the family. Mrs. R. told me that they will have chicken for their Christmas dinner. They already have the chicken—it is a live one 'living in a little box underneath the stairs in the back kitchen'. I saw it as I went out.

When Mr. R. heard me coming down the stairs he came to the bottom and held a lighted candle for me. The house has no electric light. When the household is prosperous, there is one paraffin lamp in use: when it is not, it is lit by candles. Yet as I was going tonight Mr. R. offered me 'a drop of brandy'. It was a bitter night.

There are now thirteen people living in the L. household. Mr. and Mrs. L., both aged 42, and eleven children. They have three rooms—a kitchen living-room and two bedrooms. Today Mrs. L. showed me the bedrooms and told me there is now almost complete segregation of the sexes in their sleeping arrangement. There are two beds, a double bed and single bed and a large cot, in the female bedroom. Mrs. L., Jane, aged 6, Shirley, aged 4, and Bob, aged 1, sleep in the double bed. Nancy, aged 17, and Freda, aged 13, sleep together in the single bed. The new twins sleep in the cot. The only furniture in the bedroom was the beds and cot, which indeed took up all the space. Today at 11 a.m. the beds were made and tidy, but the covering looked most inadequate. For sheets there were thin pieces of unstitched cotton, and there were two coloured blankets on each bed. Mrs. L. said, 'We're perishing for want of blankets but they're such a price.' The cot was covered with new clean baby blankets. The other bedroom was still smaller and a large double bed took up all the space in it. Mr. L., Brian, aged 14½, Jimmy, aged 11, Michael aged 9, and Joseph, aged 8, all sleep together in it.

(H) GOING TO BED

It was a Saturday night, Mrs. J. and I spent the evening out. It was 11.20 p.m. when we returned from the café. The children were still up. As soon as Mrs. J. saw them she said, 'Go to bed.' Ruth, aged 9, retorted, 'The bed's not made.' Mrs. J. asked me to help her make it and I at once accompanied her upstairs. There was a sheet over the mattress on the bed. Mrs. J. then arranged six pillows in three piles of two. Two piles at the head of the bed, and one pile at the foot of the bed but rather near the middle. The bed was a double bed. Mrs. J. and Ruth sleep with their heads at the head of the bed, Yvonne, aged 8, sleeps with her head at the foot of the bed. We then covered the bed with four large blankets, tucking them in nowhere. The bedding, and indeed the room and everything in it, was very clean. Mrs. J. explained that while her husband is away at sea the children sleep with her. When he returns, the children move into the other bedroom where they sleep together in another double bed, and she and her husband sleep together.

We then went into the kitchen living-room and Mrs. J. insisted on making tea. We all four had some. Ruth was running about still in her day clothes, but not a bit tired. Yvonne was sitting sleepily in a white flannel nightdress in the kitchen. She was tired and cold and she had tried unsuccessfully to light the kitchen fire. Her mother had asked her if she had thrown paraffin over the fire, adding to me that she hates the smell of paraffin. Yvonne said she had not. Mrs. J. had left some sausages, new potatoes and gravy in the toaster under the grill. The sausages were gone, Ruth had had them, two potatoes and gravy were left. Mrs. J. heated them up, put them on a plate and started to eat them. Ruth came over and picked off her mother's plate with her hands. Each time she deliberately picked the mouthful her mother was just about to put into her mouth. Mrs. J. got cross, Ruth laughed. Mrs. J. offered Yvonne some. Yvonne refused. Presently Yvonne came over to us, kissed us good-night and went upstairs to bed. Ruth ran up to change, came down in a good long white flannel nightdress also, shouted good-night at us and then joined her sister in bed. Tonight they fell asleep quickly. It was near 1 a.m. when I left.

(i) DEATH AND FUNERALS

The children came to tell us of the baby's death so I immediately went round to see Mr. and Mrs. O. When I got there the baby's body had been taken away for examination. There was to be a Coroner's inquest. He was only two months old. Mrs. O. told me that he had been perfectly all right up to last Saturday night. 'Then he coughed up his bottle. So the next bottle I only gave him warm water and sugar. After that he took his bottle again. On Tuesday morning when I went to give him his first bottle he didn't move. His eyes were open and I put the bottle to his mouth but he didn't suck. Then I shook him and found he was dead. It was such a shock because his eyes were open—his eyes were open.' Mrs. O. put the baby's death down to the fact that they were without coal. Some of the children had had 'flu. Today a neighbour had sent a bucket of coal.

Ida, aged 6, called to tell us of Aunt Cissy's death. The funeral was to be tomorrow morning. I went round with some flowers. Aunt Cissy, aged 79, had died of cancer in hospital. Her body was brought back and the funeral was from her home. Aunt Cissy had been much loved in the street so quite a number of children went to see her after she was laid out, in spite of their dislike and fear of seeing a dead person. Many told me that they had kept their eyes shut. A child of 13 who was no relation of Aunt Cissy's, said, 'I kept me eyes shut but I prayed.

I asked God to forgive her her sins if she had sinned and to take her to heaven.' Neighbours were at their doors crossing themselves and praying as the coffin was brought out and the hearse drove away, followed by one car of mourners.

(J) THE WEDDING

I was invited to Monica's wedding. Monica is not yet 21 and is marrying Peter, aged 24. They are both R.C. They have been courting nearly four years. Peter is her first boy friend. . . . When I arrived at the house Monica called me upstairs. She was dressed and putting make-up on her face. It was a white wedding. She was attended by four bridesmaids—three of them her younger sisters, and one cousin. Her little brother Tony, aged 3, was page-boy. He was dressed in shorts and a clean white satin blouse with frills. All the bridesmaids were with Monica in her small bedroom where some of them had dressed. Tony kept running in and out and Monica continued to look after him. Presently she asked him to bring her a gin and orange and to be careful not to spill it on himself. He ran down and fetched it up carefully for his sister. Monica gulped it down. Then Mrs. T., Monica's mother, called me down for a drink. All the brides' guests, mostly relations, had been invited to the house 45 minutes before the wedding. Drinks were laid in the back parlour and we were all given a gin and orange before going to the church. A car had been hired and all the guests and the family were taken to the church by car. Friends were taken first, then the more distant relatives, then the nearer relatives, then the bridesmaids and finally the bride and her father who gave her away. The bride's guests sat on the left of the altar, the bridegroom's on the right. The bridegroom, his best man, and all the bridegroom's guests were already in the church when I arrived. The bridegroom's mother had a girl of about 2 with her who wouldn't sit still and climbed about noisily throughout the ceremony. When the bride arrived she went straight to the altar with her father but there was no priest there to receive her so she went and sat down. When the priest arrived all the people involved got up and went to the altar. The bride's father who was giving her away took her up to the altar and then immediately went back and sat down. His reason for this was because he is not R.C. The priest hurried over the service, most of which was inaudible and in Latin. . . . After the ceremony the bride was kissed by her mother, the bridegroom by his. Then as they passed down the aisles all the people in the end seats got up and shook them by the hand, each saying in turn, 'All the best, all the best.' A photographer had been engaged to take photographs and was waiting outside the church. Quite a number were taken. As soon as we came out of the church Tony ran and spent a penny in the corner of the yard. Most of us laughed. . . . A hall had been engaged for the wedding breakfast and we were all taken to it by car in the reverse order from which we had been brought to the church. Mr. T. however remained with the last guests. Four long tables had been arranged in a T shape with the bride and groom sitting at the head of the T. The tables were decorated, the room was decorated, and each person's place was marked at the table. There was an excellent meal of ham and tongue and delicious salads; jelly, peaches and custard and tea. Monica's brother, Edward, aged 6, who knows me well came and sat on my seat with me and shared my meal. There did not appear to be a place laid for him. We took a mouthful of everything in turn—same knives and forks and spoons! The bride and groom's health was proposed by the bride's eldest paternal uncle, who made no speech, and we were all provided with a gin and orange again or a whisky and soda to drink it. The tables were then cleared, the guests sat round the room and the bride went home to change into a costume. Trays of beer were passed round from time to time, groups of people broke up and went round to the adjoining pub for drinks from time to time. . . .

It was very interesting that much of the behaviour observed, though not important in itself, stressed and confirmed information obtained from the field. A tidy, clean, efficient middle-aged woman seemed to be in charge of the catering. She looked after us all personally. I asked Mrs. T. if the woman was a relative or friend. Mrs. T. replied that she was neither but a neighbour. 'She was a lodger in me mother's house. She still lives just round the corner from us.' This woman had been responsible for getting the meal ready, laying it and serving it.

She had decorated the hall and tables. She had not been to the church but had been at the hall all day. Mrs. T. on the other hand did not go near the hall today till she arrived from the church to find the meal ready for her.

Many mothers told me that they had left their youngest children with neighbours and so had been able to come to the wedding. Mrs. T. herself had left her 10-weeks-old baby with a neighbour. In some cases, where all the family was young, Dads had stayed at home to look after the children enabling Mums to come to the wedding. Much of the crockery had been loaned by neighbours and had to be sorted out at the end of the evening.

Many new clothes had been bought for the occasion and in particular hats—which were discarded as soon as possible. One of Mr. T.'s younger married sisters went round the room dancing with the price ticket of her dress hanging out at the back of her neck. She was heartily ragged; her laughter was the loudest. She left the ticket and said she'd bought the dress on 'club money'.

As soon as the tables were cleared a girl who looked about 16 or 17 put a dance record on a gramophone standing in the corner of the room. The adolescent girls at once all got up and started dancing together. The interesting thing is that many of them had their boy friends there, but not one of them danced. They sat tightly with their girl friends, but as soon as each record started the girls got up and danced while the men watched. When the music stopped the girl flopped back beside her boy. Each girl danced with her 'mate', they knew each other's steps perfectly, they were experts together. For instance, I noticed one young girl who did not at first join in the dancing. Half-way through the evening her 'mate' came in from work. The two girls danced together non-stop for the rest of the evening. Sometimes it appeared they were showing off to their boys. When the boys wanted a look in, they carted their girl off to the pub. Even then if the 'mate' hadn't a boy with her, she went with them. Some of the older members tried to get the courting males to dance with their girls. The only one who was induced to dance, danced with his aunt, much to everybody's merriment. The adolescent girls danced the most up-to-date dances all the time, holding each other by one hand and doing the most intricate movements. Only the older women did waltzes, foxtrots, etc. They too always danced together, unless they danced with a male relative. Woman after woman told me, 'I was dancing mad, but I haven't danced since me wedding.' The whole evening I was there, the bride and bridegroom were the only non-related girl and boy who danced together. They danced one slow foxtrot.

The female members of the T. household helped the 'lodger' with the clearing away and washing up. On my many visits to the T. household, it has always been apparent that Monica, the eldest child, was her mother's right hand. She remained so today on her wedding-day. Monica spent much of the time in the kitchen drying up, while her 'dancing mad' sister, Rita, just two years younger, spent all the time dancing. Yet Rita is now seriously courting, her boy was there today. She told me that on her marriage she is prepared to give up dancing. . . .

The party broke up at about 10 p.m. The bride and bridegroom went to their new home, one minute's walk from the bride's parents' home. Mr. and Mrs. T and a small party of relatives returned to their household where 'they sent out for drinks' and sat up the whole night.

(K) THE PUB

The adults' evenings' entertainments have been described in Chapter III on recreation and those of the adolescent in Chapter VI. During the week adult males sometimes have a drink at the pub on the way home and their tea is put in the oven until they turn up. It is generally only at the weekend that they take their wives out.

'Now the children are old we both go out together for a glass of ale on a Saturday night. We never go out without the other.' (An informant married 29 years.)

'If me husband isn't working, we go to the pictures together every Saturday night.' (An informant married 23 years.)

I had invited Mrs. Y., aged 39, to go to the pub with me tonight and called for her at 8.30 p.m. I found Mr. and Mrs. Y. and Mr. Y.'s unmarried brother Gregory, aged 31, waiting for me. I was introduced to him as Greg. Mr. Y had just washed and shaved and was drying his face as I came in. The two men went off to the pub and then Mrs. Y. went into the 'back kitchen' where she took off her top clothes and washed at the kitchen sink. She came back into the kitchen living-room in a black silk dress and brushed her hair hard and long before the mirror. Then she put on a cardigan and a black coat and we went off to the pub. Mr. Y. and Greg were on the look out for us and immediately joined us and stood us drinks. The whole evening I was only allowed to stand Mrs. Y. one drink. When I was rather unhappy about this and pointed out that I had invited Mrs. Y. to come to the pub with me, Mr. Y. said, 'What are you worrying about? Everybody here has much more money than you. They have all been paid today. Every man has a fiver in his pocket.' Greg was most generous the whole evening, and Mr. Y. said, 'Don't worry, he has nobody to spend his money on.' An elderly Irishman, who at a guess I would have said was a coalman, plied me with cigarettes and drinks. He would not accept a drink from me. When I thanked him, he said, 'God bless you, I like to see a cheerful face.' I ordered and tried to drink 'milds', but was not very successful. When Mr. Y. saw this he gave Mrs. Y. £1 and told her to order gin and lime. She ordered two and left Mr. Y. to collect the change. Most of the men in the pub were dockers and we all called each other by Christian names. When Mr. and Mrs. Y. introduced me they introduced me by my Christian name. When the pub closed Mr. and Mrs. Y. invited me to return with them. The table was laid with a clean cloth and cups and saucers and biscuits. Tea was made. The Y.'s eldest daughter Sylvia, aged 18, had got it ready for her parents. She, and her three younger sisters and a cousin joined us. I left soon after 11 p.m. and I was given two slices of fresh home-made bun loaf—which proved excellent—to take home with me. Greg was delegated to see me home. The next time I saw the younger children, they asked, with their tongues in their cheek, when they could call me 'Aunty'! (The Y.'s are at the top of our income group.)

(L) INSURANCE

Other routine factors of great importance are the visits of the insurance man and the coal man. One day when I called at

Mrs. D.'s the front door was open and what I saw of the house looked polished and clean. I was closely followed by an insurance man collecting 'club money'. It appeared that David had come round and remained in to do this job for his Aunt. He paid the man with a £1 note and got little change. I think he paid 17s. and something in all.

While I was there at 10.30 a.m. today the insurance man called. Mrs. S. handed him a 10s. note saying, 'You'll only have to take 5s. this week as we're broke.' The insurance man grinned and said, 'Is that so?' He marked her book and handed her back 5s. He was obviously on quite friendly terms with the household and was given a cup of tea.

Insurance, of one kind or another, is of great importance to the North Country working class. Our informants, time after time, say that if they wish to save they have to take out some policy. These policies range from ones taken with the big insurance companies to informal 'clubs' run by someone in the street, called tontines. One woman, separated from her husband, belongs to a local tontine and saves her annual holiday money in this way. When her money is refunded her she always gives the tontine collector 4s. When it was pointed out to her that she is thus actually out of pocket she replied, 'Oh aye, but it helps you save.' Tontines, however, are not so frequent in our area. Another woman who is much younger than her husband has insured him, 'So that I can bury him and buy black when he dies.'

In the winter the weekly coal ration for the majority of our households is 1 cwt. A few get more but not many. All of them complain that they cannot manage on this cwt. a week yet only a small minority take advantage of summer rationing. Of course the poorer burn coal throughout the summer as the kitchen range or even an open fireplace is their only means of cooking; and some say that they have to keep a fire going most of the summer to keep the damp out. But very few buy coal in the summer to store for the winter. Storage space is not great, but most have facilities for 5 cwt. Yet every winter the majority start with an empty coal cupboard or cellar. Thus it is common occurrence in the winter to see Mums or children—usually boys—queueing for hours in coal merchants' yards who are selling inferior stuff off the ration. Only today two Mums said they had queued from 2 p.m. to 4 p.m. for a quarter of a cwt. of coal at 1s 7½d a quarter. 'It'll be finished by tomorrow.' The Mums or children cart the coal in old prams or sacks. The same prams that are used to transport the weekly washing to and from the washhouse. There are many reports of swindling on the part of the coalman, especially during the very cold weather and at Christmas time. The poorest Mum will tip heavily 'to get a bag of coal for Christmas'. There appears to be little class solidarity about the coalman.

APPENDIX II

RORSCHACH TABLE OF MEAN SCORES

TABLE 8

Location expressed in Means

	W	D	d	dd	de	di	dr
Means	5·16	14·96	4·25	3·49	0·75	0·39	1·02

	S	W%	D%	d%	Dd%	S%
Means	1·31	26·12	50·19	9·35	11·27	2·88

Determinants expressed in Means and Percentages of total Number of Responses

	M	FM	m	k	K	FK	F
Ship Street Means	2·65	4·1	0·43	0·04	0·45	0·53	16·47
Ship Street Percentages	8·46	13·1	1·38	0·13	1·44	1·69	60·84

	Fc	c	C¹	FC	CF	C
Ship Street Means	0·84	0·47	0·84	0·92	0·35	0·63
Ship Street Percentages	2·69	1·50	2·69	6·70	1·13	2·01

Total No. of Children in Group, 51

INDEX

Founded by KARL MANNHEIM
Late Professor of Education in the University of London

Edited by W. J. H. SPROTT
Professor of Philosophy in the University of Nottingham

The International Library

of

Sociology and Social

Reconstruction

ROUTLEDGE & KEGAN PAUL

BROADWAY HOUSE, CARTER LANE, LONDON, E.C.4

SOCIOLOGY OF EDUCATION

Mission of the University
JOSÉ ORTEGA Y GASSET. Translated and introduced by Howard
Lee Nostrand   *Second Impression.* 12*s.* 6*d.*

Total Education
A Plea for Synthesis
M. L. JACKS, *Director of the Institute of Education, Oxford*
Fourth Impression. 16*s.*

The Social Psychology of Education
An Introduction and Guide to its Study
C. M. FLEMING, *Reader in Education, Institute of Education, London* 10*s.*

Education and Society in Modern Germany
R. H. SAMUEL, *Professor of Germanic Languages, Melbourne,* and
R. HINTON THOMAS, *Lecturer in German, Birmingham*   16*s.*

The Museum
Its History and Its Tasks in Education
ALMA S. WITTLIN   *Illustrated.* 28*s.*

The Educational Thought and Influence of Matthew Arnold
W. F. CONNELL, *Senior Lecturer in Education, Sydney.* With an Introduction by Sir Fred Clarke   23*s.*

Comparative Education
A Study of Educational Factors and Traditions
NICHOLAS HANS, *Reader in Education, Institute of Education, London*
Fourth Impression. 23*s.*

New Trends in Education in the 18th Century
NICHOLAS HANS   21*s.*

From School to University
A Study, with special reference to University Entrance
R. R. DALE, *Lecturer in Education, University College, Swansea*   21*s.*

Adult Education
A Comparative Study
ROBERT PEERS   *In Preparation*

2

Education and Society

An Introduction to the Sociology of Education

A. K. C. OTTAWAY, *Lecturer in Education, Leeds.* With an Introduction by W. O. Lester Smith   *Second Impression.* 18s.

German Youth: Bond or Free

HOWARD BECKER   18s.

Parity and Prestige in English Secondary Education

OLIVE BANKS, *Lecturer in Sociology, Liverpool*   25s.

Helvetius

His Life and Place in the History of Educational Thought

IAN CUMMING, *Senior Lecturer in Education, Auckland*   25s.

Adolescence

Its Social Psychology: With an Introduction to recent findings from the fields of Anthropology, Physiology, Medicine, Psychometrics and Sociometry

C. M. FLEMING, *Reader in Education, Institute of Education, London*   18s.

Studies in the Social Psychology of Adolescence

J. E. RICHARDSON, J. F. FORRESTER, J. K. SHUKLA and P. J. HIGGINBOTHAM
Edited by C. M. FLEMING   23s.

From Generation to Generation

Age Groups and Social Structure

S. N. EISENSTADT, *Head of the Department of Sociology, Hebrew University, Jerusalem*   42s.

SOCIOLOGY OF RELIGION

Sociology of Religion

JOACHIM WACH, *Professor of the History of Religions, Chicago*   30s.

The Economic Order and Religion

FRANK KNIGHT, *Professor of Social Science, Chicago,* and
THORNTON W. MERRIAM   18s.

3

SOCIOLOGY OF ART AND LITERATURE

Chekhov and His Russia: A Sociological Study
W. H. BRUFORD, *Schröder Professor of German, Cambridge* 18s.

The Sociology of Literary Taste
LEVIN L. SCHÜCKING *Third Impression.* 9s. 6d.

Men of Letters and the English Public in the 18th Century, 1660-1744, Dryden, Addison, Pope
ALEXANDRE BELJAME, Edited with an Introduction and Notes by Bonamy Dobrée. Translated by E. O. Lorimer 28s.

SOCIOLOGICAL APPROACH TO THE STUDY OF HISTORY

The Aftermath of the Napoleonic Wars
The Concert of Europe—An Experiment
H. G. SCHENK, *Lecturer in Political Economics, Fellow of Exeter College, Oxford* *Illustrated.* 18s.

Military Organization and Society
STANISLAW ANDRZEJEWSKI, *Simon Fellow, Manchester*. Foreword by A. Radcliffe-Brown 21s.

Population Theories and the Economic Interpretation
SYDNEY COONTZ, *Assistant Professor in Forest Economics, State University of New York, Syracuse* 25s.

SOCIOLOGY OF LAW

Sociology of Law
GEORGES GURVITCH, *Professor of Sociology, Sorbonne.* With an Introduction by Roscoe Pound *Second Impression.* 21s.

The Institutions of Private Law and their Social Functions
KARL RENNER. Edited with an Introduction and Notes by O. Kahn-Freund 28s.

Legal Aid
ROBERT EGERTON. With an Introduction by A. L. Goodhart
Second Impression. 12s. 6d.

4

Soviet Legal Theory: Its Social Background and Development
RUDOLF SCHLESINGER, *Lecturer in Soviet Social and Economic Institutions, Glasgow*   *Second Edition.* 28s.

CRIMINOLOGY

Juvenile Delinquency in an English Middletown
HERMANN MANNHEIM, *Reader in Criminology, London School of Economics*   14s.

Criminal Justice and Social Reconstruction
HERMANN MANNHEIM   *Second Impression.* 20s.

Group Problems in Crime and Punishment
HERMANN MANNHEIM   28s.

The Psycho-Analytical Approach to Juvenile Delinquency: Theory, Case Studies, Treatment
KATE FRIEDLANDER   *Fourth Impression.* 23s.

The English Prison and Borstal Systems
LIONEL FOX, K.C.B., M.C., *Chairman of the Prison Commission for England and Wales*   32s.

Crime and the Services
JOHN SPENCER, *Director of the Bristol Social Project*   28s.

Delinquent Boys: The Culture of the Gang
ALBERT K. COHEN, *Assistant Professor of Sociology, Indiana*   21s.

The Criminal Area
A Study in Social Ecology
TERENCE MORRIS   *In preparation*

THE SOCIAL SERVICES

Social Service and Mental Health
An Essay on Psychiatric Social Workers
M. ASHDOWN and S. C. BROWN   18s.

The Social Services of Modern England
M. PENELOPE HALL, *Lecturer in Social Science, Liverpool*
Third Edition (Revised). 28s.

Lunacy, Law and Conscience, 1744-1845
The Social History of the Care of the Insane
KATHLEEN JONES   21s.

British Social Work in the 19th Century
A. F. YOUNG and E. T. ASHTON, *Department of Social Studies,*
Southampton University   25s.

Social Policies for Old Age
B. E. SHENFIELD, *Lecturer in Social Studies, University of Birmingham*   25s.

Voluntary Societies and Social Policy
MADELINE ROOFF, *Lecturer in Social Policy and Social Administration at*
Bedford College, London   35s.

· SOCIOLOGY AND POLITICS

Social-Economic Movements
An Historical and Comparative Survey of Socialism, Communism, Co-
operation, Utopianism; and Other Systems of Reform and Reconstruction
H. W. LAIDLER, *Executive Director, League for Industrial Democracy*
                         Second Impression. Illustrated. 37s. 6d.

Dictatorship and Political Police
The Technique of Control by Fear
E. K. BRAMSTEDT   20s.

Nationality in History and Politics
A Psychology and Sociology of National Sentiment and Nationalism
FRIEDRICH HERTZ   *Third Impression.* 30s.

The Logic of Liberty: Reflections and Rejoinders
MICHAEL POLANYI, F.R.S., *Professor of Social Studies, Manchester*
                                                                  18s.

Power and Society
A Framework for Political Inquiry
HAROLD D. LASSWELL, *Professor of Law, Yale,* and
A. KAPLAN, *Professor of Liberal Studies, Indiana*   25s.

The Political Element in the Development of Economic Theory

GUNNAR MYRDAL, *Professor of Economics, Stockholm*. Translated from the German by Paul Streeten 25*s.*

Higher Civil Servants in Britain

From 1870 to the Present Day

R. K. KELSALL, *Head of the School of Social Studies, Sheffield* 25*s.*

Democracy and Dictatorship: Their Psychology and Patterns of Life

Z. BARBU, *Lecturer in Social Psychology, Glasgow* 28*s.*

How People Vote: A Study of Electoral Behaviour in Greenwich

MARK BENNEY, A. P. GRAY, and R. H. PEAR 25*s.*

Economy and Society

A Study in the Integration of Economic and Social Theory

TALCOTT PARSONS, *Chairman of the Department of Social Relations, Harvard*, and NEIL J. SMELSER 35*s.*

The Functions of Social Conflict

LEWIS COSER, *Associate Professor of Sociology, California* 18*s.*

FOREIGN AFFAIRS, THEIR SOCIAL, POLITICAL & ECONOMIC FOUNDATIONS

Patterns of Peacemaking

DAVID THOMSON, *Research Fellow, Sidney Sussex College, Cambridge*, E. MEYER and ASA BRIGGS, *Professor of History, Leeds* 25*s.*

French Canada in Transition

EVERETT C. HUGHES, *Professor of Sociology, Chicago* 16*s.*

State and Economics in the Middle East

A Society in Transition

A. BONNÉ, *Professor of Economics. Director, Economic Research Institute, Hebrew University, Jerusalem* *Second Edition (Revised)*. 40*s.*

The Economic Development of the Middle East
An Outline of Planned Reconstruction
A. BONNÉ
Third Impression. 16*s.*

Studies in Economic Development
With special reference to conditions in the Underdeveloped Areas in Western Asia and India
ALFRED BONNÉ
32*s.*

Peasant Renaissance in Yugoslavia, 1900-1950
A Study of the Development of Yugoslav Peasant Society as Affected by Education
RUTH TROUTON
28*s.*

Transitional Economic Systems
The Polish-Czech Example
DOROTHY W. DOUGLAS
25*s.*

Political Thought in France from the Revolution to the Fourth Republic
J. P. MAYER
14*s.*

Central European Democracy and its Background
Economic and Political Group Organization
RUDOLF SCHLESINGER
30*s.*

ECONOMIC PLANNING

Private Corporations and their Control
A. B. LEVY
Two Volumes. 70*s. the set*

The Shops of Britain
A Study of Retail Distribution
HERMANN LEVY
Second Impression. 21*s.*

SOCIOLOGY OF THE FAMILY AND ALLIED TOPICS

The Family and Democratic Society
J. K. FOLSOM, *Professor of Economics, Vassar College*
35*s.*

Nation and Family
The Swedish Experiment in Democratic Family and Population Policy
ALVA MYRDAL, *Swedish Ambassador to India* 28s.

The Deprived and the Privileged
Personality Development in English Society
B. M. SPINLEY, *Educational Psychologist, Sheffield Child Guidance Clinic* 20s.

Prosperity and Parenthood
J. A. BANKS, *Lecturer in Sociology, Liverpool* 21s.

Family, Socialization and Interaction Process
TALCOTT PARSONS and ROBERT F. BALES, *Lecturer in Sociology, Harvard University* 30s.

The Home and Social Status
DENNIS CHAPMAN, *Senior Lecturer in Social Science, Liverpool University*
119 tables, diagrams and plates, 35s.

Women's Two Roles
Home and Work :
ALVA MYDAL, and VIOLA KLEIN 25s.

TOWN AND COUNTRY PLANNING. HUMAN ECOLOGY

The Social Background of a Plan: A Study of Middlesbrough
Edited by RUTH GLASS. With Maps and Plans 42s.

City, Region and Regionalism
A Geographical Contribution to Human Ecology
ROBERT E. DICKINSON. With Maps and Plans 25s.

The West European City: A Study in Urban Geography
ROBERT E. DICKINSON. With Maps and Plans 42s.

Revolution of Environment
E. A. GUTKIND *Illustrated.* 32s.

The Journey to Work
Its Significance for Industrial and Community Life
K. LIEPMANN, *Research Fellow in Economics, Bristol.* With a Foreword
by Sir Alexander Carr-Saunders *Second Impression* 16s.

Stevenage: A Sociological Study of a New Town
HAROLD ORLANS   30s.

The Genesis of Modern British Town Planning
A Study in Economic and Social History of the Nineteenth and Twentieth
Centuries
W. ASHWORTH, *Professor of History, London School of Economics*   21s.

SOCIOLOGICAL STUDIES OF MODERN COMMUNITIES

Negroes in Britain
A Study of Racial Relations in English Society
K. L. LITTLE, *Reader in Anthropology, Edinburgh*   25s.

Co-operative Living in Palestine
HENRIK F. INFIELD. With a Foreword by General
Sir Arthur Wauchope   *Illustrated.* 12s. 6d.

Co-operative Communities at Work
HENRIK F. INFIELD   18s.

Colour Prejudice in Britain
A Study of West Indian Workers in Liverpool, 1941-1951
ANTHONY H. RICHMOND, *Lecturer in Social Theory, Edinburgh*   18s.

Social Mobility in Britain
Edited by DAVID V. GLASS, *Professor of Sociology, London School of
Economics*   36s.

The Absorption of Immigrants
S. N. EISENSTADT   25s.

Studies in Class Structure
G. D. H. COLE   21s.

The Study of Groups
JOSEPHINE KLEIN, *Lecturer in Social Studies, Birmingham*   21s.

SOCIOLOGY OF INDUSTRY

Mobility in the Labour Market
MARGOT JEFFERYS, *Lecturer, London School of Hygiene and Tropical Medicine* 15s.

Patterns of Industrial Bureaucracy
ALVIN W. GOULDNER, *Professor of Sociology, Illinois* 21s.

Wildcat Strike
A Study of an Unofficial Strike
ALVIN W. GOULDNER 16s.

Recruitment to Skilled Trades
GERTRUDE WILLIAMS, *Professor of Social Economics, Bedford College, London* 23s.

ANTHROPOLOGY & RURAL SOCIOLOGY

The Sociology of Colonies: An Introduction to the Study of Race Contact
RENÉ MAUNIER, *Member of the French Academy of Colonial Sciences.* Translated from the French by E. O. Lorimer *Two volumes. 63s. the set*

A Chinese Village: Taitou, Shantung Province
MARTIN C. YANG 23s.

A Japanese Village: Suye Mura
JOHN F. EMBREE, *Associate Professor of Anthropology, California.* With an Introduction by A. R. Radcliffe-Brown *Illustrated.* 21s.

The Golden Wing: A Sociological Study of Chinese Familism
YUEH-HWA LIN, *Professor of Social Anthropology, Yenching.* Introduction by Raymond Firth 18s.

Earthbound China: A Study of Rural Economy in Yunnan
HSIAO-TUNG FEI and CHIH-I CHANG *Illustrated.* 20s.

Under the Ancestors' Shadow: Chinese Culture and Personality
FRANCIS L. K. HSU, *Professor of Anthropology, College of Liberal Arts, North Western University* *Illustrated.* 21s.

SOCIOLOGY AND PSYCHOLOGY OF THE PRESENT CRISIS

Diagnosis of Our Time
Wartime Essays of a Sociologist
KARL MANNHEIM   18s.

Farewell to European History or the Conquest of Nihilism
ALFRED WEBER   18s.

The Fear of Freedom
ERICH FROMM   21s.

The Sane Society
ERICH FROMM   25s.

Freedom, Power, and Democratic Planning
KARL MANNHEIM. Edited by Hans Gerth and E. K. Bramstedt   28s.

Essays on Sociology and Social Psychology
KARL MANNHEIM. Edited by Paul Kecskemeti   28s.

Essays on the Sociology of Culture
KARL MANNHEIM. Edited by Ernest Manheim and Paul
Kecskemeti   28s.

SOCIAL PSYCHOLOGY AND PSYCHO-ANALYSIS

Psychology and the Social Pattern
JULIAN BLACKBURN, *Associate Professor of Psychology, McGill University, Canada*   *Fifth Impression.* 14s.

The Framework of Human Behaviour
JULIAN BLACKBURN   *Second Impression.* 15s.

A Handbook of Social Psychology
KIMBALL YOUNG, *Professor of Sociology, North-western University*
                                                                35s.

Solitude and Privacy
A Study of Social Isolation, Its Causes and Therapy
PAUL HALMOS, *Lecturer in Social Psychology, Social Studies Dept., South West Essex Technical College*   21s.

The Human Group
GEORGE C. HOMANS, *Associate Professor of Sociology, Harvard* 28s.

Sigmund Freud: An Introduction
A Presentation of his Theories and a Discussion of the Relationship between Psycho-analysis and Sociology
WALTER HOLLITSCHER, *Professor of Philosophy and Sociology, Humboldt University, Berlin* *Second Impression.* 12s.

The Social Problems of an Industrial Civilization
ELTON MAYO, *Late Professor of Industrial Research, Harvard Business School* *Second Impression.* 15s.

Oppression
A Study in Social and Criminal Psychology
TADEUSZ GRYGIER. Foreword by Hermann Mannheim 28s.

Mental Health and Mental Disorder
A Sociological Approach
Edited by ARNOLD M. ROSE, *University of Minnesota* 40s.

APPROACHES TO THE PROBLEM OF PERSONALITY

The Cultural Background of Personality
RALPH LINTON, *Professor of Anthropology, Yale*
Third Impression. 12s. 6d.

The Feminine Character: History of an Ideology
VIOLA KLEIN. With an Introduction by Karl Mannheim 16s.

A History of Autobiography in Antiquity
GEORG MISCH, *Professor of Philosophy, Göttingen,* Translated by E. W. Dickes. *Two volumes.* 45s. *the set*

Personality and Problems of Adjustment
KIMBALL YOUNG *Second Edition (Revised).* 35s.

Towards a Measure of Man
The Frontiers of Normal Adjustment
PAUL HALMOS 28s.

PHILOSOPHICAL AND SOCIAL FOUNDATIONS OF THOUGHT

Homo Ludens: A Study of the Play Element in Culture
J. HUIZINGA   18s.

The Ideal Foundations of Economic Thought
Three Essays on the Philosophy of Economics
WERNER STARK, *Reader in Economics, Manchester*
Third Impression.   16s.

The History of Economics in its Relation to Social Development
WERNER STARK   *Third Impression.*   12s.

America: Ideal and Reality
The United States of 1776 in Contemporary European Philosophy
WERNER STARK   12s.

The Decline of Liberalism as an Ideology
With Particular Reference to German Politico-Legal Thought
J. H. HALLOWELL   14s.

Society and Nature: A Sociological Inquiry
HANS KELSEN, *Department of Political Science, California*   25s.

Marx: His Time and Ours
R. SCHLESINGER   *Second Impression.*   32s.

The Philosophy of Wilhelm Dilthey
H. A. HODGES, *Professor of Philosophy, Reading*   30s.

Essays on the Sociology of Knowledge
KARL MANNHEIM   28s.

The Sociology of Knowledge
W. STARK   *In preparation*

GENERAL SOCIOLOGY

A Handbook of Sociology
W. F. OGBURN, *Professor of Sociology, Chicago,* and
M. F. NIMKOFF, *Professor of Sociology, Bucknell*
Third Edition (Revised).   30s.

Social Organization
ROBERT H. LOWIE, *late Professor of Anthropology, Chicago*   35s.

15

Professional Ethics and Civic Morals
EMILE DURKHEIM. Translated by Cornelia Brookfield   30s.

Systematic Sociology
KARL MANNHEIM
Edited by W. A. C. STEWART and J. S. EROS   24s.

Value in Social Theory
GUNNAR MYRDAL   *In preparation*

FOREIGN CLASSICS OF SOCIOLOGY
Wilhelm Dilthey: An Introduction
A comprehensive account of his sociological and philosophical work,
with translations of selected passages.
H. A. HODGES   *Second Impression.* 14s.

From Max Weber: Essays in Sociology
Translated, Edited and with an Introduction by H. H. GERTH and
C. W. MILLS   *Second Impression.* 28s.

Suicide: A Study in Sociology
EMILE DURKHEIM. Translated by J. A. Spaulding and George
Simpson   28s.

Community and Association
FERDINAND TONNIES. Edited and supplemented by Charles P.
Loomis   21s.

DOCUMENTARY
Changing Attitudes in Soviet Russia
Documents and Readings. Edited with an Introduction by
RUDOLF SCHLESINGER
Volume 1: *The Family in the U.S.S.R.*   30s.
Volume 2: *The Nationalities Problem and Soviet Administration* 30s.

Psychology in the Soviet Union
BRIAN SIMON, *Lecturer in Education, University College, Leicester*   32s

Soviet Youth: Some Achievements and Problems
Excerpts from the Soviet Press
Edited and translated by DOROTHEA L. MEEK   28s.

All prices are net

1.11.57   Clarke, Doble & Brendon, Ltd., Oakfield Press, Plymouth